IMAGES
of America

WILLIAMSPORT

THE DUG-OUT

A MORALE-BUILDER FOR THE ARMED FORCES

Vol. II — No. 7 WILLIAMSPORT, MD., U. S. A., MARCH 10, 1944 Price: Ten Cents

WILLIAM D. BYRON LIBERTY SHIP

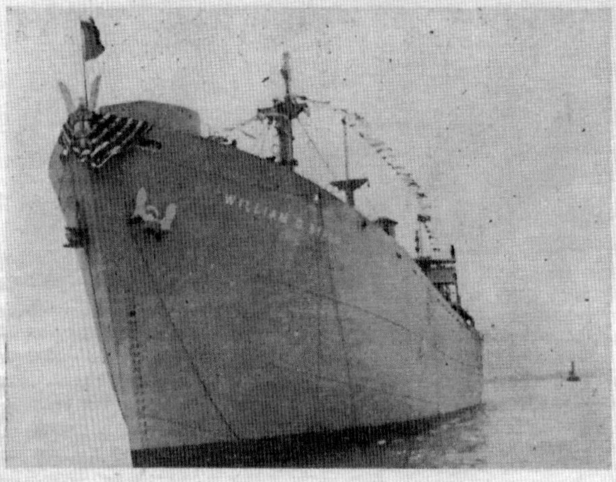

The Liberty Ship, William D. Byron just after she had slid down the ways at the Bethlehem - Fairfield shipyards at Baltimore. Named in honor of Williamsport's late Congressman, the William D. Byron will soon be carrying vital war material to our boys on the fighting fronts. The vessel was launched by Mrs. Katherine E. Byron, with a number of Williamsport citizens witnessing the ceremonies.

INCREASE GRANTED WORKERS AT THE LOCAL TANNERY

At the request of the company, the Reigonal War Labor Board in Philadelphia has granted wage increases averaging approximately five per cent to all employees of W. D. Byron and Sons of Maryland tannery at Williamsport, these increases to be reactroactive to November 9, 1943.

RETURNS TO CAMP

Pfc. Harold C. Kinser has returned to Camp Cooke, Calif.fl, after spending a 17-day furlough with his wife, Mrs. Edna Kinser and son, Duane, also his parents, Mr. and Mrs. Charles Kinser and family, Williamsport.

The flag poles at City Hall and the World War I Memorial are flying new flags, replacing those that were slightly worn.

COMPLETES TRAINING

Aviation Cadet Raymond H. Miller, Jr., 21, of Clear Spring, has completed his basic flight training at the Coffeyville, Kan., Army Air Field and has gone on to an advanced field where he will finish his cadet training and win his wings in the AAF. Cadet Miller attended Lehigh University at Bethlehem, Pa., 1941-1943. He is the son of Mr. and Mrs. Raymond H. Miller, Sr., of Clear Spring.

EIGHT CALLED—EIGHT IN

Eight of our citizens (all married) were called for induction the last week of February and all went thru the mill with flying colors. Five were assigned to the Army; three to the Navy. Where is that guy who said the cream of the crop left last year?

Subscribe to The Dug-Out!

WILLIAM SHIPLEY NAMED PATROLMAN

Citizens of Williamsport will receive a two-fold measure of protection against violators of the law, beginning in March, according to a recent announcement of the Town Council. William Shipley has been named patrolman to fill a position that has been vacant two months because of the induction of Officer Elwood Davis. Bill, who is local Boy Scout leader and a former Navy man handled the duties of this position several years ago, but resigned to go into defense work.

In addition to this the community will have the permanent services of a State patrolman who will have his office in the City Hall. This marks the first time that we have had this extra protection and our folks are quite appreciative to those responsible for obtaining it.

FURLOUGH PARTY HELD

Mr. and Mrs. Charles A. Myers entertained at their home in Williamsport in honor of their son, Corporal Wilbur J. Myers, who has been spending a two-week furlough with his parents. He has now returned to Camp Campbell, Ky. Guests at the party were: Mr. and Mrs. Voss Moser, Mr. and Mrs. Pete Stenger, M.r and Mrs. Richard Kesselring, Corporal and Mrs. W. J. Myers and son, Ronnie; Mr. and Mrs. James Fazenbaker, Mrs. Dorine M. Herbert, Ivy, Bobbie, Jim, Bill, Harriette and Tom Myers; H. C. Stenger, Elaine Moser, Margie and Dixie Lee Stenger, Dick and June Kesselring and Jack Fazenbaker.

SUCKERS RUNNING

The mild weather on tap at the opening of the dip-net season found the finny tribe quite plentiful and some nice catches were reported out of the Antietam and Potomac.

The front page of this March 10, 1944, issue of *The Dug-Out* highlights a picture of a Liberty ship named for one of Williamsport's own. The *William D. Byron* Liberty ship was launched by Katherine E. Byron at the Bethlehem-Fairfield shipyards in Baltimore with a number of Williamsport citizens there to watch the ceremonies. The rest of this front page also makes entertaining reading about local goings-on in Williamsport. (Courtesy Williamsport Town Museum.)

IMAGES
of America

WILLIAMSPORT

Mary H. Rubin

ARCADIA
PUBLISHING

ISBN 978-0-7385-4176-1

Published by Arcadia Publishing
Charleston, South Carolina

Printed in the United States of America

Library of Congress Catalog Card Number: 2005926758

For all general information contact Arcadia Publishing at:
Telephone 843-853-2070
Fax 843-853-0044
E-mail sales@arcadiapublishing.com
For customer service and orders:
Toll-Free 1-888-313-2665

Visit us on the Internet at www.arcadiapublishing.com

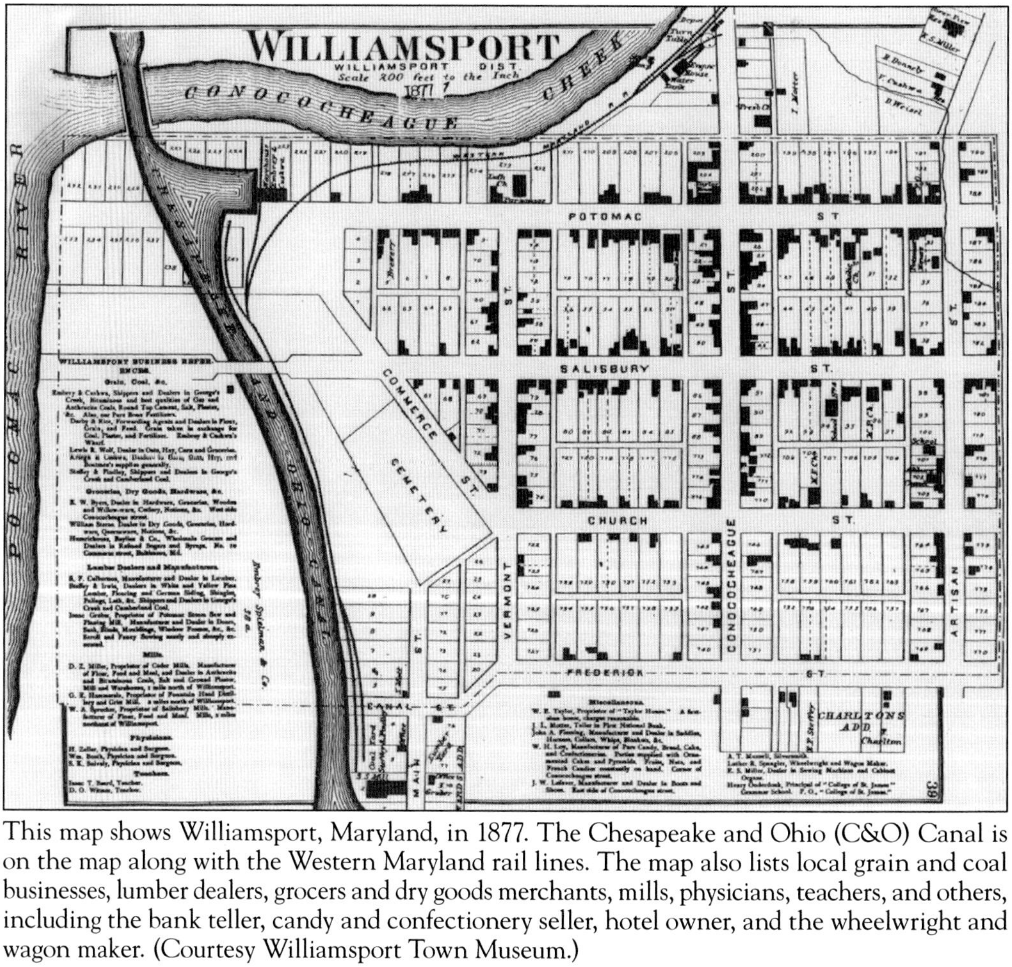

This map shows Williamsport, Maryland, in 1877. The Chesapeake and Ohio (C&O) Canal is on the map along with the Western Maryland rail lines. The map also lists local grain and coal businesses, lumber dealers, grocers and dry goods merchants, mills, physicians, teachers, and others, including the bank teller, candy and confectionery seller, hotel owner, and the wheelwright and wagon maker. (Courtesy Williamsport Town Museum.)

Contents

ACKNOWLEDGMENTS

The author wishes to gratefully acknowledge all the help provided by everyone at the Williamsport Town Museum, in particular Gerald and Joan Knode and Maurice Snyder. Their generosity in opening their collection to me made this title possible, and their stories of years and times past helped bring the photographs to life. They also provided invaluable time and services as proofreaders of the text for accuracy. Also grateful thanks go to Frank Woodring for providing additional photographs and information from the *Maryland Cracker Barrel* magazine. The C&O Canal National Historical Park, as well as the Western Maryland Room of the Washington County Free Library, were also very generous in opening their collections to allow the utmost range of sources for this title. The author would also like to thank Kay Rubin for ongoing and continuous enthusiastic assistance in helping gather and research information. Last but not least, thanks to everyone in the community for continued support of my efforts to document our region's history.

INTRODUCTION

If you've taken a close look at Washington County's flag, you'll note that it bears the head of George Washington. The initial "W" is included in the design in honor of the man for whom the county was named. The flag also includes nine stars representing the nine incorporated towns in the county. The largest star represents Hagerstown, the county seat, but the next star represents Williamsport, incorporated in 1823, the second of the nine towns.

Williamsport holds the honor of being the site of Washington County's first settlement, known as Conococheague, dating back to the late 1730s. The small settlement, situated on the banks of the Potomac River and Conococheague Creek, served as a trading post, one of the last vestiges of civilization for those heading out to explore and settle the great untamed West. The locale is named from the Native American terms "Conococheague," meaning "a long way," and "Potomac," meaning "among the black walnuts" (also meaning "trading place" in the Algonquin tongue). Spelling of the word Conococheague varied greatly in early years, when standardized spelling was not given the importance it holds today. Variations included the Conogsgee and Conegocheagh spellings used by early Maryland governor Horatio Sharpe, the spelling Connogogee and Conogogee used by Gen. Edward Braddock during the French and Indian War, and finally, an early newspaper that used today's current spelling.

George Washington was one of the area's honored visitors over the years, and, having been given permission to locate the new nation's capital along the Potomac, he gave heavy consideration to the town that Otho Holland Williams had laid out, then known as Williams-Port. Unfortunately areas such as Great Falls made the river unnavigable along its full length, and the capital was duly situated in Washington, D.C., instead. Washington, however, had additional interests in the region, including the possibility of a canal running west to meet the Ohio River.

The Chesapeake and Ohio Canal was designed to meet the need for a faster method of transporting goods to and from the West. So named because it was intended to begin at the Chesapeake Bay and continue on to the Ohio River, the canal follows the route of the Potomac River. The first spade of dirt for the canal was turned on July 4, 1828, and the canal arrived in Williamsport in 1834. The town became a boomtown with the arrival of the canal and grew to be the county's second largest town. Business and industry flourished in this major port along the canal. Citizens became known as "river rats" in this true canal town. The railroad opened lines into Washington County with the intention of competing with the canal for the transportation of both goods and passengers. The Baltimore and Ohio (B&O) Railroad, the first railroad in the United States, was also begun in 1828 and, in fact, reached Cumberland, Maryland, the terminus of the canal, before the canal construction reached that point. The coming of the railroads spelled the beginning of the end for the canal, and, after damage from floods and financial difficulties, the canal closed in 1924. Highway development then encroached on the heyday of the railroads. After World War II, the region became more "suburbanized," the population began to look to areas outside Williamsport and Washington County itself for employment, and the town's "boom" was something fading into the past.

Other history of national significance has also taken place in and near Williamsport. With the 20/20 hindsight given after the fact, Williamsport was in a position to have played a role in perhaps ending the Civil War two years early. After Gettysburg, the Confederate troops retreated to Williamsport, where high waters on the Potomac prevented them from crossing back into Virginia. With the Confederate army trapped between the flooded Potomac and the oncoming Union forces, Lincoln tried to get Union commanders to deliver the final blow that might have been the deciding blow in the war. However, the commanders did not have a clear appreciation of what their victory at Gettysburg meant and knew only that their troops needed rest. The commanders hesitated to risk their weary men again, and while they were deliberating, the river receded enough to allow Lee to escape to the other side.

This is just the beginning of the rich history associated with Williamsport. Historical accounts tell stories of the affluent lifestyles of those living in large homes in the area and of imported furniture and costly coaches traveling the early roads with English coach dogs running alongside. Other accounts document the accomplishments of George Williamson (grandson of Eli Whitney of cotton gin fame) the railroad engineer who actually cut through the mountains. Williamson ended his career as a teacher in Williamsport and is buried in Riverview Cemetery.

So the sound of clip-clopping mules along the towpath has faded into the past now, the train whistle no longer blows, and Williamsport has reverted to the quintessential American small hometown. But size does not dictate history, and Williamsport can be deservedly proud of the role it has played in shaping our great nation. Now let's turn the pages of time back and revisit Williamsport's past.

One

The Early Years

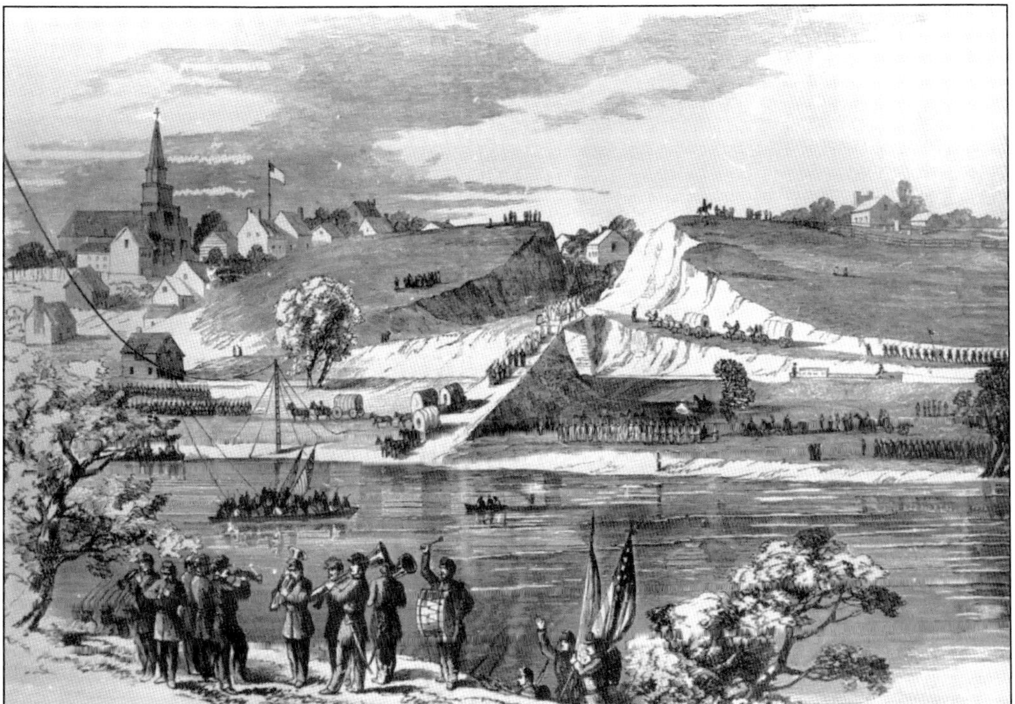

This sketch is from a drawing made by Edwin Forbes that was published in *Frank Leslie's Illustrated Newspaper* on July 5, 1862. The sketch is of a division of the National army under Gen. Nathaniel P. Banks recrossing the Potomac River from Williamsport to attack the Rebel army under Gen. Stonewall Jackson. A canal boat passes on the right, and the band of the 46th Pennsylvania Volunteers is playing the National Airs on what was at that time the Virginia (now West Virginia) shore. (Courtesy Williamsport Town Museum.)

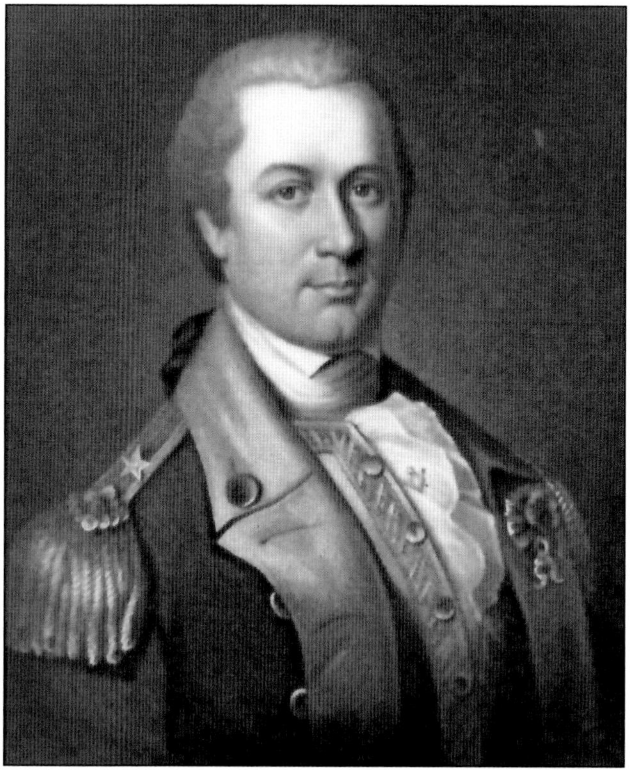

This painting portrays Gen. Otho Holland Williams, the founder of Williams-Port (later truncated to simply Williamsport). The Revolutionary War hero had plans to make his town a great city on the banks of the Potomac and, with this in mind, laid out wide main streets for the town. Williams is buried in Riverview Cemetery in the town he gave his name to, and there is a monument there that was erected to his memory in 1882. (Courtesy Williamsport Town Museum.)

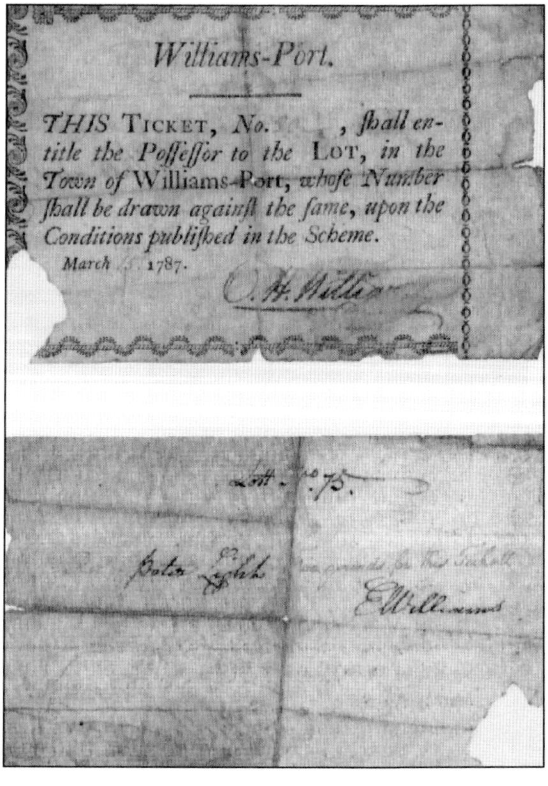

Williams-Port.

THIS TICKET, *No.*   , *ſhall entitle the Poſſeſſor to the* LOT, *in the Town of* Williams-Port, *whoſe Number ſhall be drawn againſt the ſame, upon the Conditions publiſhed in the Scheme.*

March . 1787.

O. H. Willia

Lott No. 75

Peter Light

E Williams

This rare item, shown front and back, is a lottery ticket from March 15, 1787, when Otho Holland Williams was parceling out the various lots he had segmented his grant into. The signatures on the back appear to be Peter Light and E. Williams. (Courtesy Williamsport Town Museum.)

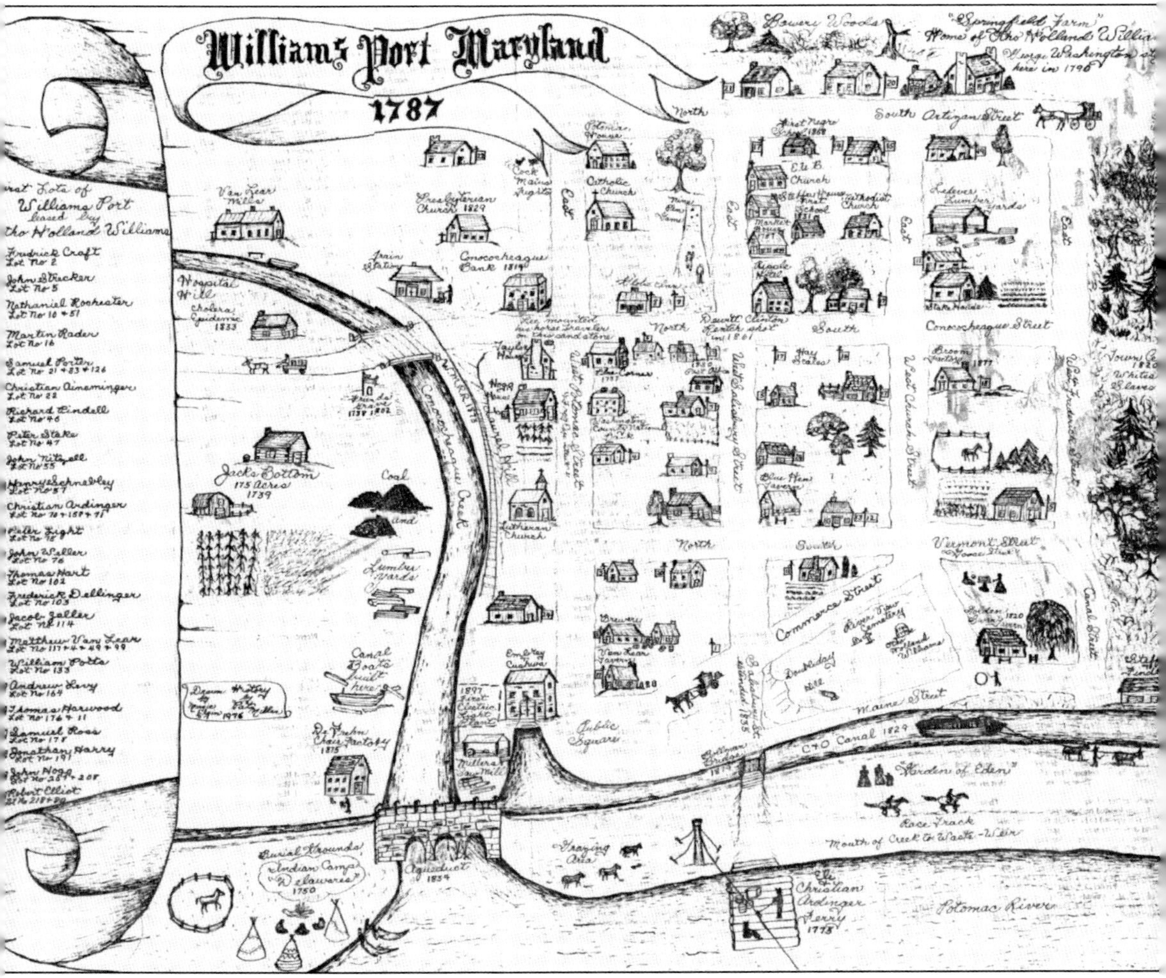

This hand-drawn map by Margie Elgin and Pat Miller from 1976 shows a lot of important dates and places in Williamsport's history along with a list of tenants of the first lots leased by Otho Holland Williams. The broom factory from 1877 is shown on W. Church Street. The first African American school in Washington County, from 1868, is on Artizan Street. The market house, Washington County National Bank, the Hotel Ripple, the train station, Hospital Hill (site of the burial of many canal workers who died during the construction from a cholera outbreak in 1833), and much, much more are all here. (Courtesy Williamsport Town Museum.)

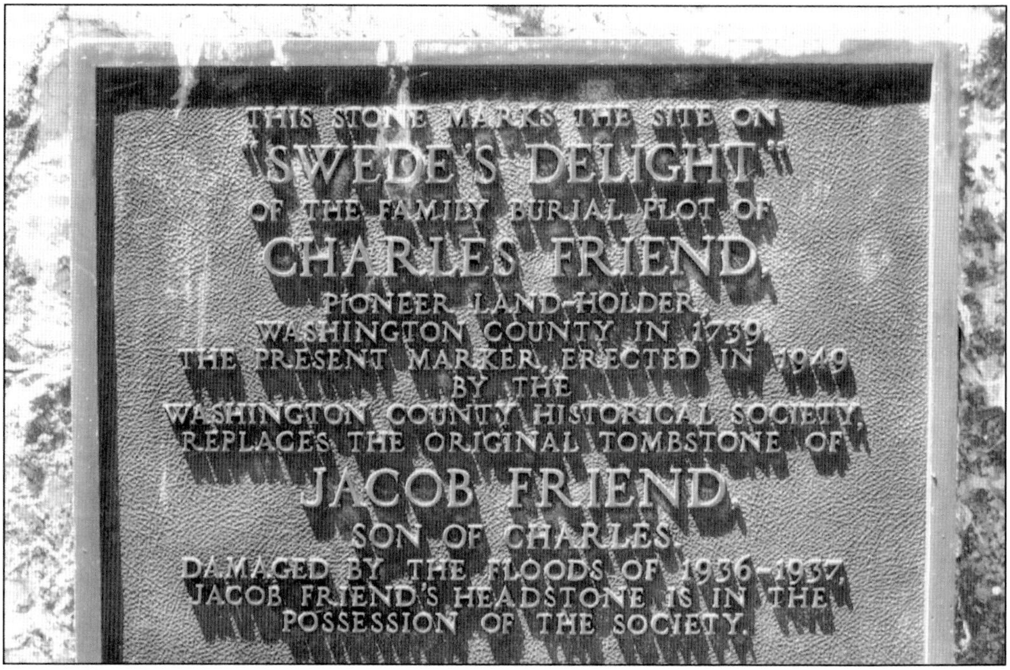

Generally acknowledged as Washington County's first permanent resident, Charles Friend settled with his family at the mouth of the Conococheague Creek in 1732 and named his home Swede's Delight. Rival Delaware and Catawba tribes battled constantly in the region, which explains in part why the western part of the state was settled so long after Eastern Maryland was flourishing. Friend's location on the Conococheague was considered a strategic outpost, and General Braddock used it as base to store ammunition during his advance to Fort Duquesne. (Courtesy Mary H. Rubin.)

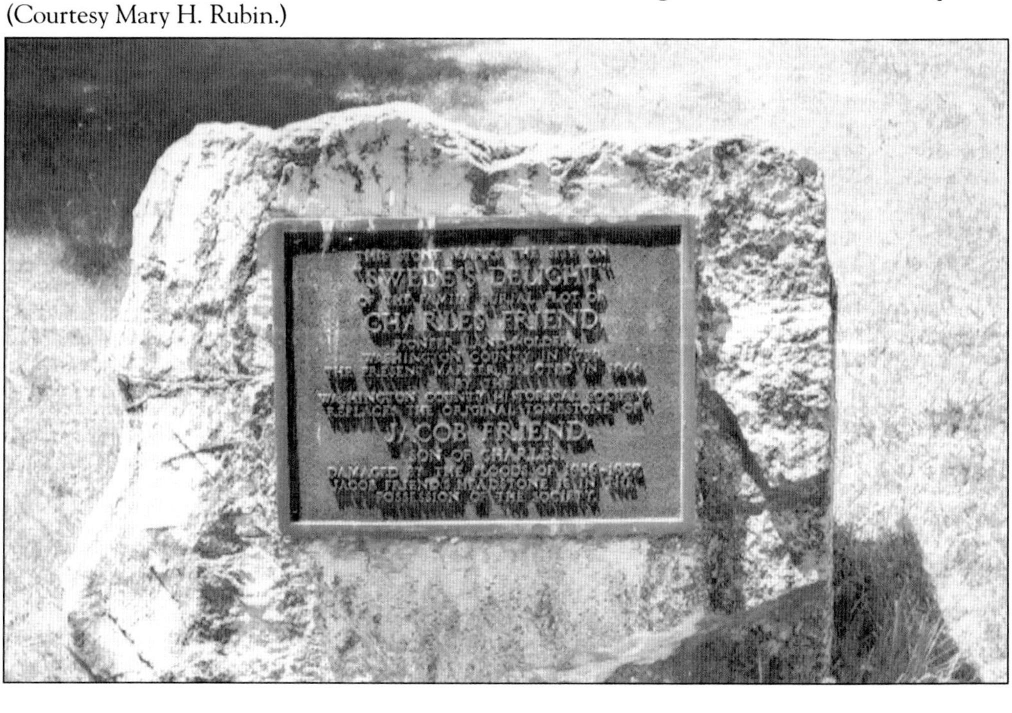

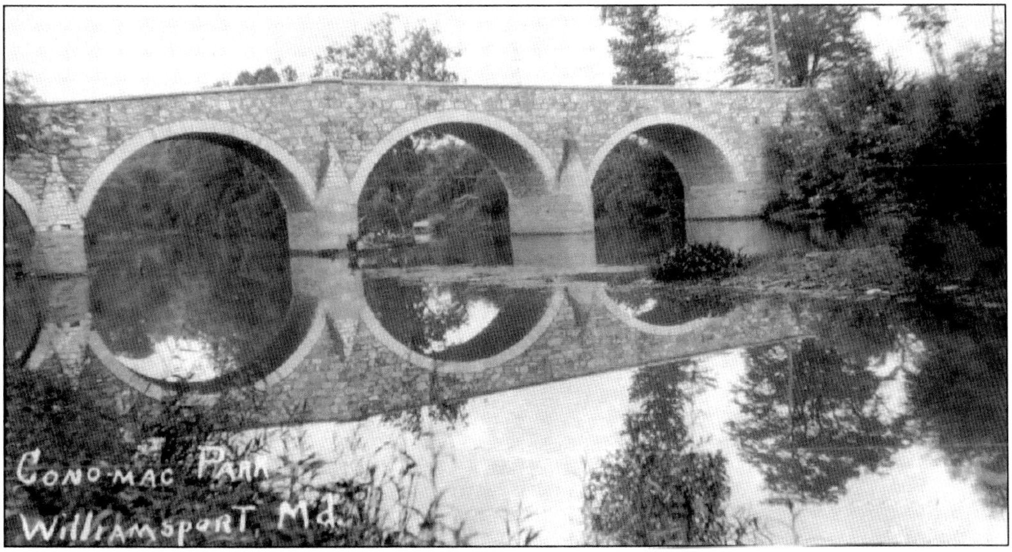

This 1879 photograph shows the stone Conococheague Creek Bridge near Conomac Park. The four-arch bridge was constructed in 1829 by Charles Wilson and Company. The west end of the bridge rests on land that was part of Swede's Delight, the tract of land granted to Charles Friend. Regarded as "wonders of their day" at the time of construction, the stone bridges of the county were nevertheless objects of much speculation as to their durability. The Conococheague Creek Bridge has survived major remodeling to widen the roadbed but is still resting firmly on the original arches first erected over 170 years ago. (Courtesy Williamsport Town Museum.)

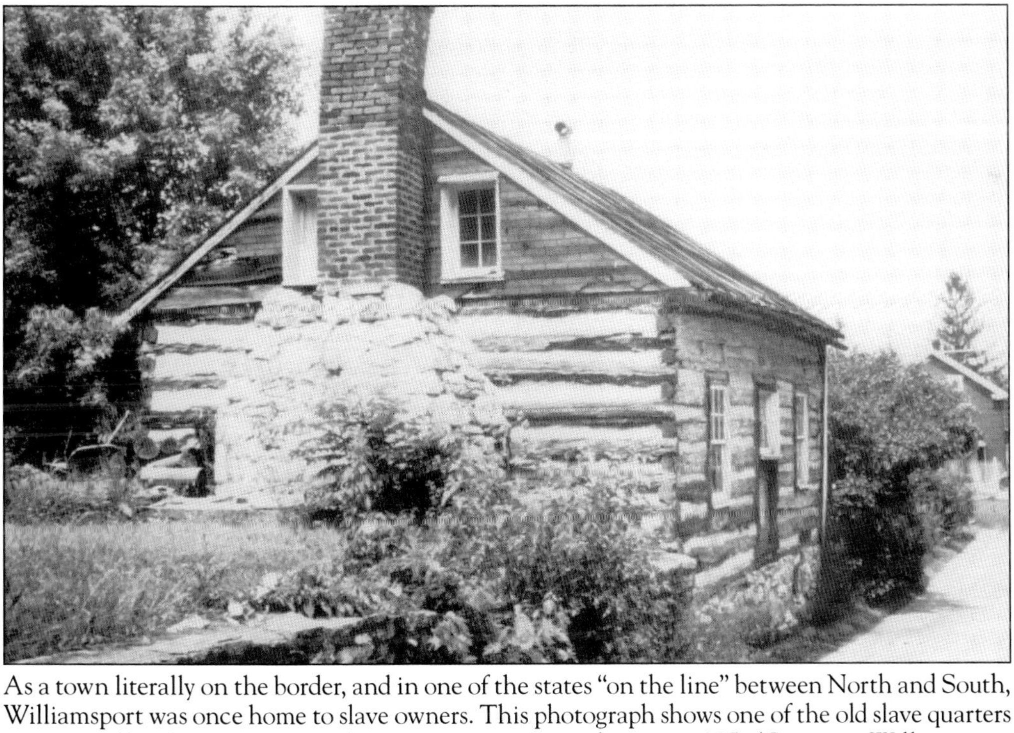

As a town literally on the border, and in one of the states "on the line" between North and South, Williamsport was once home to slave owners. This photograph shows one of the old slave quarters in town off Salisbury Street. The structure was torn down in 1995. (Courtesy Williamsport Town Museum.)

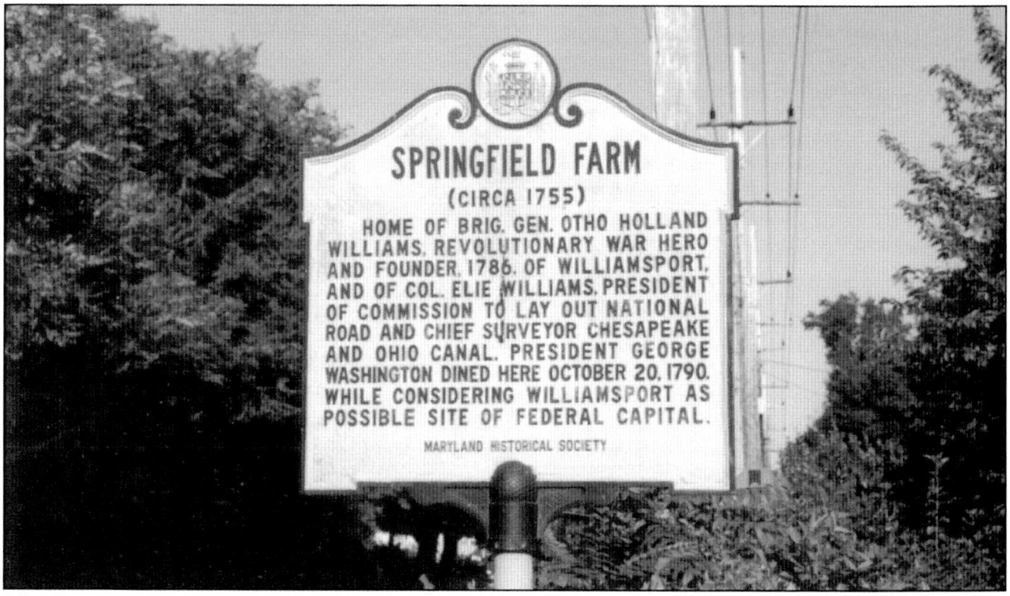

This historical marker is located on U.S. Route 11 near the lane leading to Springfield Farm. As the marker indicates, the farm predates the town of Williamsport itself. At one time, a drive-in movie theater was located near the entrance lane along the Williamsport-Hagerstown Highway (U.S. Route 11). The drive-in was still in operation into the 1960s. (Courtesy Williamsport Town Museum.)

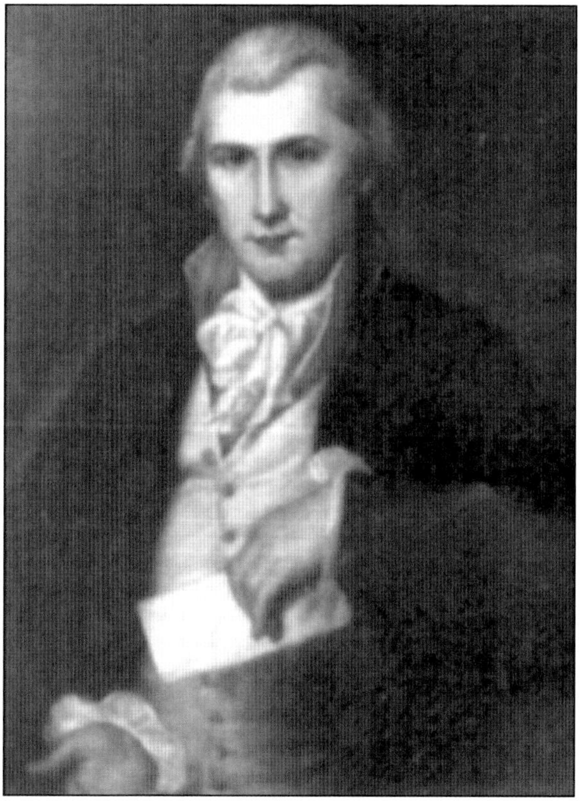

This image shows Col. Elie Williams, the brother of Williamsport's founder, Otho Holland Williams. Elie lived in Springfield during the late 18th century and was host to Pres. George Washington on his visits to the region. Elie also served as clerk of Washington County Court until 1800. (Courtesy *Maryland Cracker Barrel.*)

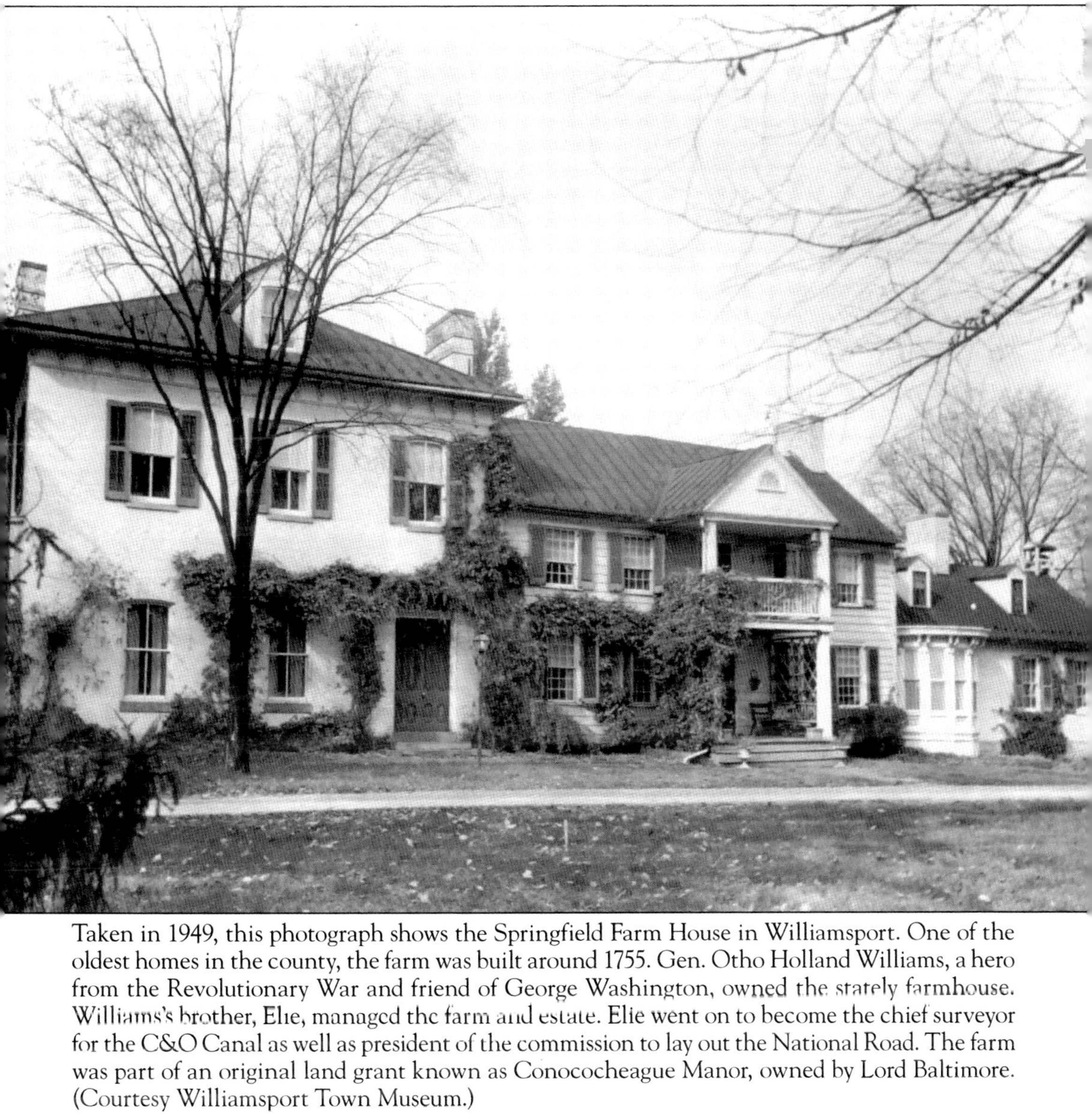

Taken in 1949, this photograph shows the Springfield Farm House in Williamsport. One of the oldest homes in the county, the farm was built around 1755. Gen. Otho Holland Williams, a hero from the Revolutionary War and friend of George Washington, owned the stately farmhouse. Williams's brother, Elie, managed the farm and estate. Elie went on to become the chief surveyor for the C&O Canal as well as president of the commission to lay out the National Road. The farm was part of an original land grant known as Conococheague Manor, owned by Lord Baltimore. (Courtesy Williamsport Town Museum.)

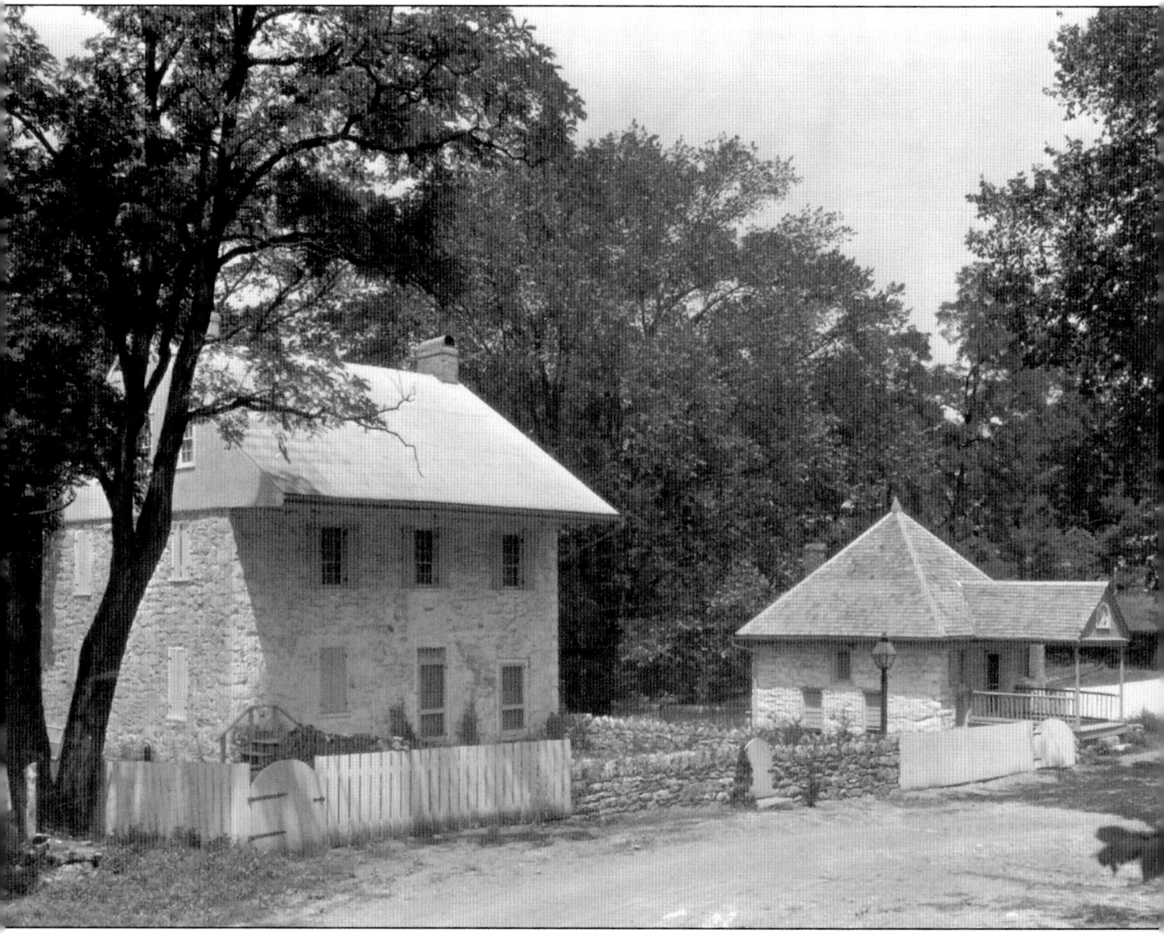

This 1941 photograph shows the Springhouse and Still House at Springfield Farm. The Springhouse was built by Thomas Cresap (founder of Cresaptown in Allegany county) over the spring from which Springfield derives its name. Built of local limestone, the upper-story contained Cresap's living quarters. The spring provided a source of fresh water in the event of any attacks from natives in the area. George Washington visited Washington County in October 1790 and after visiting Hagerstown on October 20, traveled on to Williamsport the next day to dine at Springfield Farm. Washington was seriously considering locating the capital of the new nation here in Williamsport. He also was interested in the Potomac River's navigational possibilities, which would later lead to the C&O Canal. The Still House was used to convert local grain into rye whiskey, which was a major source of income to the county (a gallon of whiskey was valued at the equivalent of a shilling). It is thought that Pres. George Washington visited Williamsport and stayed at Springfield Farm for a second time on October 13, 1793, during the Whiskey Rebellion. (Courtesy Washington County Historical Society.)

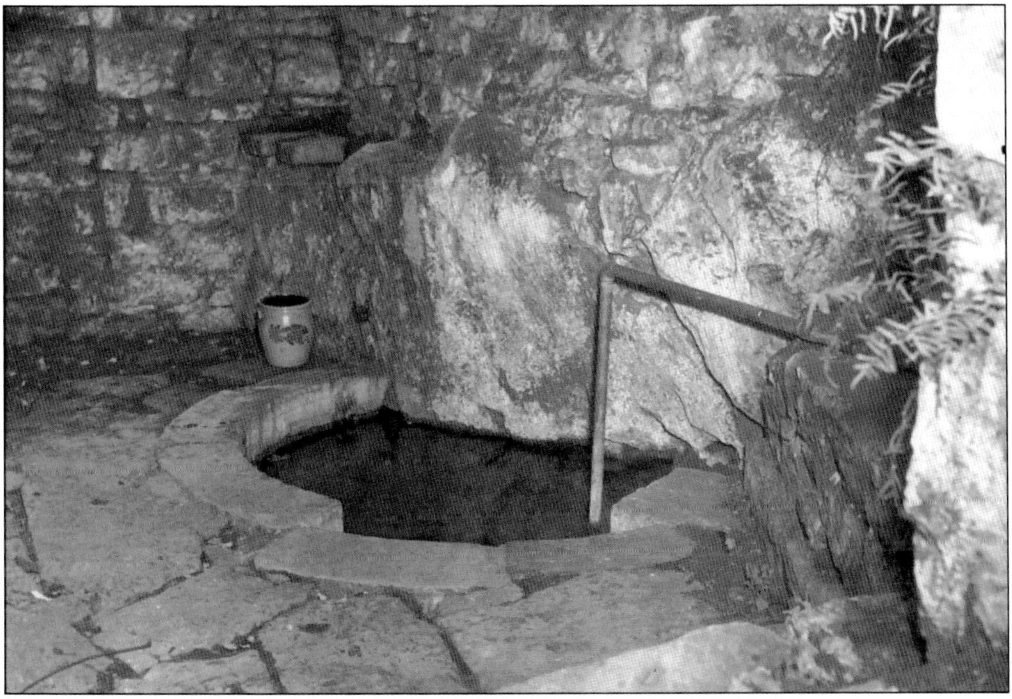

This 1949 photograph depicts the spring at Springfield Farm that George Washington and General Braddock reportedly drank from upon a visit. (Courtesy Washington County Historical Society.)

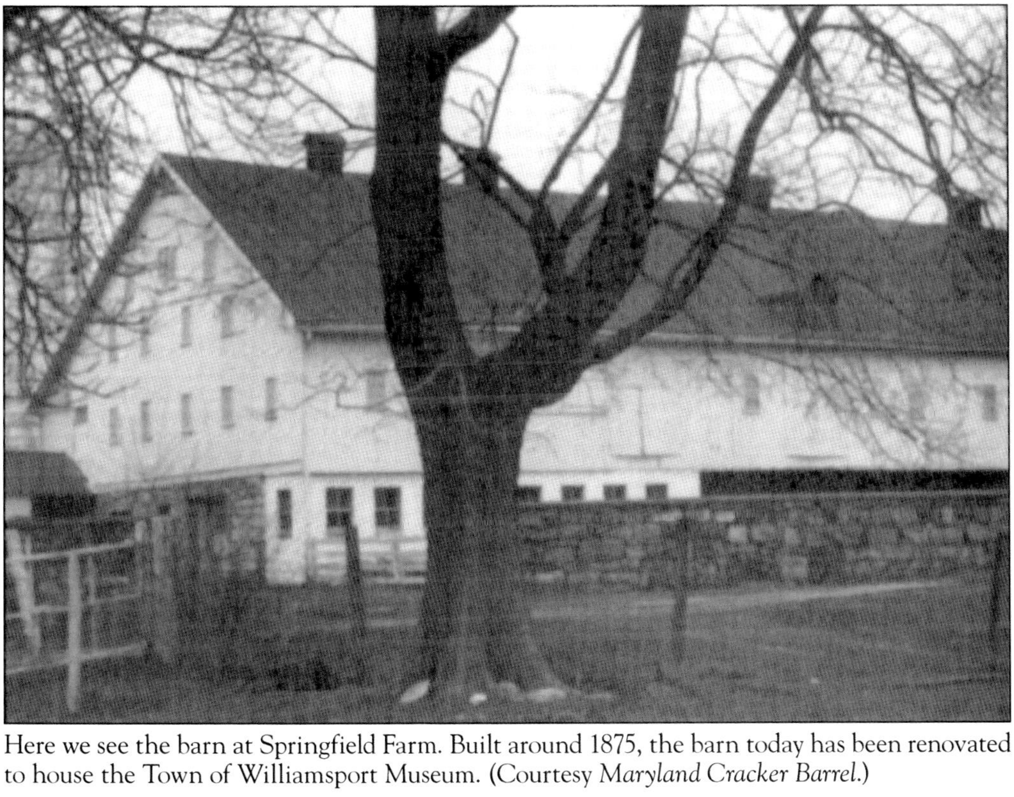

Here we see the barn at Springfield Farm. Built around 1875, the barn today has been renovated to house the Town of Williamsport Museum. (Courtesy *Maryland Cracker Barrel*.)

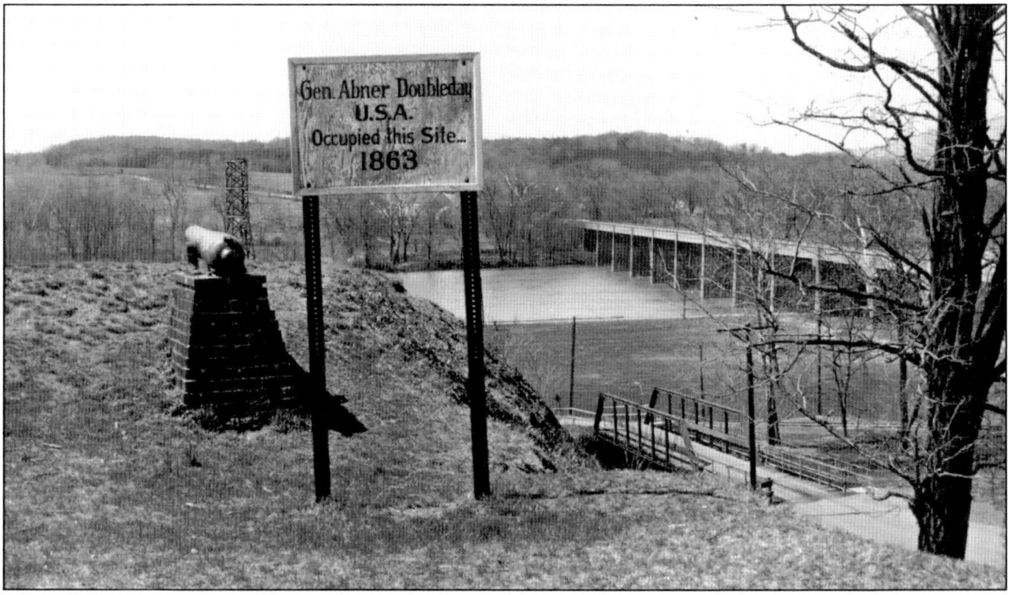

This photograph shows Doubleday Hill in Williamsport. It was occupied by Gen. Abner Doubleday, and the first shots across the Potomac during the Civil War were fired from here. Doubleday is often credited with creating the game of baseball in 1839, and his name has stuck with the public, though authoritative sources do not uphold this theory. (Courtesy Western Maryland Room Washington County Free Library.)

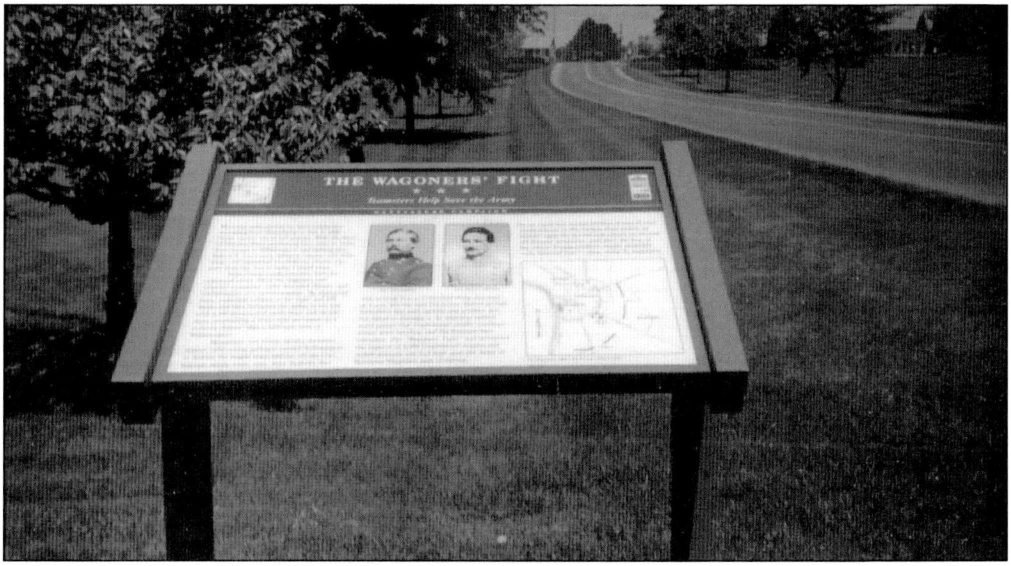

This historic marker along the Gettysburg Campaign Civil War Trail is located just inside the entrance to the Red Men facilities on U.S. Route 68. The marker details information on the Wagoners' Fight on July 6, 1863. During their retreat from Gettysburg, Confederate troops guarded a 17-mile long column of wagons carrying several thousand wounded soldiers back to Virginia. Union cavalry arrived and tried to stop the retreat but the Confederates, along with 700 wagoners pressed into service, held back the Union troops and prevented the capture of not only the wounded but also almost all of Lee's transportation of 4,000 wagons and 10,000 horses. (Courtesy Mary H. Rubin.)

Two

People, Places, and Events

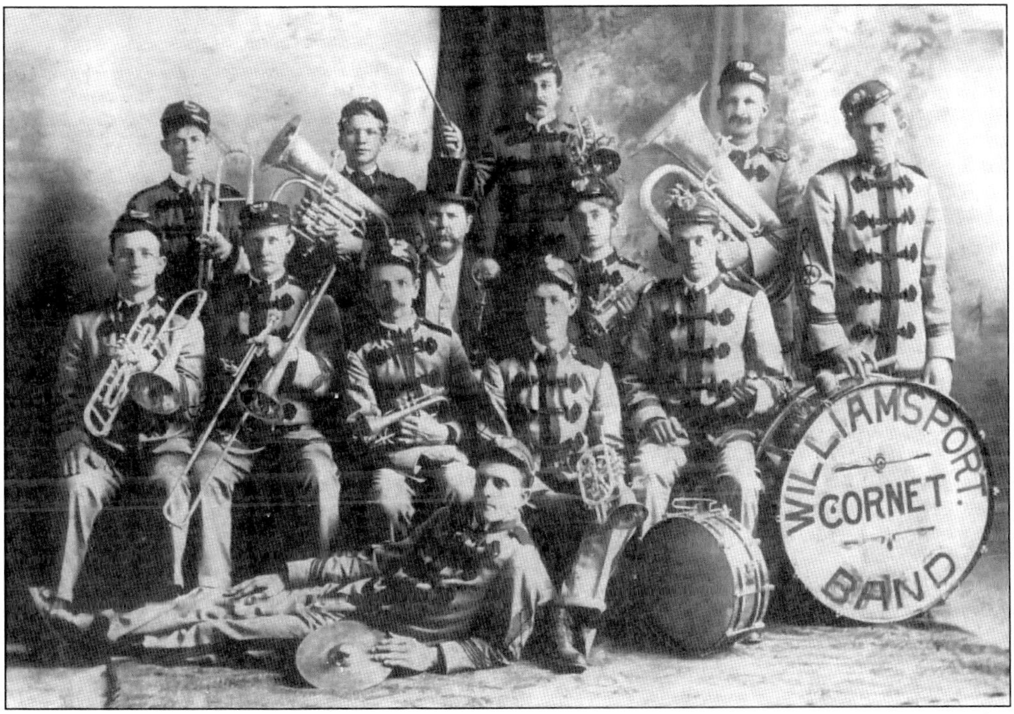

This photograph depicts Williamsport's Cornet Band. Town bands have always been popular throughout Washington County, and in the days before modern roads and transportation made travel between towns quick and easy, even small communities had their own band. In 1928, the Williamsport Community Band traveled to Houston, Texas, to represent the state of Maryland at the Democratic National Convention. (Courtesy Williamsport Town Museum.)

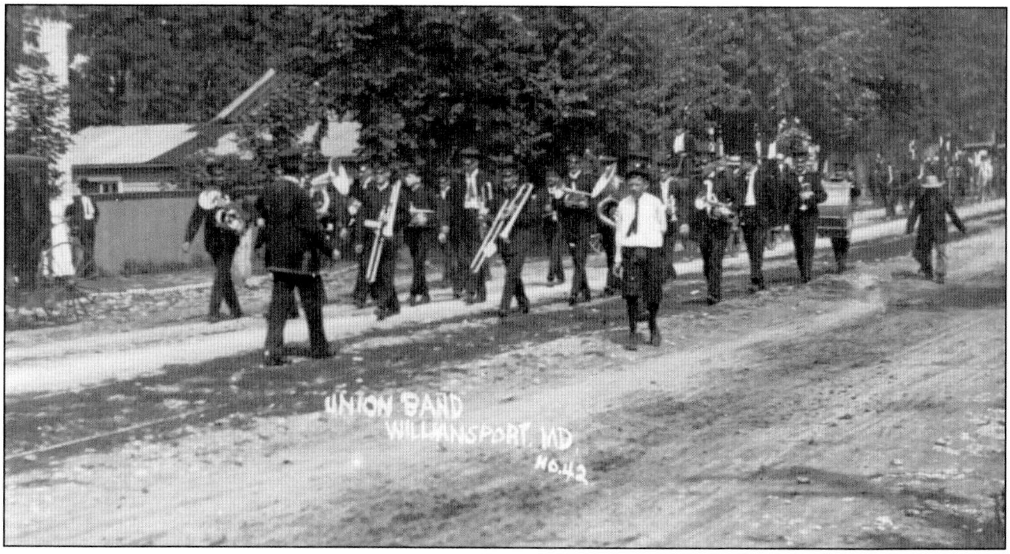

Here is a view of the town's popular Union Band marching along. Note the streets appear to be unpaved at the time of this photograph, and a horse-drawn buggy can be seen off to the left. Old records show that Williamsport's town band tradition dates back quite a number of years; in 1837, the town is said to have owned a bassoon, a bugle, two French horns, and four clarinets. (Courtesy Williamsport Town Museum.)

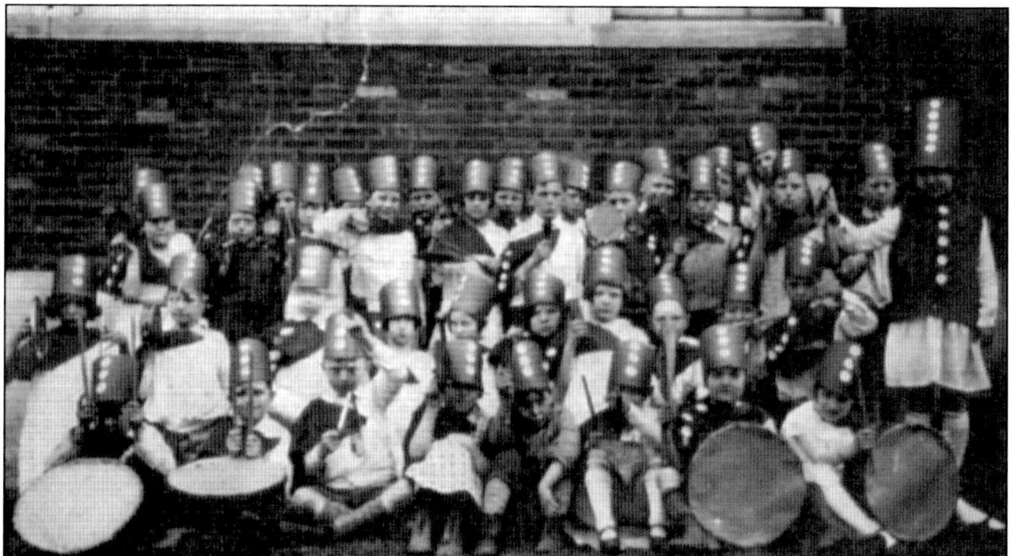

The youngsters weren't left out of the town's musical affairs, as we see in this image. The school photograph from Lola Myers Kesselring shows the Primary School Band complete with uniforms and drum major. (Courtesy Williamsport Town Museum.)

Here is a copy of the front and back, as well as an interior page, detailing part of the program from a February 5, 1898, concert given by the Williamsport Cornet Band. The band's officers and members are listed on the back cover. The concert included piano and voice solos, as well as a solo on the euphonium—an tuba-like instrument of the brass family. (Courtesy Williamsport Town Museum.)

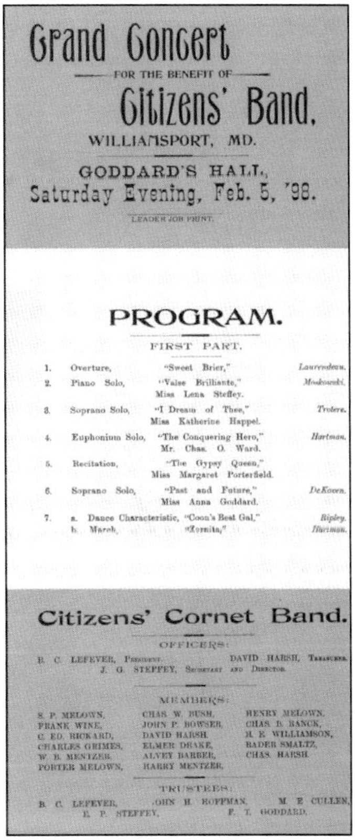

Grand Concert
FOR THE BENEFIT OF
Citizens' Band,
WILLIAMSPORT, MD.
GODDARD'S HALL,
Saturday Evening, Feb. 5, '98.
LEADER JOB PRINT.

PROGRAM.

FIRST PART.

1. Overture, "Sweet Brier," *Laurendeau.*
2. Piano Solo, "Valse Brilliante," Miss Lena Steffey. *Moskowski.*
3. Soprano Solo, "I Dream of Thee," Miss Katherine Happel. *Trotere.*
4. Euphonium Solo, "The Conquering Hero," Mr. Chas. O. Ward. *Hartman.*
5. Recitation, "The Gypsy Queen," Miss Margaret Porterfield.
6. Soprano Solo, "Past and Future," Miss Anna Goddard. *DeKoven.*
7. a. Dance Characteristic, "Coon's Best Gal," *Ripley.*
   b. March, "Zormita," *Hartman.*

Citizens' Cornet Band.

OFFICERS:

B. C. LEFEVER, President. DAVID HARSH, Treasurer.
J. G. STEFFEY, Secretary and Director.

MEMBERS:

S. P. MELOWN,	CHAS. W. BUSH,	HENRY MELOWN,
FRANK WINE,	JOHN P. BOWSER,	CHAS. B. BANCK,
C. ED. RICKARD,	DAVID HARSH,	H. E. WILLIAMSON,
CHARLES GRIMES,	ELMER DRAKE,	BADER SMALTZ,
W. B. MENTZER,	ALVEY BARBER,	CHAS. HARSH.
PORTER MELOWN,	HARRY MENTZER,	

TRUSTEES:

B. C. LEFEVER, JOHN H. HOFFMAN, M. E. CULLEN,
E. P. STEFFEY, F. T. GODDARD.

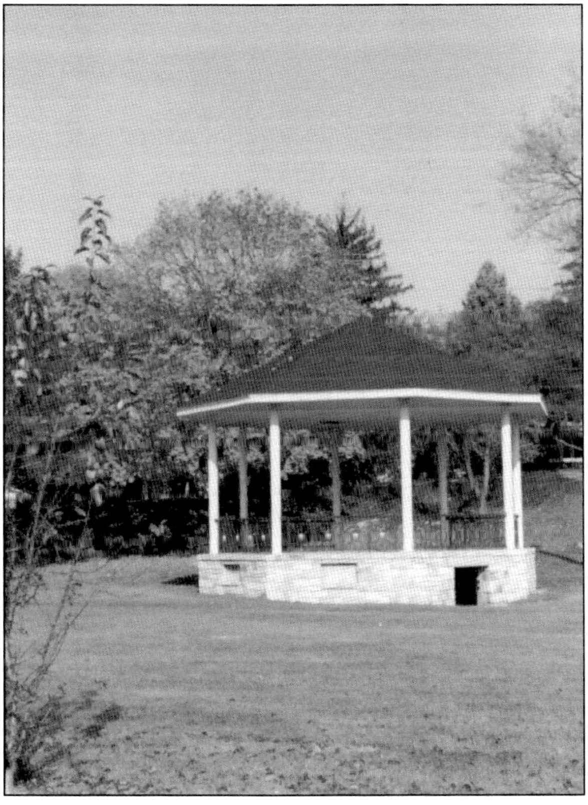

What's a town band without a place to play? Here is the gazebo-like bandstand located in Byron Memorial Park. At one time, the World War I memorial stood here before moving to its present location at the American Legion. (Courtesy Williamsport Town Museum.)

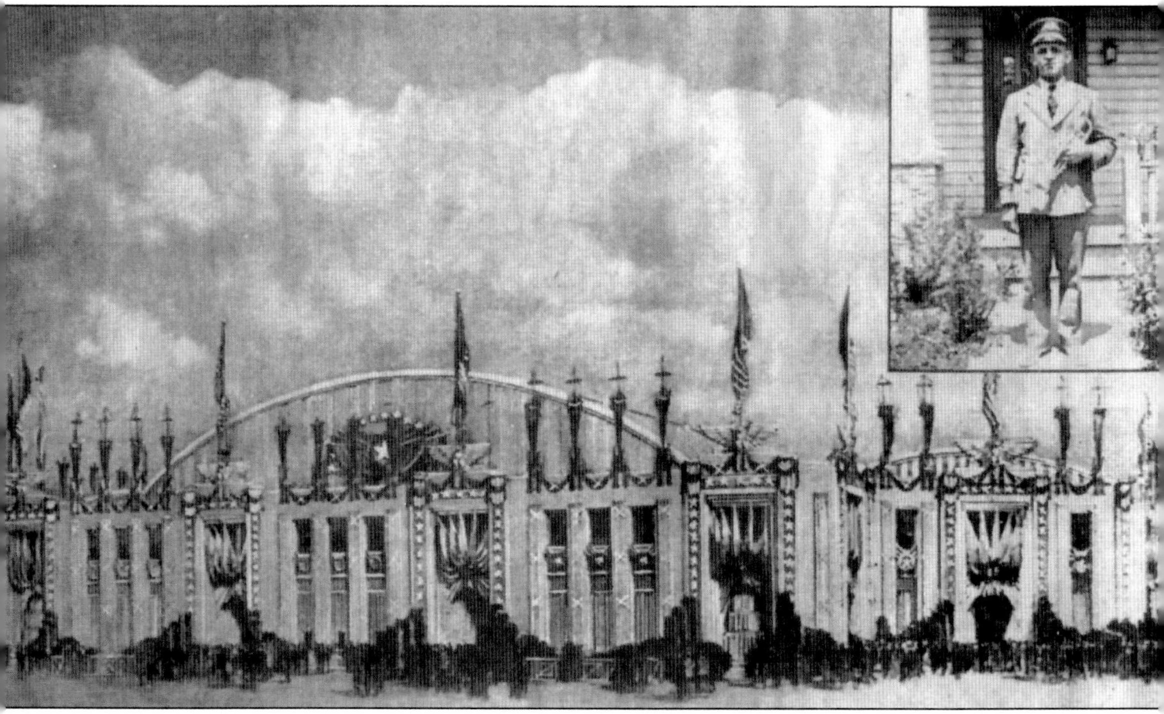

The Williamsport Community Band went to the Democratic Convention in Houston, Texas, in 1928 in support of then-Maryland governor Albert Ritchie, who was running for the presidential nomination on the Democratic ticket. The band traveled and lived on a special railroad car while in Texas. Just a few of the popular tunes the band played to great acclaim included *Maryland, My Maryland*, *Dixie*, and *The Sidewalks of New York*. The convention center in Houston is shown in this photograph along with an inset photograph of Beckley Harsh, a member of the band, standing proudly in his uniform just before leaving for the trip. The band was the only one from east of the Mississippi in attendance at the gala event. (Courtesy Williamsport Town Museum.)

The 50th Anniversary of Bryon Memorial Park was in 1999. A 1941 photograph of the park highlights this cover from the May 15, 1999, rededication program. The park was named in memory of former Williamsport mayor William D. Byron. Bryon also served as the Maryland Sixth District U.S. Congressman. (Courtesy Williamsport Town Museum.)

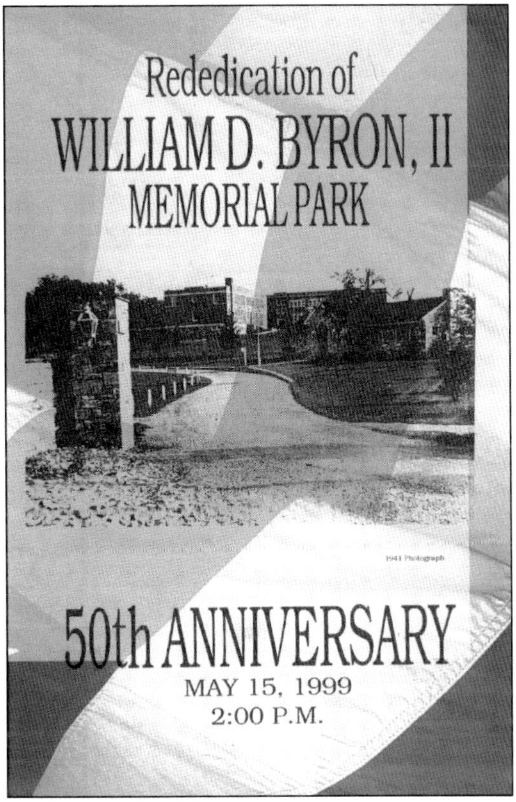

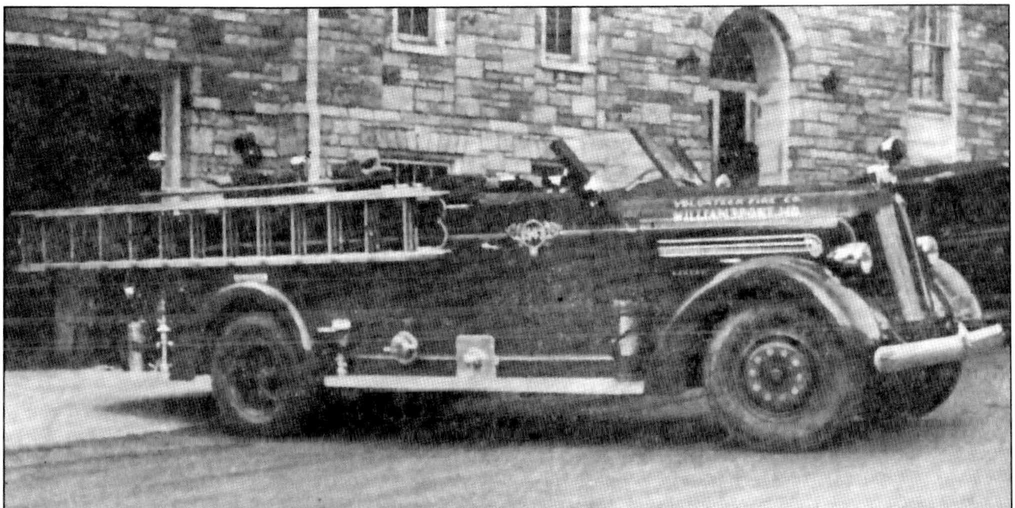

Williamsport has had several fire companies over the years. The first, known as the Williamsport Fire Company, was formed on November 14, 1839. The company engine, called the "Lark," was destroyed during the Civil War. Today's Volunteer Fire Company is housed in a modern firehouse on Conococheague Street, and when the fire whistle blows in town calling the volunteers to work, everyone hears it! (Courtesy Williamsport Town Museum.)

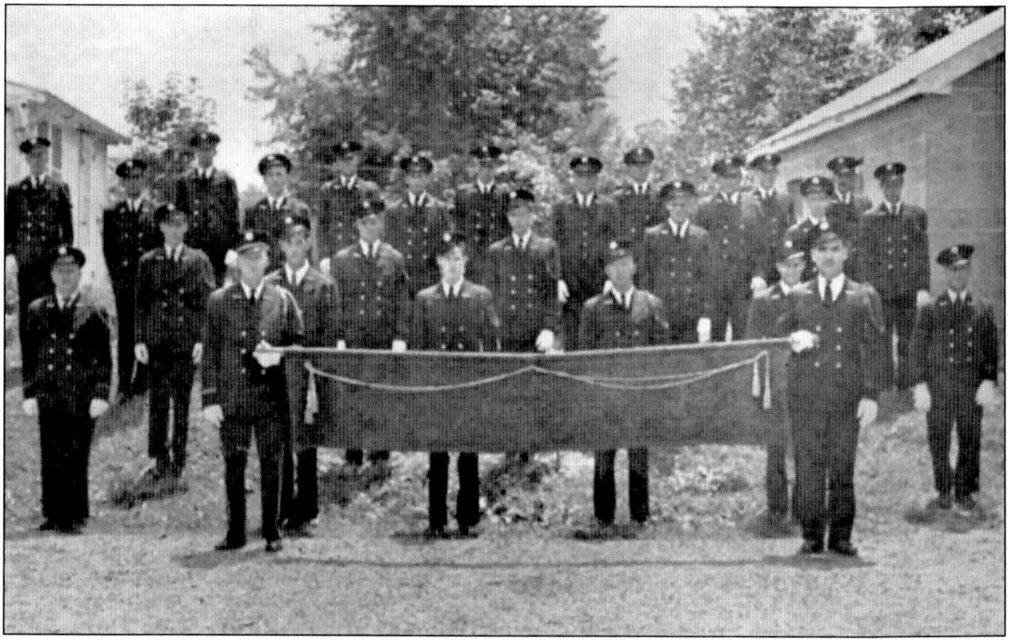

The Williamsport Volunteer Fire Company Drill Team was organized in August 1946 and had 40 members just two short months later. The team entered six parades right away in 1946 and was awarded two first and two third prizes. This 1948 photograph shows the team in their navy blue uniforms trimmed with red cord. (Courtesy Williamsport Town Museum.)

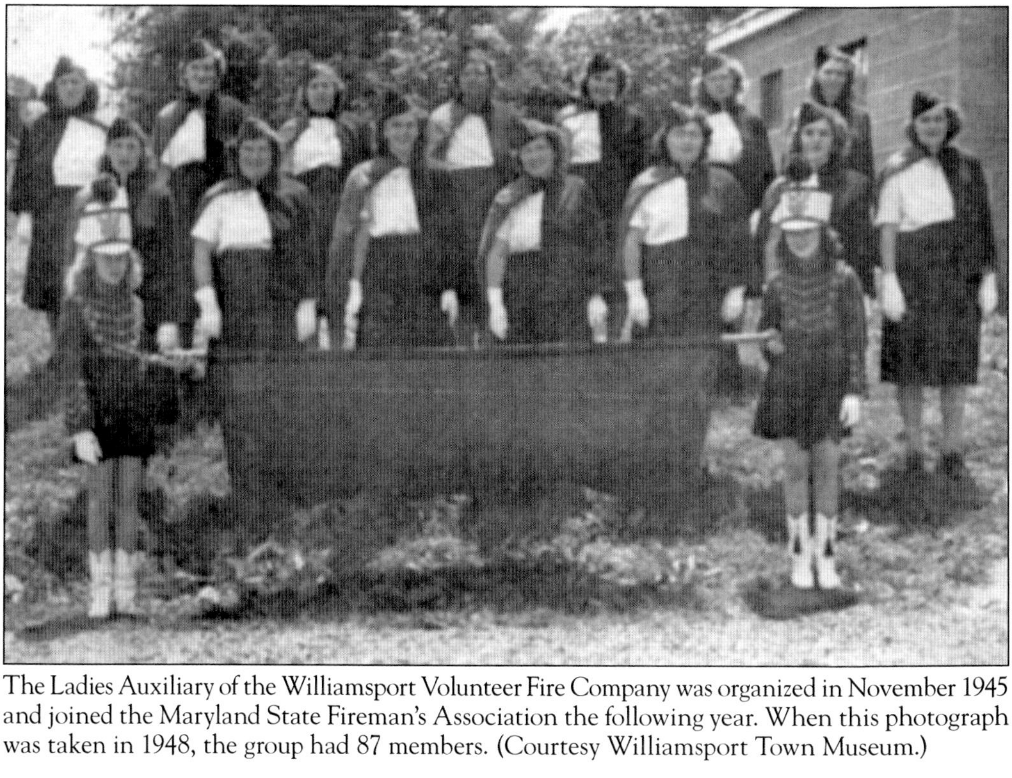

The Ladies Auxiliary of the Williamsport Volunteer Fire Company was organized in November 1945 and joined the Maryland State Fireman's Association the following year. When this photograph was taken in 1948, the group had 87 members. (Courtesy Williamsport Town Museum.)

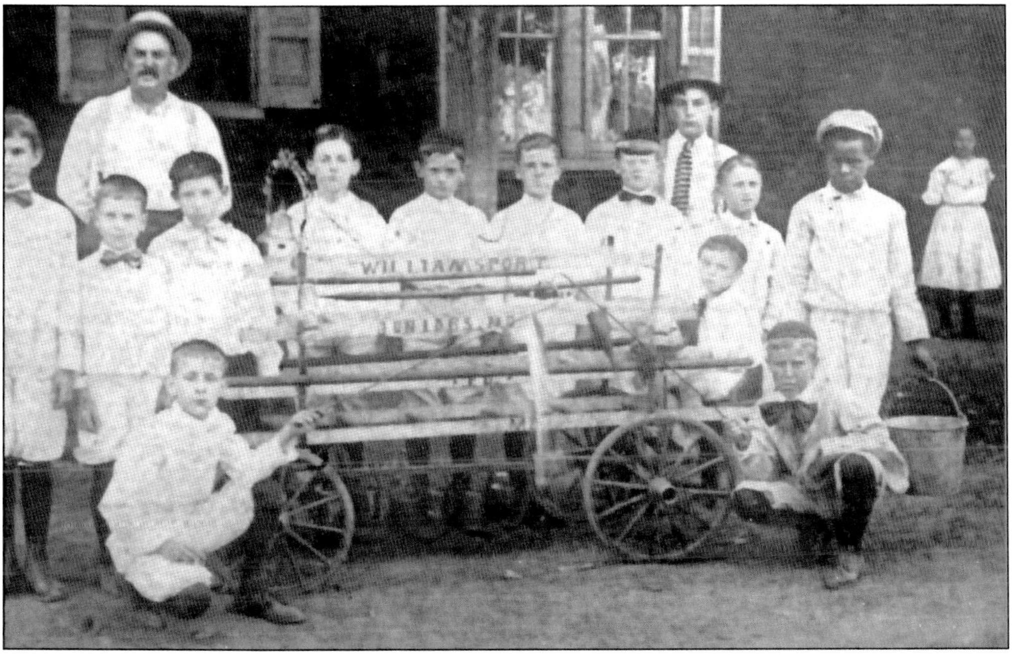

Just like the youth band, youngsters wanted to emulate their parents by being part of other civic affairs. This photograph shows a group of town youths in 1920 who belonged to the Williamsport Juniors of the Fire Department. Note the bell they have rigged to their fire wagon. (Courtesy Williamsport Town Museum.)

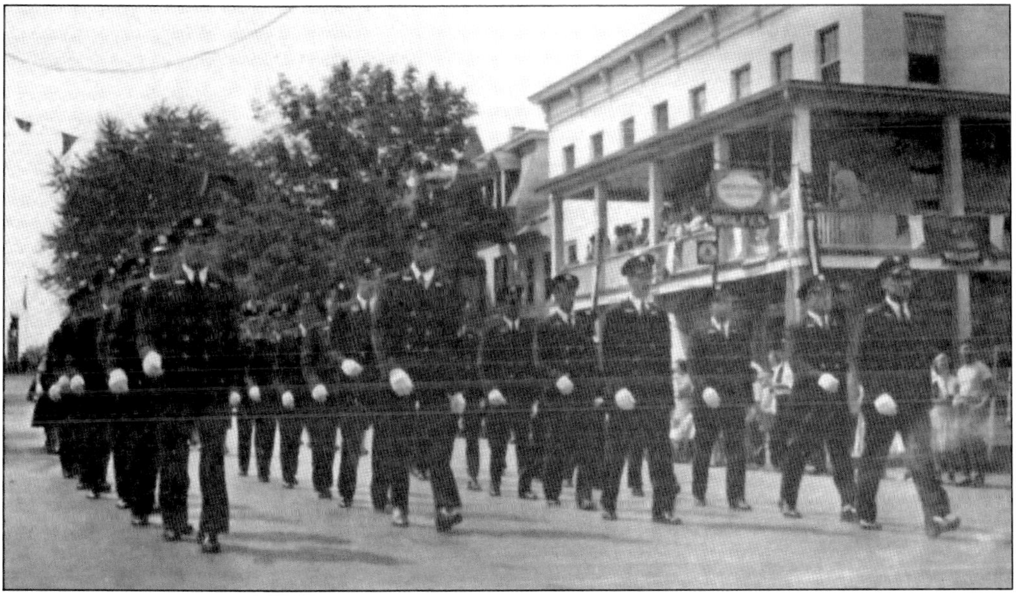

This photograph shows the Williamsport firemen marching in a parade down Potomac Street. Early firefighting in Williamsport, as in many communities, consisted of the bucket brigade. Note that Wolfe's On The Square can be seen in the background. This store was the livelihood of the legendary local canaller George "Hooper" Wolfe. The book *I Drove Mules on the C&O Canal*, written by Hooper, is highly prized by those that have a copy. Many were autographed by Hooper with ink derived from water taken from the canal itself. (Courtesy *Maryland Cracker Barrel.*)

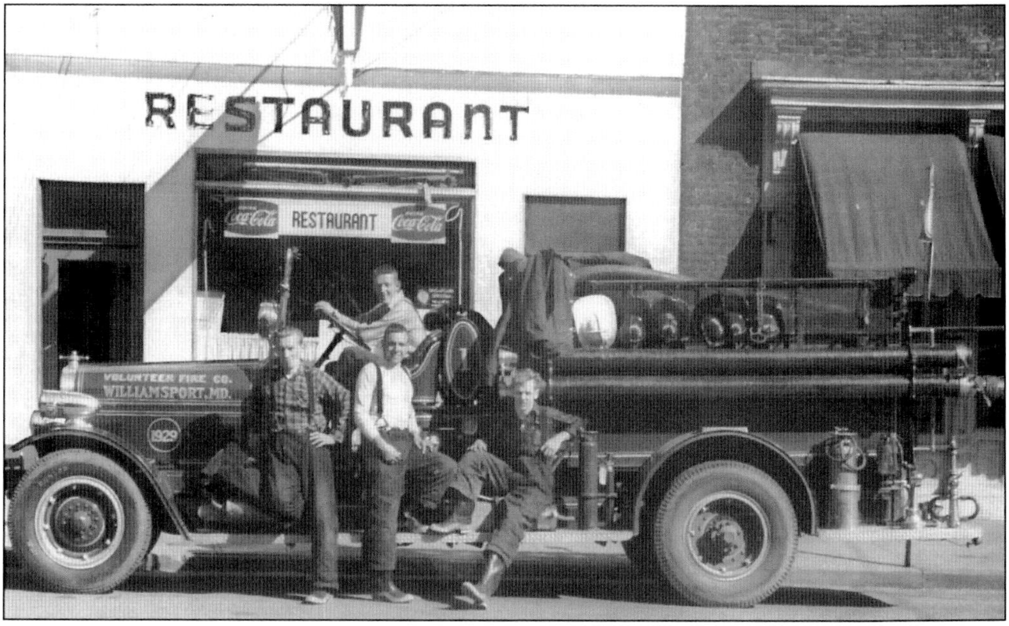

This 1929 truck, the first Seagrave model brought into town, is a far cry from today's large fire engines that use cutting-edge technology, but this was state of the art for its time. This photograph shows volunteers from Williamsport Company No. 2 outside The Grill restaurant. Pictured from left to right are Billy Turner, John Hetzer, Len McCardell, and Mac Rohrer. (Courtesy Williamsport Town Museum.)

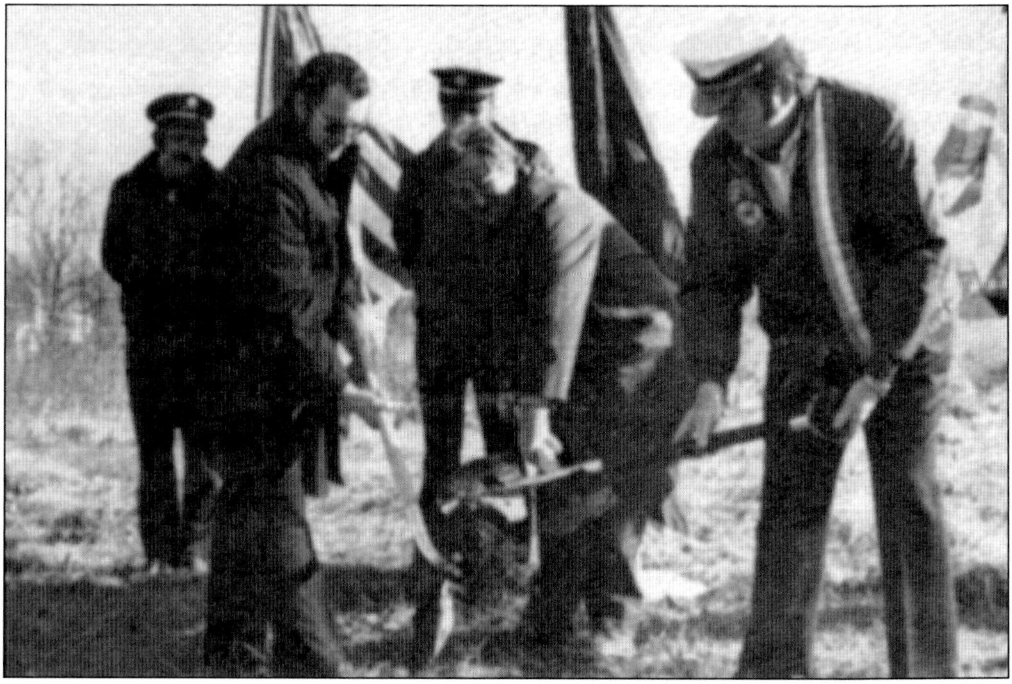

This photograph was taken on December 19, 1977, during the ground-breaking ceremony for a new fire department building complete with facilities for not only the fire fighting equipment but also space for training, administration, and recreation. (Courtesy *Maryland Cracker Barrel.*)

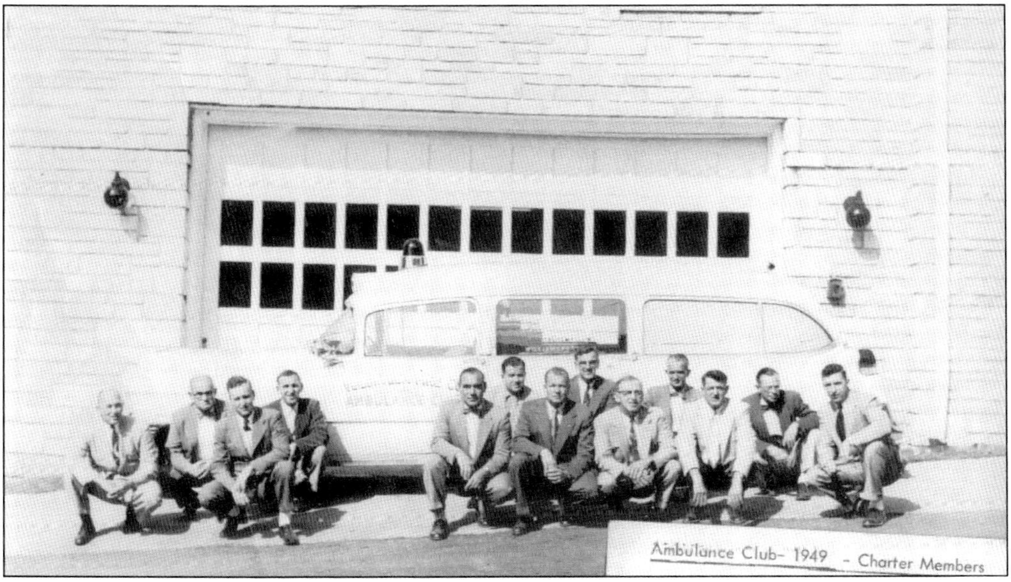

This photograph was taken c. 1950 and shows the Williamsport Volunteer Ambulance Club. Charter members of the club pictured from left to right in the photo are Admiral Britton, Edward Shank, Charles South, Beckley Harsh, ? Whipp, Brandy Zimmerman, Mason Gigeous, Woodrow Grove, Adam Harsh, Maurice Miller, Benjamin Garrish, Warren Seymour, and Maurice Snyder. (Courtesy Williamsport Town Museum.)

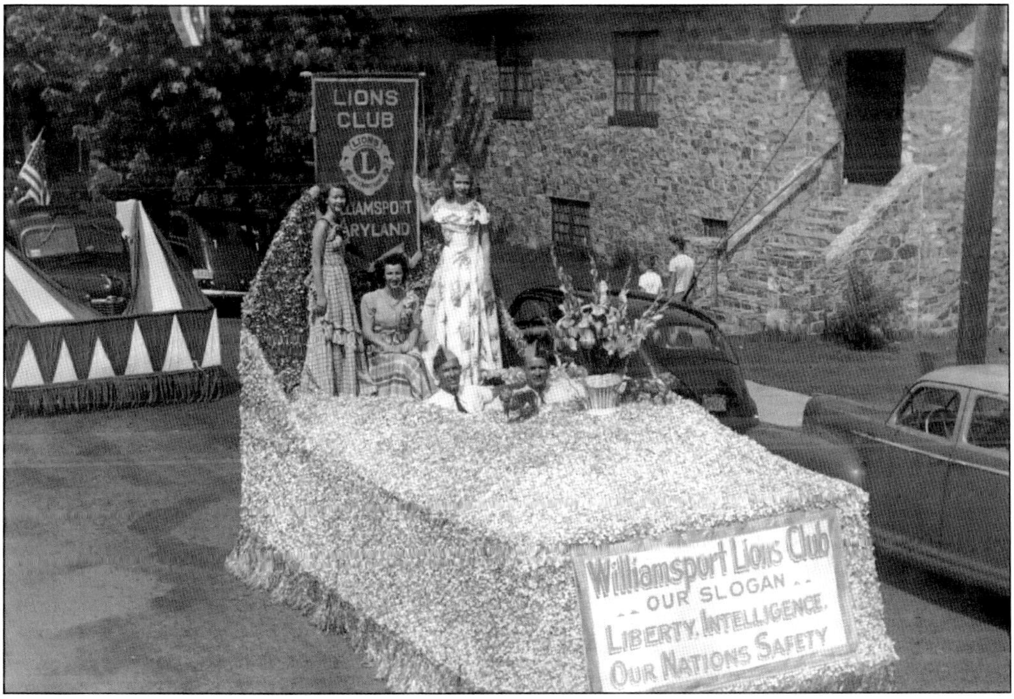

This photograph, taken in 1942, shows a parade float from the Williamsport Lions Club, another of the civic groups in town. Pictured from left to right are (standing) Katherine Kretsinger, Loraine Grove, and Betsy Newcomer; seated in the car on the left is Ms. Kretsinger's father, Glenn Kretsinger. (Courtesy Morrison Photographers, Williamsport Town Museum.)

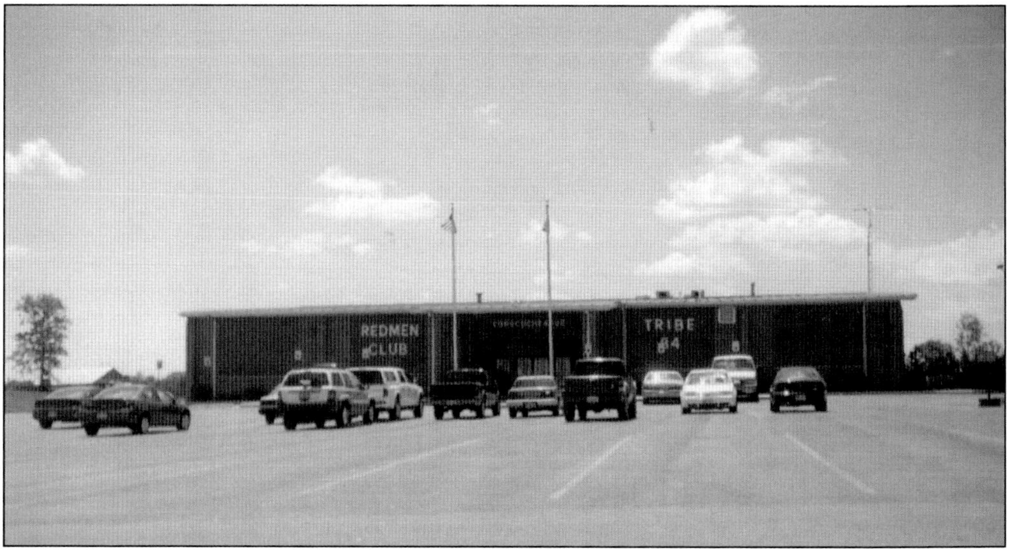

Williamsport is home to Tribe No. 84 of the Improved Order of Red Men. The Order of Red Men is a national fraternal organization. Founded in 1765, the group was originally known as the Sons of Liberty. The group patterns themselves after the Native American Iroquois and uses their system of democratic governance. The Williamsport Conococheague Tribe was founded on November 17, 1886, with the following officers: Robert DeFrehn, sachem; W. H. Z. King, keeper of records; and Charles J. Davis, keeper of wampum. The brick building that currently houses the tribe was originally home to a Presbyterian church. (Courtesy Mary H. Rubin.)

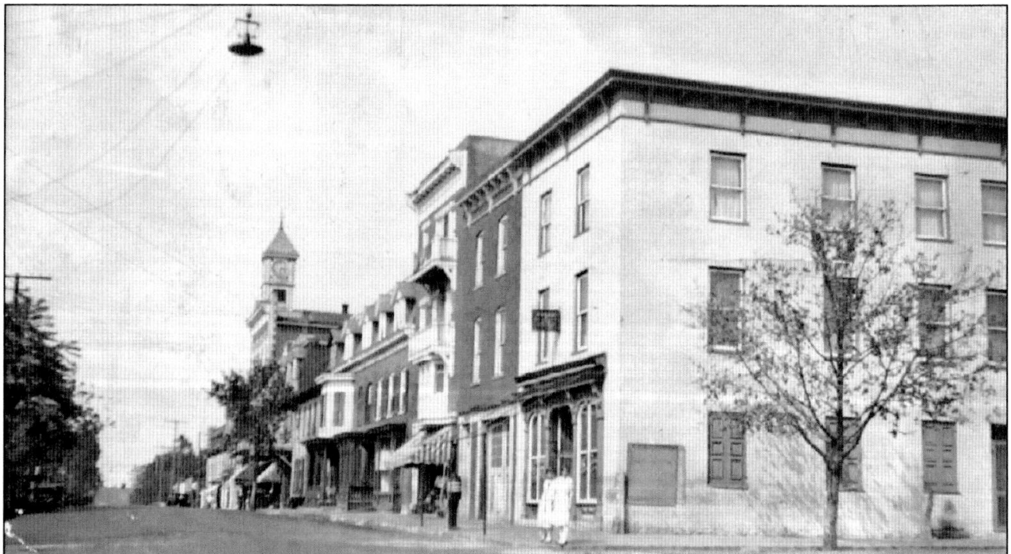

Here is a photograph of the Odd Fellows Building on Conococheague Street. The first Washington County fatality of the Civil War happened outside this building on June 5, 1861. DeWitt Clinton Rench, a local citizen with a reputation as a Confederate spy and a friend of Henry Kyd Douglas (the youngest member of Stonewall Jackson's staff), was a little too vocal about his Confederate sympathies, and a pro-Union mob accosted and killed him as he tried to leave town. (Courtesy Williamsport Town Museum.)

These photographs are from a real-estate listing when the Fleming Hospital was put up for sale. Note the list of the number of rooms and the medical equipment of the day offered for sale. The building was next to the Lutheran church on Potomac Street and is believed to have closed sometime in the 1950s. (Courtesy Williamsport Town Museum.)

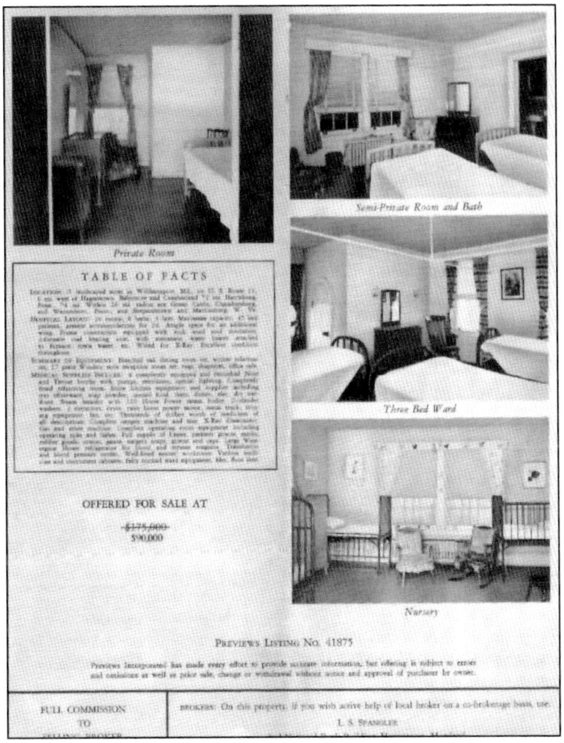

Private Room

Semi-Private Room and Bath

Three Bed Ward

Nursery

TABLE OF FACTS

OFFERED FOR SALE AT

~~$175,000~~
$90,000

PREVIEWS LISTING No. 41875

Previews Incorporated has made every effort to provide accurate information, but offering is subject to errors and omissions as well as prior sale, change or withdrawal without notice and approval of purchaser by owner.

FULL COMMISSION TO

BROKERS: On this property, if you wish active help of local broker on a co-brokerage basis, use:

L. S. SPANGLER

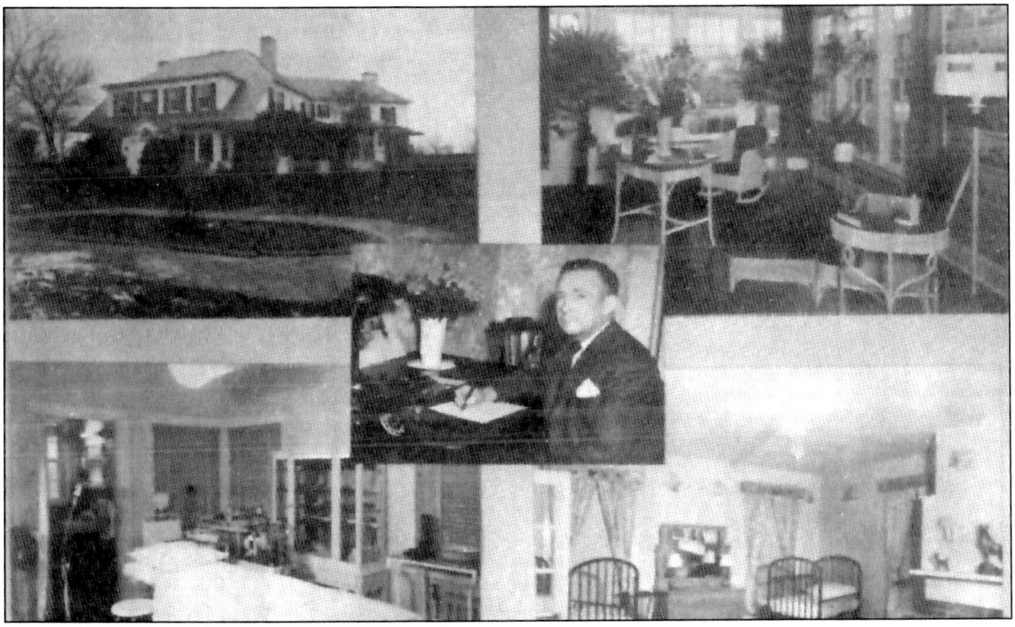

Here is another series of photos showing various rooms, including an operating room, at the privately owned Fleming Hospital, which once operated in Williamsport. A small news clipping attached to the real estate brochure mentions a 22-month old child, Thomas Wallace, son of Mr. and Mrs. Lindsay Wallace of Hedgesville, West Virginia, being in critical condition after being operated on at the hospital to remove a peanut that lodged in his lung on December 24, 1943. (Courtesy Williamsport Town Museum.)

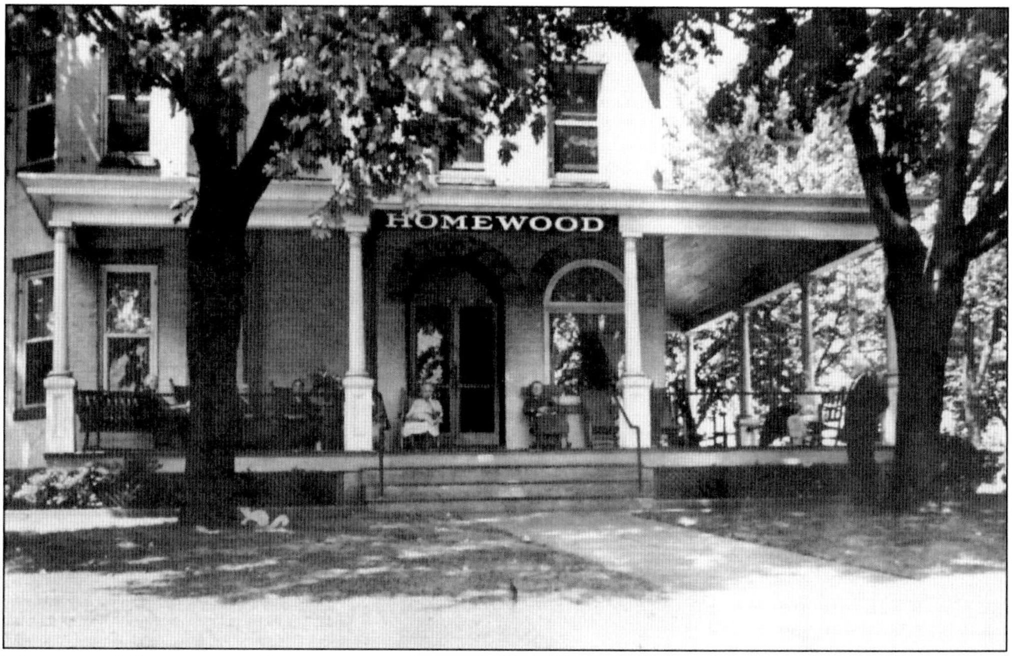

Homewood Retirement Home is a staple in Williamsport, but the first Homewood was actually located outside Williamsport on the corner of Virginia Avenue and Halfway Boulevard, where St. Joseph's Catholic Church is now located. It was in this house that 11 men and women resided when Homewood first opened in 1932. (Courtesy *Maryland Cracker Barrel.*)

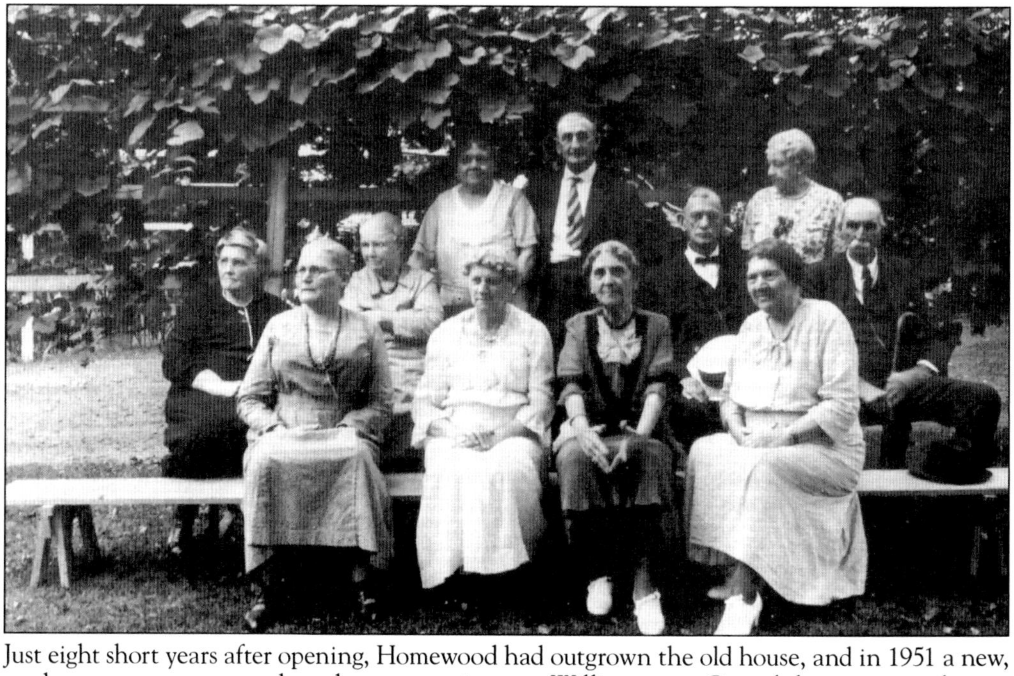

Just eight short years after opening, Homewood had outgrown the old house, and in 1951 a new, modern center was opened on the current site near Williamsport. Growth has continued since that time, and Homewood is now well known throughout the region. This photograph shows the original residents of the Homewood that started it all. (Courtesy *Maryland Cracker Barrel.*)

Formerly the Byron home, this series of photographs shows various views of what later became Williamsport Retirement Home. Located on N. Artizan Street, the house was originally the Darby home (owner of the Darby Mill) and was sold to the Byrons in 1897. (Courtesy Western Maryland Room Washington County Free Library.)

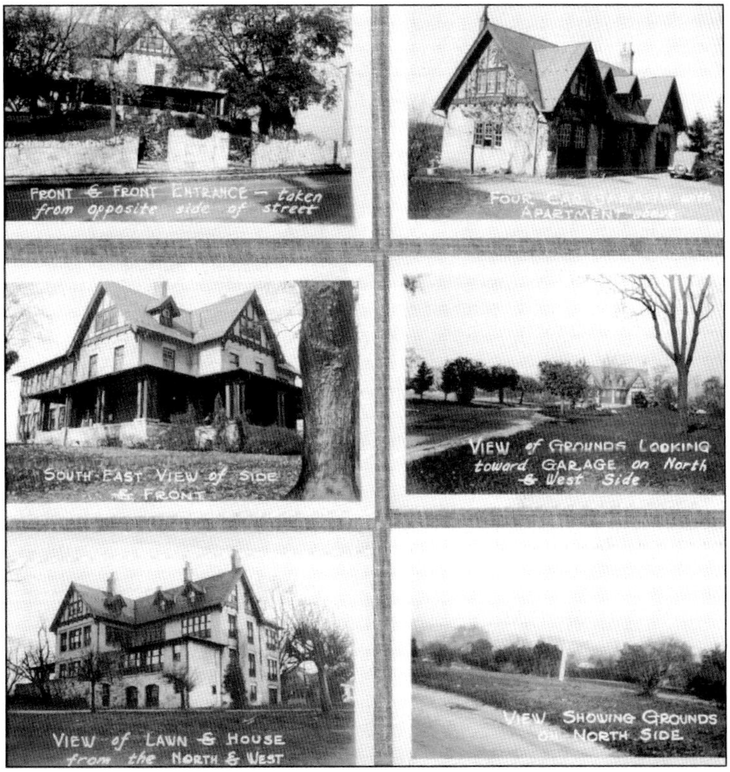

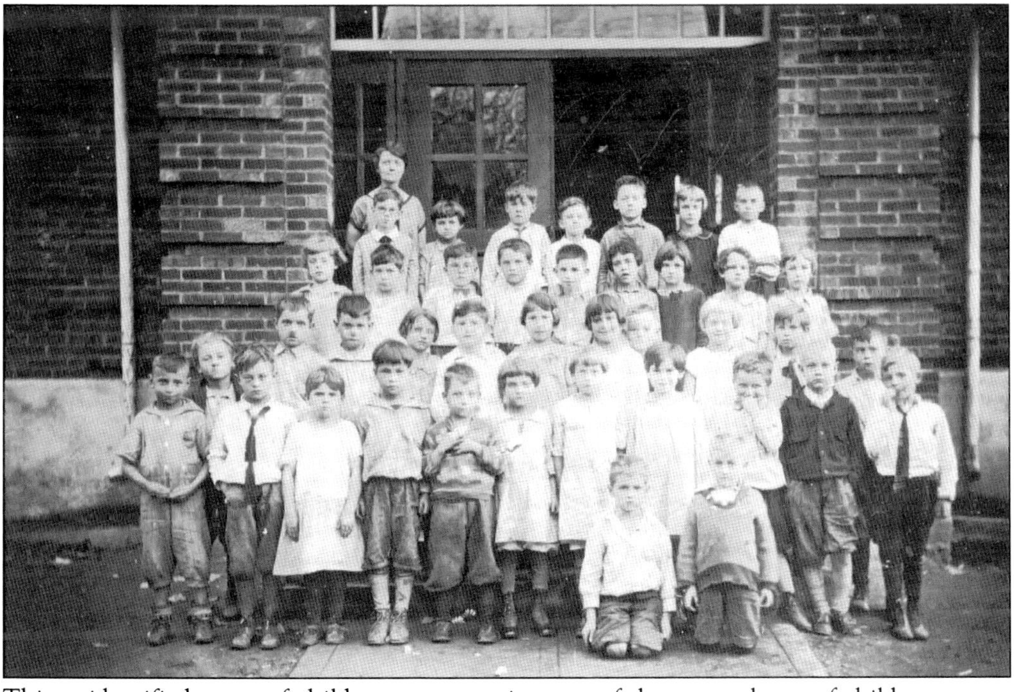

This unidentified group of children represents just one of the many classes of children to pass through Williamsport schools. This class of about 40 young children is a pretty hefty number for the one teacher to handle. (Courtesy Williamsport Town Museum.)

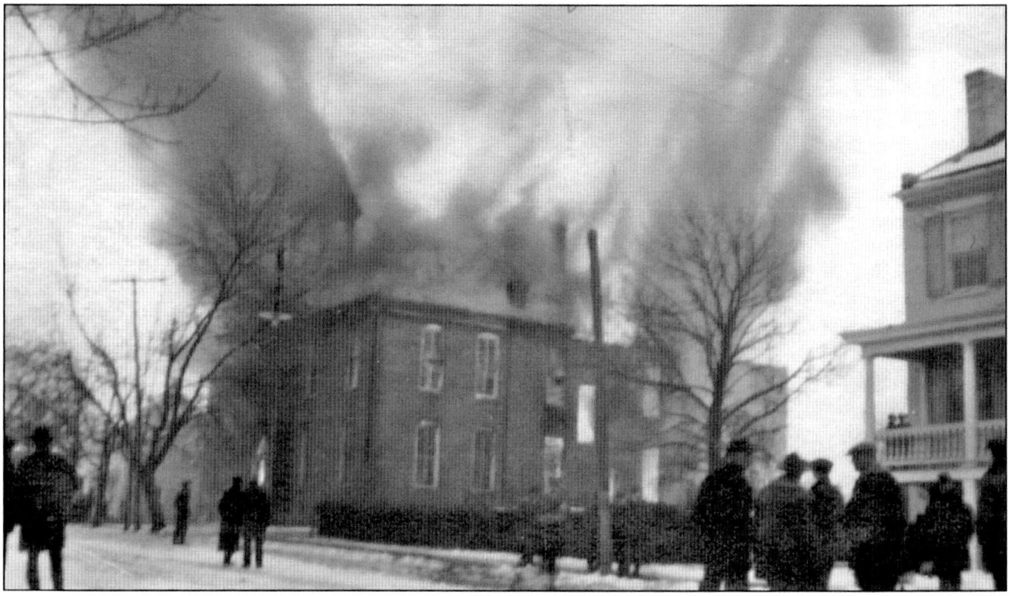

This photograph was taken on January 9, 1923, at 10:15 a.m., when fire broke out at the Williamsport Elementary School on Church Street. Mamie Schnebly, the fourth grade teacher at the time, got everyone out of the building unharmed. Flames from the fire were severe enough to scorch the bell tower of the nearby Methodist Church. This building, constructed in 1897, replaced an earlier school building on E. Salisbury Street. That building, built in 1867, was outgrown by the large influx of pupils during rapid growth in town. (Courtesy Williamsport Town Museum.)

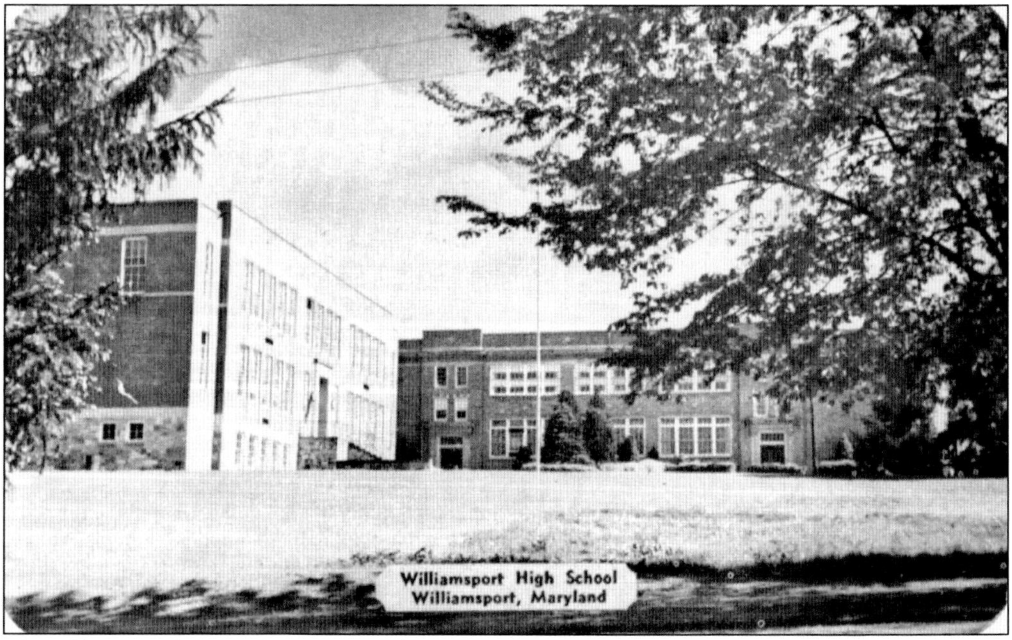

This old postcard shows the "new" Williamsport High School that was constructed between 1920 and 1921. It was located on the site of what later became Pine View Senior Housing. The original school building is on the right, while the section on the left was a later addition. Williamsport's current high school is located on Clifton Street. (Courtesy Williamsport Town Museum.)

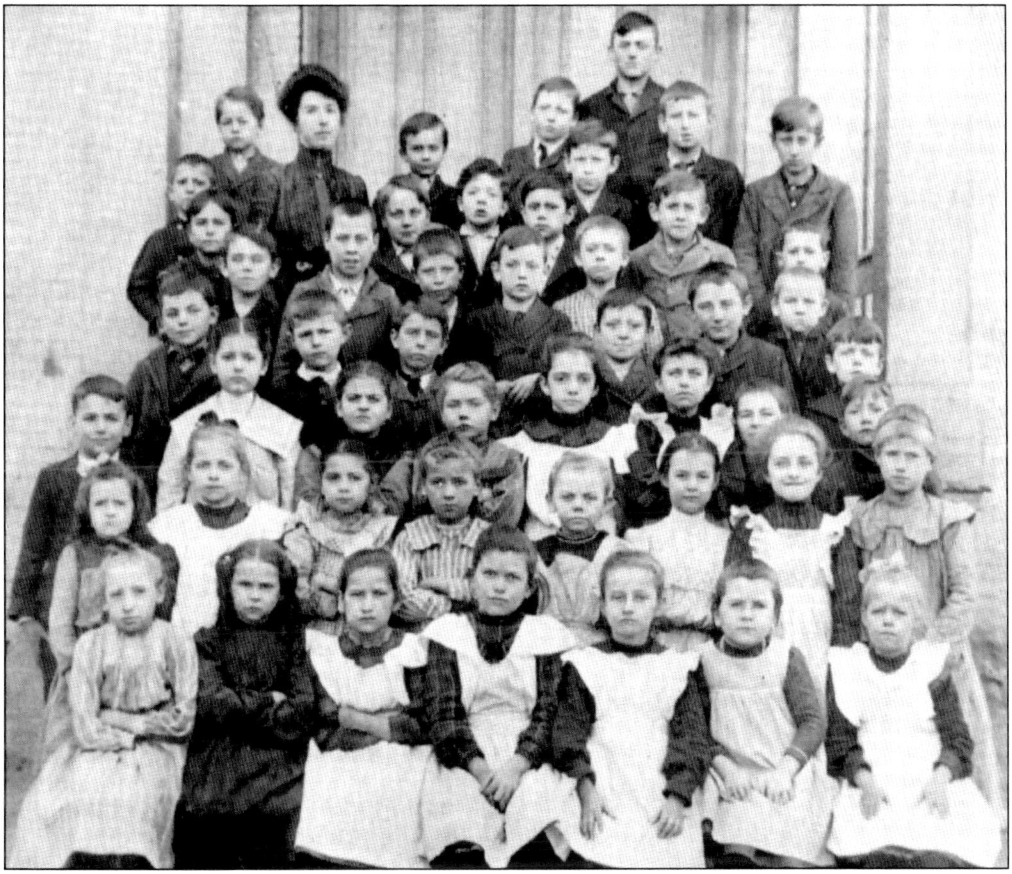

Here is another Williamsport school group, this time the third and fourth grades from 1903 to 1904. In the photograph, from left to right, are the following: (first row) Mary Kreps, Blanche Miller, Grace Jessup, Edith Banzhoff, Elizabeth Long, Melva Hoffman, and Edith Taylor; (second row) Ella Hoover, Nancy Beard Davis, Alma Keller, Grace Johnson, Lutie Buchanan, Grace Mentzer, and Jesse Keller; (third row) Edward Patton, Emily Steffy, Leah Bell, Charlotte Guessford, Josephine Cullen, Lucy Poffenberger, George Wolf, and Lesher Kreps; (fourth row) Cushen Forsythe, Robert Sheetz, Hubert Spangler, Harry Grimes, Harry Hull, and Alvey Guessford (son of Martin Guessford); (fifth row) Alvey Guessford (son of Harry Guessford), Stuart Ardinger, James Straitiff, Jesse Ghompson, Frank Long, Leslie Stenger, and Bernard Taylor; (sixth row) McAfee Riley, John Wine, Frank Kesselring, and James Long; (seventh row) Carl Gaver, Harry Hoffman, teacher Nellie Reed, Beale Harsh, Frank Shafer, Neal Kelly, Arthur Wolf, Charles Mullinex, and Howard Forsyth. (Courtesy *Maryland Cracker Barrel.*)

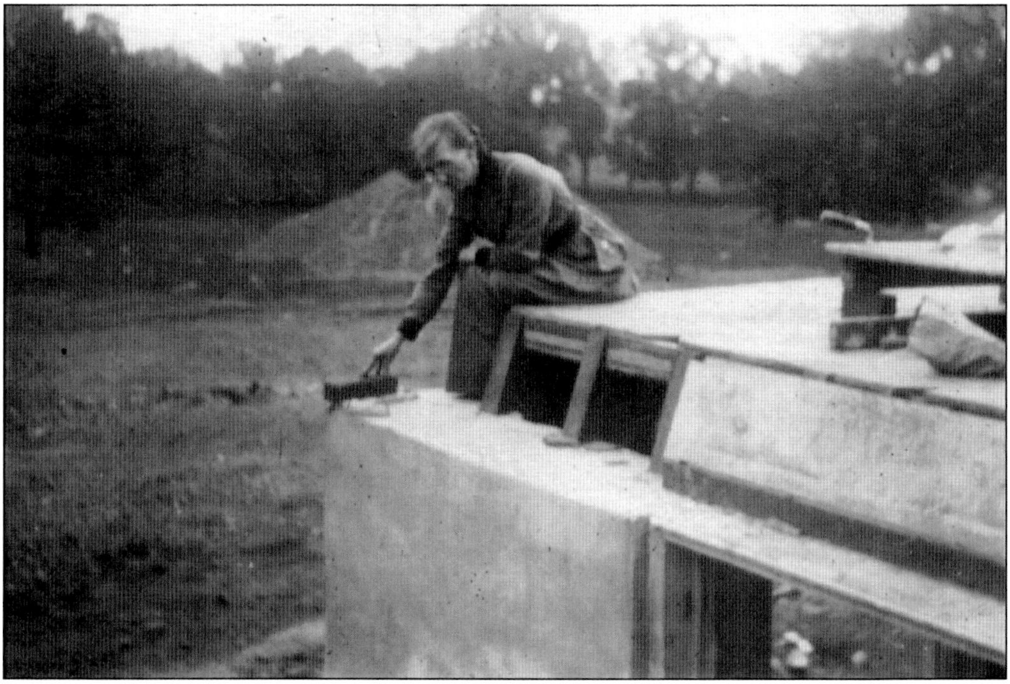

Here is Miss Mamie Schnebly, the oldest schoolteacher at the school at the time, laying the cornerstone for the new high school on October 1, 1920. Virtually every student beginning school in the county for a 35-year span began their school days under Miss Schnebly. The building was completed and ready for classes in the spring of 1921. (Courtesy Williamsport Town Museum.)

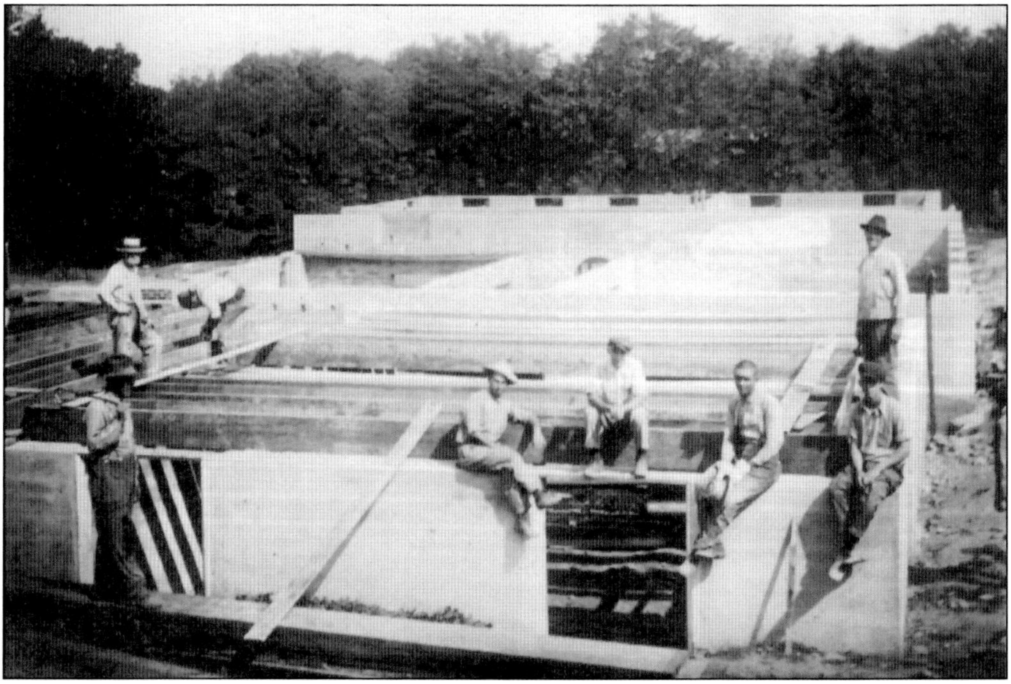

Here is a view of the construction crew taking a break to pose for the camera while working on the new high school. (Courtesy Western Maryland Room Washington County Free Library.)

Here is one of the three cannons mounted on Doubleday Hill. On July 4, 1897, Williamsport held a celebration during which the cannons were installed in the cemetery to mark the site where Union soldiers were situated. Note that Riverview Cemetery, final resting place of Otho Holland Williams and many other early town residents, is in the background. (Courtesy *Maryland Cracker Barrel.*)

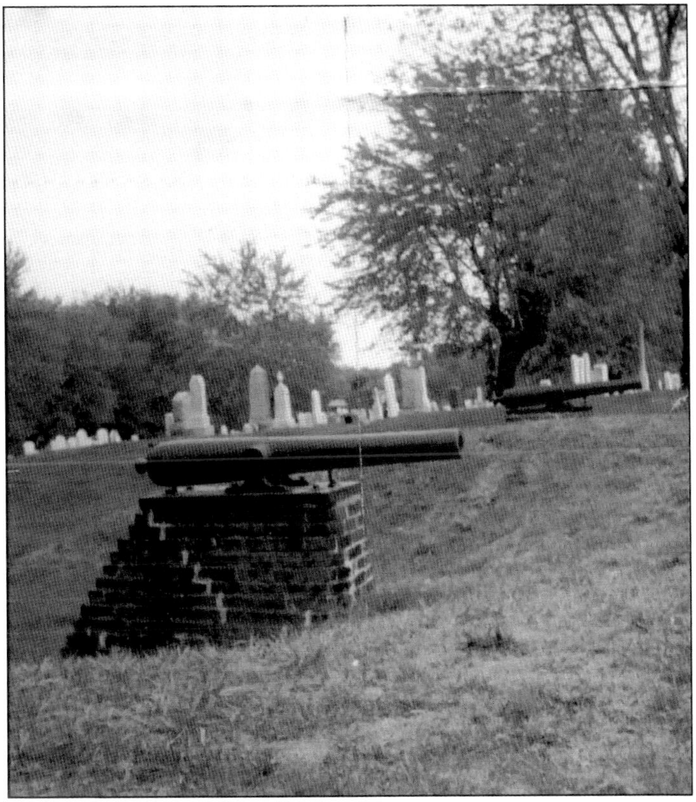

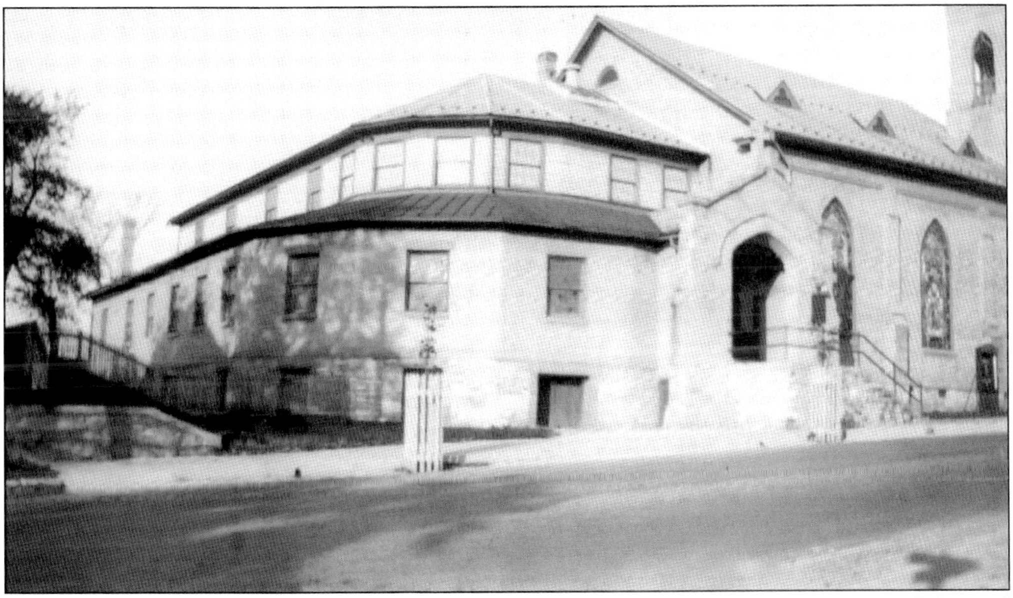

This photograph shows one of the churches in Williamsport, the Zion Lutheran Church located on Potomac Street. This church and others, such as St. Augustine's Catholic Church, also on Potomac Street, were among the many buildings in town forced into use as hospitals during the Confederate retreat from Gettysburg. (Courtesy Western Maryland Room Washington County Free Library.)

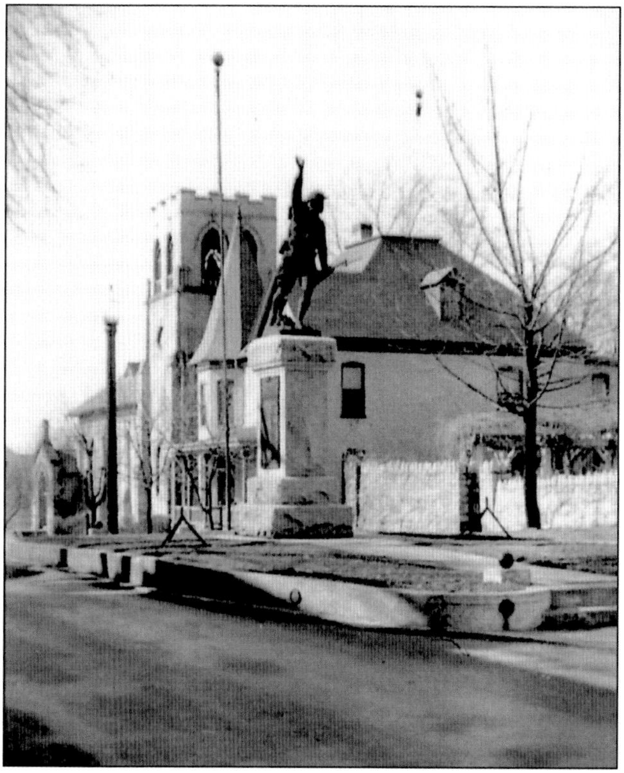

This photograph shows the World War I Memorial in Williamsport in front of the Lutheran Church. To the left of the memorial in the distance, across the Potomac, is the tract known as Maidstone on the Potomac in West Virginia. Lord Fairfax of Virginia set the land for Maidstone apart in the 1740s for a manor adjacent to Evan Watkins's ferry that ran across the Potomac to Conococheague. Located on part of the land is Maidstone Manor, which was built in 1847 and was the childhood home of William Robinson Leigh, an artist well known for his depictions of the Old West. (Courtesy Western Maryland Room Washington County Free Library.)

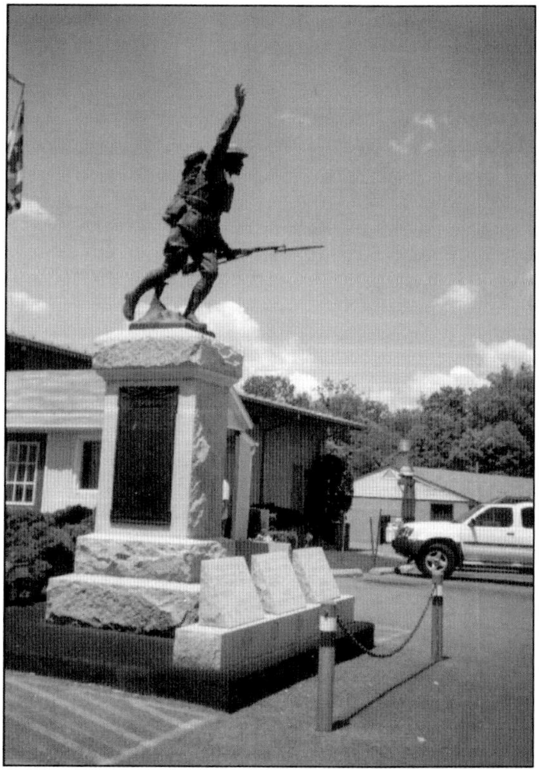

Here is the same World War I monument at its current home in front of the American Legion Potomac Post 202 on Conococheague Street. The monument has been enhanced to include memorial plaques to soldiers serving in other conflicts including World War II, the Korean War, and Vietnam. (Courtesy Mary H. Rubin.)

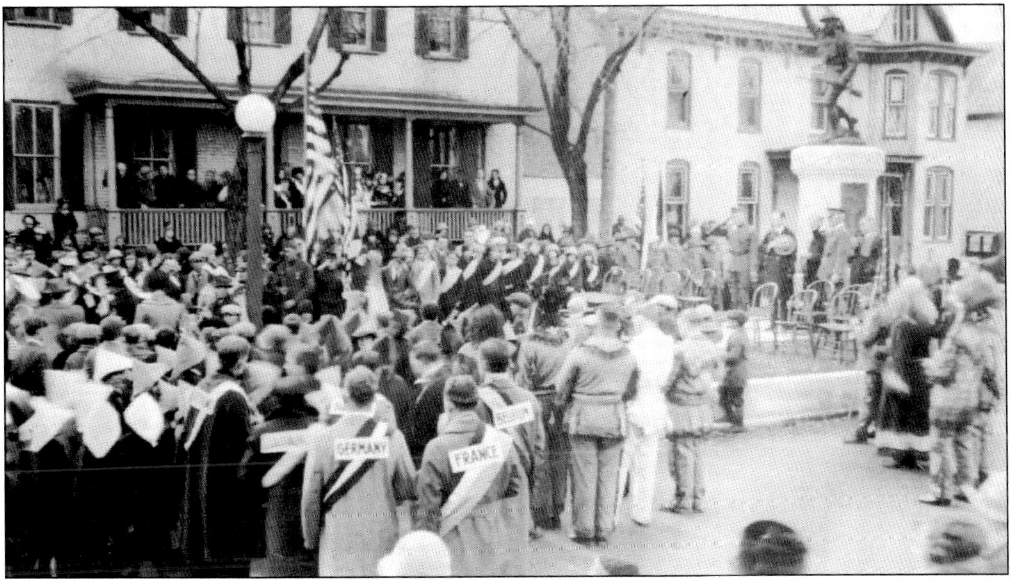

This 1926 photograph was taken on Armistice Day during the town commemoration events. Note the men standing in the back of the crowd wearing sashes and the names of countries involved in the Great War. There was no World War I nomenclature yet—it was simply the "war to end all wars." In 1926, no one planned on the next war, which would change the Great War to World War I. The world wars and the wars that followed ultimately led Armistice Day to be renamed Memorial Day. (Courtesy Williamsport Town Museum.)

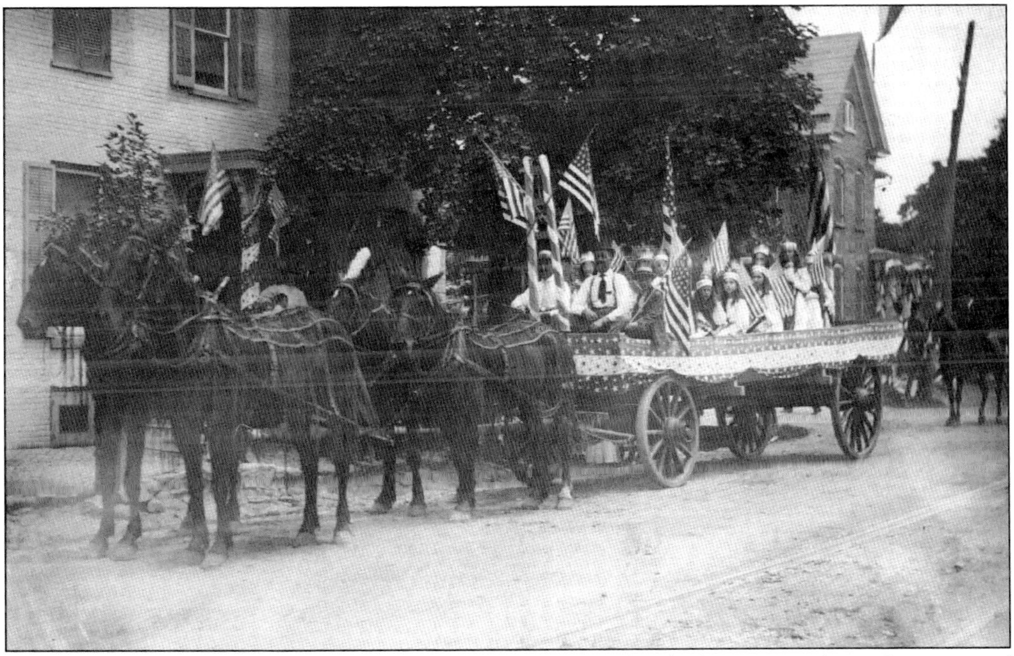

No one remembers just what this event was, but this wagonload of townspeople, at the corner of Artizan and E. Potomac Street, are all decked out in their patriotic best. Perhaps it was a parade or a town picnic? (Courtesy Western Maryland Room Washington County Free Library.)

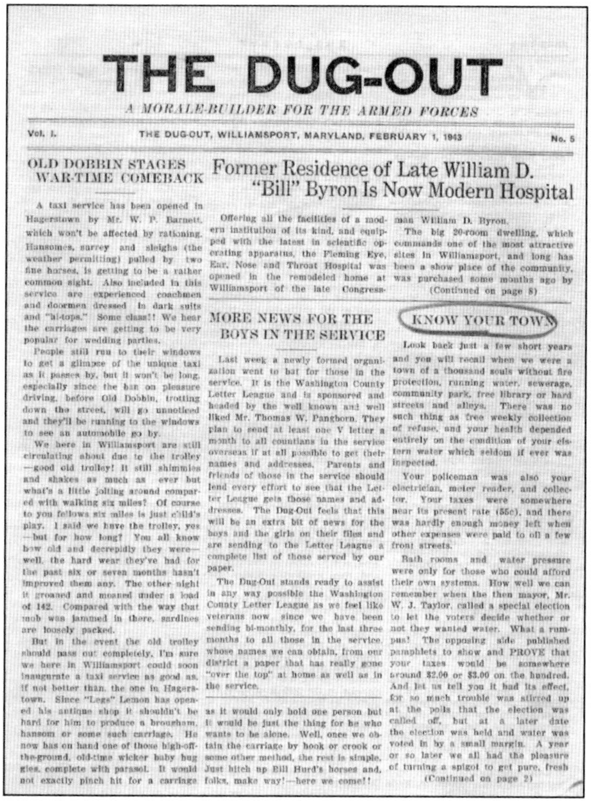

THE DUG-OUT

A MORALE-BUILDER FOR THE ARMED FORCES

Vol. I. THE DUG-OUT, WILLIAMSPORT, MARYLAND, FEBRUARY 1, 1943 No. 5

OLD DOBBIN STAGES WAR-TIME COMEBACK

A taxi service has been opened in Hagerstown by Mr. W. P. Barnett, which won't be affected by rationing. Hansomes, surrey and sleighs (the weather permitting) pulled by two fine horses, is getting to be a rather common sight. Also included in this service are experienced coachmen and doormen dressed in dark suits and "hi-tops." Some class!! We hear the carriages are getting to be very popular for wedding parties.

People still run to their windows to get a glimpse of the unique taxi as it passes by, but it won't be long, especially since the ban on pleasure driving, before Old Dobbin, trotting down the street, will go unnoticed and they'll be running to the windows to see an automobile go by.

We here in Williamsport are still circulating about due to the trolley—good old trolley! It still shimmies and shakes as much as ever but what's a little jolting around compared with walking six miles? Of course to you fellows six miles is just child's play. I said we have the trolley, yes—but for how long? You all know how old and decrepidly they were—well, the hard wear they've had for the past six or seven months hasn't improved them any. The other night it groaned and moaned under a load of 142. Compared with the way that mob was jammed in there, sardines are loosely packed.

But in the event the old trolley should pass out completely, I'm sure we here in Williamsport could soon inaugurate a taxi service as good as, if not better than, the one in Hagerstown. Since "Legs" Lemon has opened his antique shop it shouldn't be hard for him to produce a brougham, hansom or some such carriage. He now has on hand one of those high-off-the-ground, old-time wicker baby buggies, complete with parasol. It would not exactly pinch hit for a carriage as it would only hold one person but it would be just the thing for he who wants to be alone. Well, once we obtain the carriage by hook or crook or some other method, the rest is simple. Just hitch up Bill Hurd's horses and, folks, make way!—here we come!!

Former Residence of Late William D. "Bill" Byron Is Now Modern Hospital

Offering all the facilities of a modern institution of its kind, and equipped with the latest in scientific operating apparatus, the Fleming Eye, Ear, Nose and Throat Hospital was opened in the remodeled home at Williamsport of the late Congressman William D. Byron.

The big 20-room dwelling, which commands one of the most attractive sites in Williamsport, and long has been a show place of the community, was purchased some months ago by

(Continued on page 8)

MORE NEWS FOR THE BOYS IN THE SERVICE

Last week a newly formed organization went to bat for those in the service. It is the Washington County Letter League and is sponsored and headed by the well known and well liked Mr. Thomas W. Pangborn. They plan to send at least one V letter a month to all countians in the service overseas if at all possible to get their names and addresses. Parents and friends of those in the service should lend every effort to see that the Letter League gets those names and addresses. The Dug-Out feels that this will be an extra bit of news for the boys and the girls on their files and are sending to the Letter League a complete list of those served by our paper.

The Dug-Out stands ready to assist in any way possible the Washington County Letter League as we feel like veterans now since we have been sending bi-monthly, for the last three months to all those in the service, whose names we can obtain, from our district a paper that has really gone "over the top" at home as well as in the service.

KNOW YOUR TOWN

Look back just a few short years and you will recall when we were a town of a thousand souls without fire protection, running water, sewerage, community park, free library or hard streets and alleys. There was no such thing as free weekly collection of refuse, and your health depended entirely on the condition of your cistern water which seldom if ever was inspected.

Your policeman was also your electrician, meter reader, and collector. Your taxes were somewhere near its present rate (55c), and there was hardly enough money left when other expenses were paid to oil a few front streets.

Bath rooms and water pressure were only for those who could afford their own systems. How well we can remember when the then mayor, Mr. W. J. Taylor, called a special election to let the voters decide whether or not they wanted water. What a rumpus! The opposing side published pamphlets to show and PROVE that your taxes would be somewhere around \$2.00 or \$3.00 on the hundred. And let us tell you it had its effect, for so much trouble was stirred up at the polls that the election was called off, but at a later date the election was held and water was voted in by a small margin. A year or so later we all had the pleasure of turning a spigot to get pure, fresh

(Continued on page 2)

The Dug-Out was a newsletter put together by Williamsport citizens during the bleak years of World War II. The newsletter was sent free of charge to local residents serving their country in the armed forces overseas and was sold for 10¢ locally. The paper billed itself as "A Morale Builder for the Armed Services," and that it was. The newsletter highlighted all sorts of information about goings-on in town (such as when fish started running), news of local servicemen honors, deployments, and activities, and some much-needed comic relief. (Courtesy Williamsport Town Museum.)

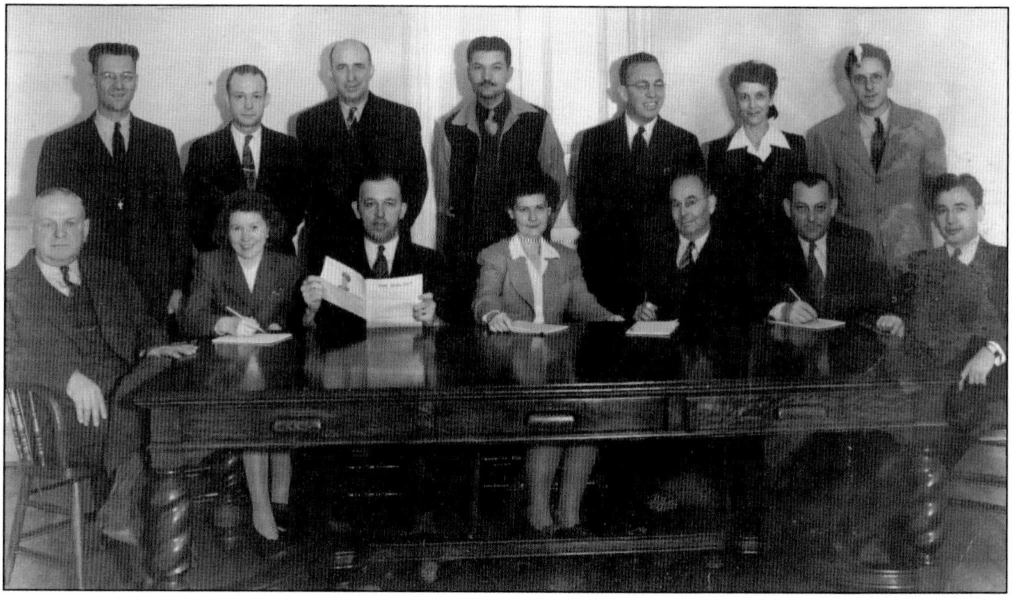

Here is a photograph of the staff of *The Dug-Out* newsletter. Pictured from left to right are (first row) Lester Swain, Leila Emerson, Adam Harsh, Margaret Jenkins, George W. Wolfe, F. E. Coakley, and Abner Kaplan; (second row) Rev. W. C. Huddle, Charles Adams, Brewer L. Stouffer, Irvin Traver, Charles N. Harsh, Naomi Harsh Taylor, and Wallace Taylor. One other staff member, D. K. Cushwa Jr., was out of town when this photograph was taken. (Courtesy Williamsport Town Museum.)

THE DUG-OUT

A MORALE-BUILDER FOR THE ARMED FORCES

Vol. III — No. 5 WILLIAMSPORT, MD., U.S.A., FEBRUARY 28, 1945 Price: Ten Cents

FRIEND BURIAL PLOT DEEDED TO SOCIETY

The plot known in Williamsport as the "Friend Burying Ground" was recently deed to the Washington County Historical Society by John E. Hoffman and wife, owners of the historical spot. Present plans call for the Society to develop the spot as a shrine honoring the Friend family, who were among the earliest white settlers in this county.

Located along the Williamsport-Clear Spring road, on the north side of Conococheague Creek, the tenth of an acre has been used of late as pasture. There are occasional depressions in the earth to indicate that it was once a burial ground and one tombstone was recently removed by the Historical Society.

This stone, the only one on which the inscription was legible, marked the grave of Jacob Friend, 1758-1802. The epitaph ends with the pious warning: "Prepare to meet thy God."

Flooded countless times by an overflowing creek, the plot lies only 200 feet north of Williamsport, yet many residents of the town are unaware of its existence.

The Friends called their village along the Conococheague "Swede's Delight" and this settlement antedated the founding of Williamsport in 1787 by Otho Holland Williams. The present bridge across the Conococheague was not built until 1829, historical records indicate.

Jacob Friend is said to have been a forceful character and this is proven by the fact that he and his party ventured into the wilderness at a time when many red-skinned inhabitants were belligerent. Said to have taken part in Indian parleys, Friend apparently lived amicably with his savage neighbors.

"When you asked her to dance did she accept quickly?

"Did she! Why she was on my feet in an instant."

SEEN (AND SCENE) ABOUT TOWN

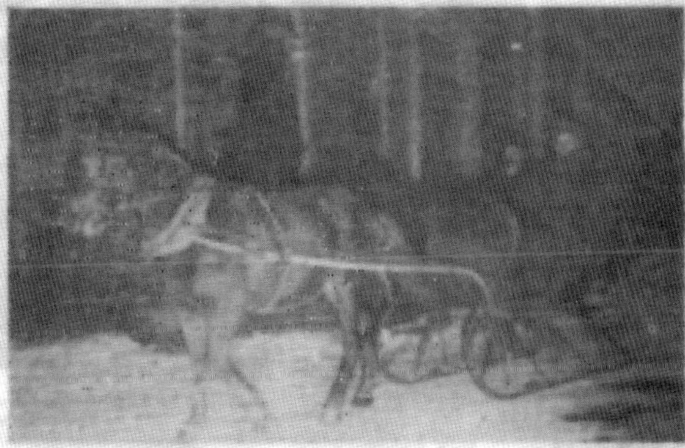

Constable Jesse Shank and Mayor Richard G. Hawken go a-sleighin'

BEAGLE CLUB BEING FORMED IN COUNTY

Owners of beagle hounds throughout this section are organizing a Beagle Club under the sponsorship of the Mason and Dixon Kennel Club, and if present plans are realized the beagle fanciers will hold a "fun" trial this spring on the grounds of the Potomac Fish and Game Club, near Williamsport.

All beagle owners whose dogs measure 13 inches and not more than 15 inches are invited to join the club by first becoming members of the Mason - Dixon Club. Application blanks may be secured from the president of the later club, Walter Ryan, who lives along the Dual Highway, or from Dr. R. C. Gale, Harvey Smith or J. Clarke Wilson, all of Hagerstown; Preston Howard, near Williamsport.

Although the Mason-Dixon Club is interested chiefly in "bench" shows, where dogs are shown only in the ring, the Beagle Club will sponsor field work for the dogs, in addition to supporting the bench shows. At the projected trial, speakers experienced in field work will talk and local men will learn how to put on a trial and what to expect of their dogs.

If there is sufficient interest in this preliminary trial, the club will apply to the American Kennel Club for a sanction match next fall. Chairman of the Beagle Committee is Lloyd Winebrenner of Hagerstown.

Sees Liberty Ship, "Wm. D. Byron," In An English Port

There was a longing look in the eyes of S 1/c Martin D. Harsh, as he stood by in an English port recently and watched a Liberty Ship nose its way out into the harbor and head for home. The vessel was the William D. Byron, named for Williamsport's late Congressman, and launched about a year ago from the Bethlehem-Fairfield shipyards in Baltimore. Marty says, in a letter to his parents that the sight of the ship brought back nostalgic memories of the old home town, but he was glad to learn that the William D. Byron was still faithfully "carrying on." This is the first report we have had of the William D Byron's whereabouts since it went into service.

This February 28, 1945, issue of *The Dug-Out* was full of information from home to keep those serving abroad up to date on all the happenings. There was a beagle club being formed in the county, the Jacob Friend burial plot was deeded to the Washington County Historical Society, there was a photograph of Mayor Richard Hawken and Constable Jesse Shank going for a horse-drawn sleigh ride, and the first report of the whereabouts of the Liberty ship *William D. Byron* since it went into service was noted. (Courtesy Williamsport Town Museum.)

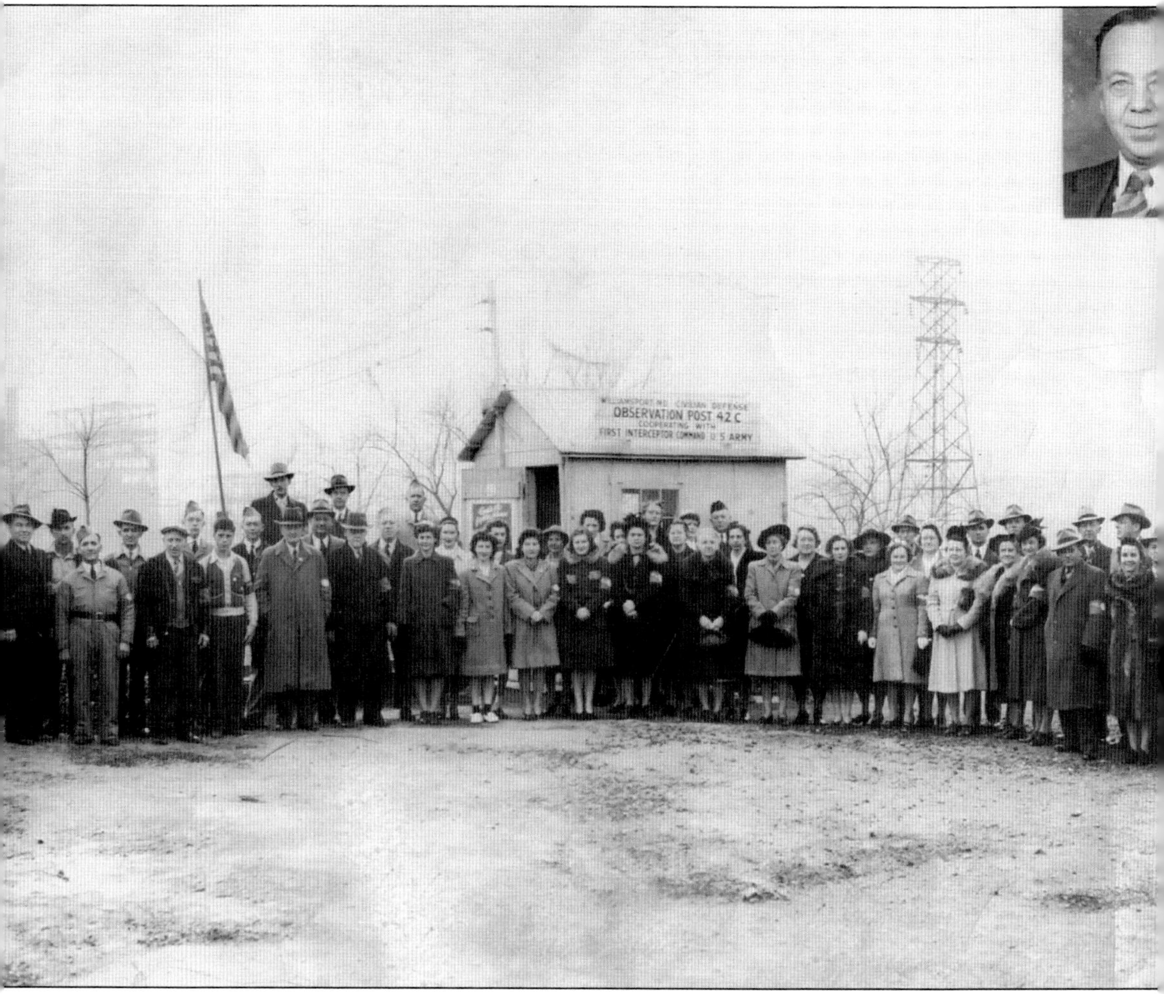

This group photograph of World War II airplane spotters from Williamsport was taken in late 1942. An important part of civilian defense on the home front, airplane spotters watched the skies up and down the coast looking for any possible enemy planes. The observation post would have included a communications radio as well as posters depicting the silhouettes of various kinds of aircraft. R. H. Miller, in the inset photo, was the chief observer. Others, from left to right, are: Jean Lizer, Theo Lizer, Howard Forsythe, Adam Harsh, Hooper Wolfe, Lloyd Stevens, Banny Banzhoff, Maurice Miller, Buddy Lizer, D. K. Poole Jr., Norman Bowers, Bill Taylor, Scott Bounds, George Bowser, William Fridinger, J. B. Poffenberger, Scott Robinson, Charles Harsh, Joe Hoffman (or possibly Johnny Corby), Margaret Jenkins, Edith Harsh, Faye Wiley, Annabelle Ditto, Phoebe Winters, Edna McCardell, Margaret Shipley Scharer, Ida Grimes, Jeanette W. Harsh, Mrs. William Fridinger, Mrs. D. K. Poole Sr., Margaret Wine, Virginia Miller, Emma Castle, Dr. I. M. Zimmerman, Edna Reichter, Ida Cushwa, Lena Burke, Francis Grimes, Aurelia Ritter, Daisy-Irene Zimmerly, Paul Garish, Nora Zimmerly, Effie Harsh, Roy Hoover Sr., Lucy Martin, William Doub (or possibly James Fearnow), Mrs. Denton Shupp, Francis Coakley, D. W. Newcomer, Margaret Coakley, Joe Forsythe, Keller Bell, Chlorine "Queenie" Newcomer, Donald Ebersole, and James L. Madison. (Courtesy Williamsport Town Museum.)

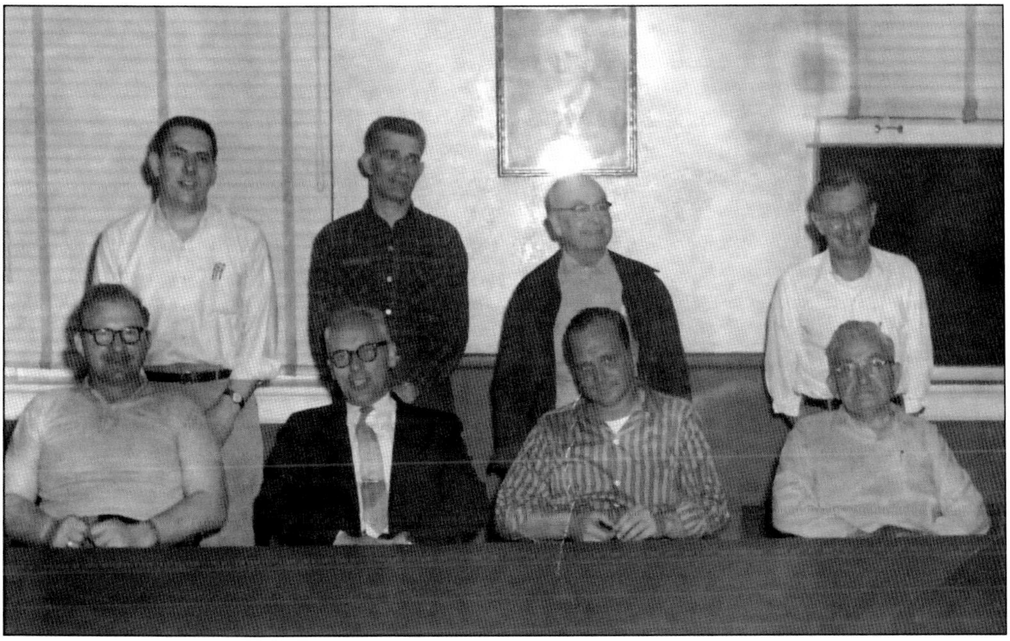

Here are the mayor and town council in 1961. Pictured are, from left to right, (first row) Charles Miller, Lewis Phelps, Hooper Wolfe, and Buss Seymour; (second row) Dutch Frederick, Beard Miller (mayor), Don Ardinger, and Charles Madison. (Courtesy Williamsport Town Museum.)

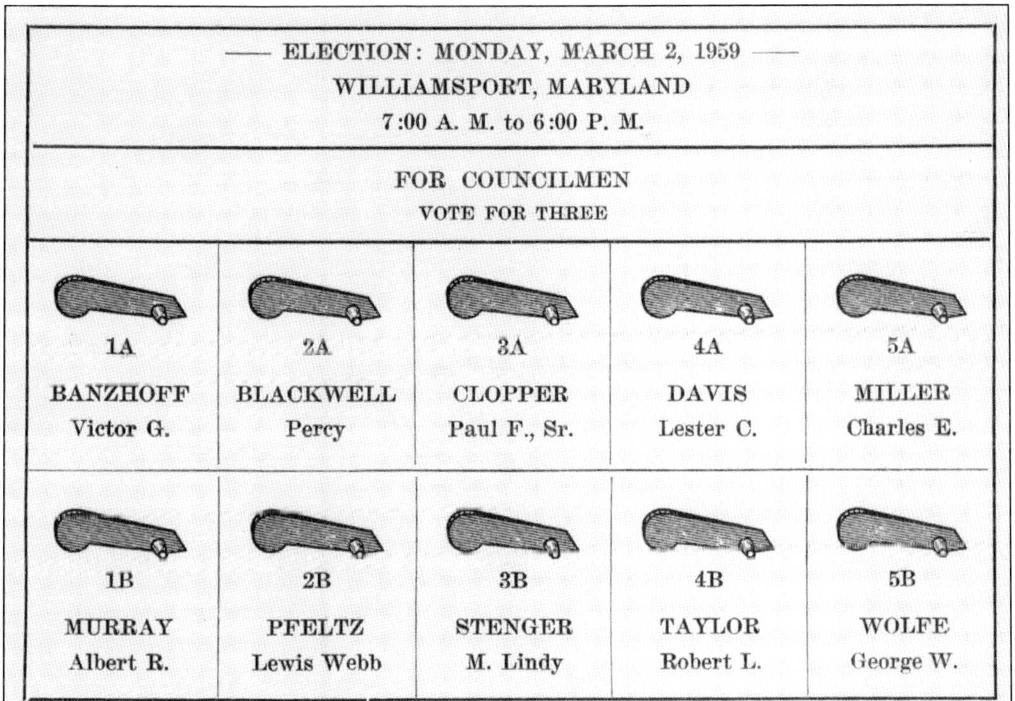

— ELECTION: MONDAY, MARCH 2, 1959 —
WILLIAMSPORT, MARYLAND
7:00 A. M. to 6:00 P. M.

FOR COUNCILMEN
VOTE FOR THREE

1A	2A	3A	4A	5A
BANZHOFF Victor G.	BLACKWELL Percy	CLOPPER Paul F., Sr.	DAVIS Lester C.	MILLER Charles E.
1B	2B	3B	4B	5B
MURRAY Albert R.	PFELTZ Lewis Webb	STENGER M. Lindy	TAYLOR Robert L.	WOLFE George W.

Here is an unusual piece of history in the form of an election ballot for the Williamsport City Council from March 2, 1959. Lever 5B was for George Wolfe, perhaps better known to some as "Hooper" of the C&O Canal. (Courtesy Williamsport Town Museum.)

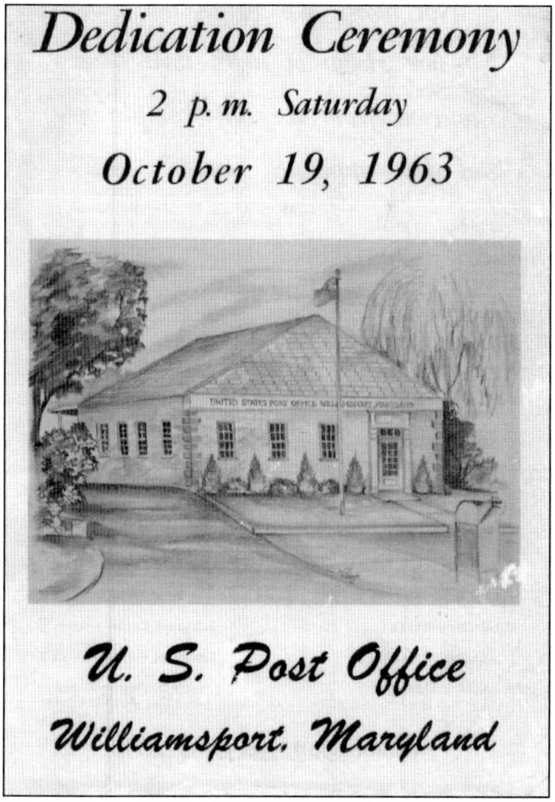

In 1963, the post office moved from its old location on the corner of N. Conococheague and W. Potomac Streets to a new building on W. Salisbury Street. This is the cover from the official dedication ceremony held on October 19, 1963. (Courtesy Williamsport Town Museum.)

Williamsport citizens are known for their community spirit that, in this photo, takes the form of a March of Dimes drive. Pictured from left to right are David Cushwa III, Maurice Miller, and Maurice Snyder. (Courtesy Williamsport Town Museum.)

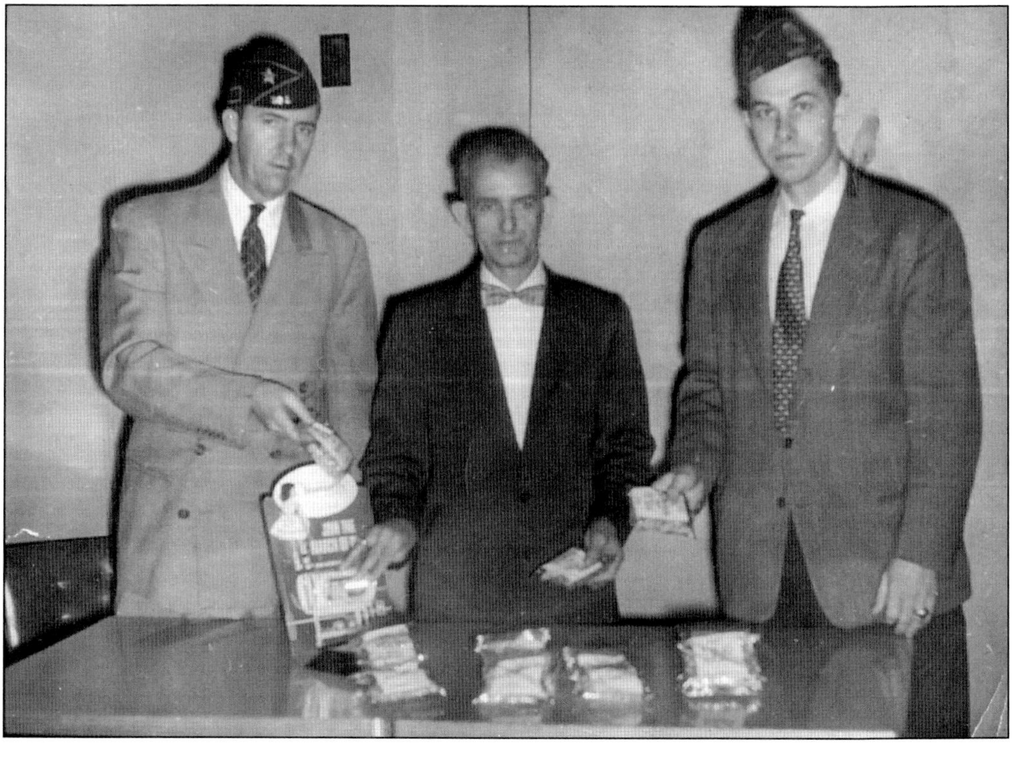

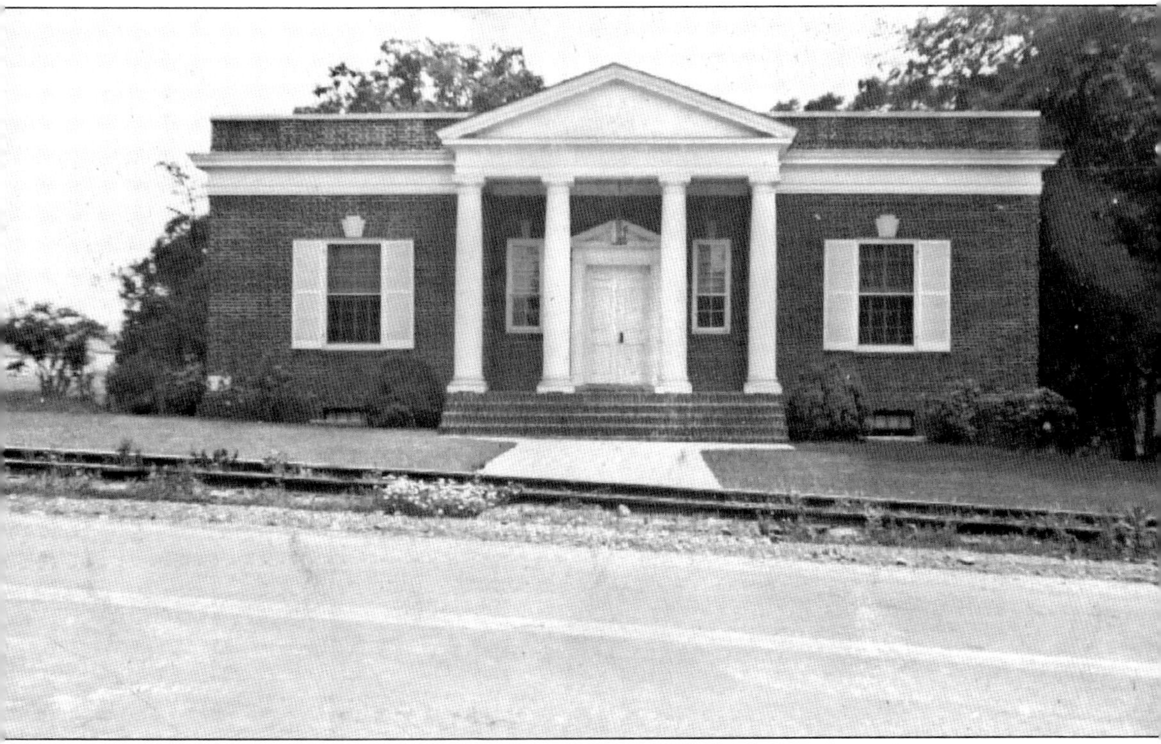

Here is an early photograph of the Williamsport Memorial Library with the trolley tracks running right in front of it. Ground was broken for the library on July 25, 1936. It was erected in memory of the students who were killed in the Rockville bus and train accident. Late on the night of April 11, 1935, a school bus carrying 26 students and their teacher, Louise Funk, was traveling back to Williamsport from a science exhibit at the University of Maryland in College Park. At 11:26 p.m., the bus, thinking the tracks clear in the damp, foggy night, headed across. The oncoming B&O Railroad express westbound from Washington, D.C., to St. Louis rammed into the bus at 58 miles per hour. The entire community was rocked by this tragic event, and 14 students lost their lives. A plaque on the left as you enter the library honors their names: Carl Brindel, Bertha Castle, Mary Louise Downs, Norris Downs, Pearl Emerson, James Flurie, Elva Harsh, Phoebe Kelley, Leroy Kendall , Paul McElroy, Claude Myers, Virginia Myers, Lois Winters, and Margaret Eva Zimmerman. To this day, Montgomery County school buses are prohibited from passing over at-grade crossings. (Courtesy Williamsport Town Museum.)

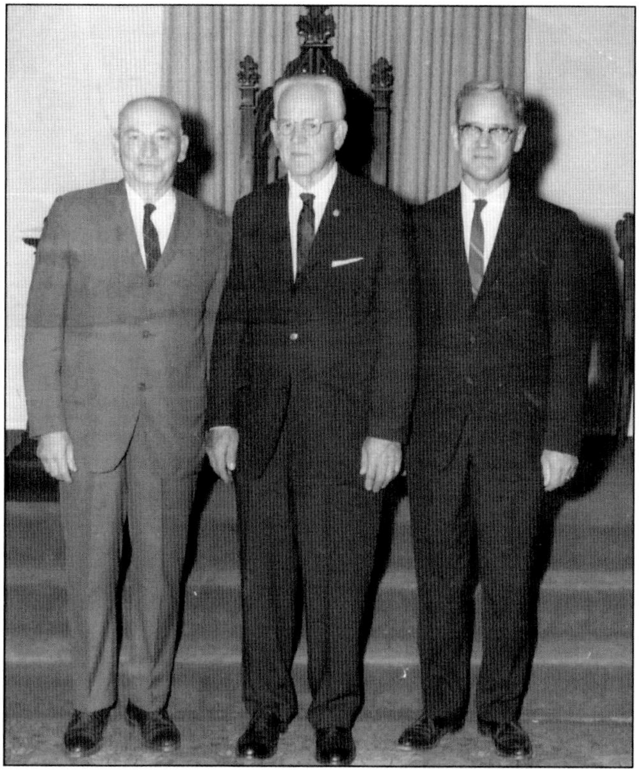

This photograph shows several of the scoutmasters from the Boy Scouts of Williamsport, including the very first scoutmaster of this historic troop, Rev. Milton Petzold. Shown here, from left to right, are: Reverend Michael, scoutmaster 1960–1971, Reverend Petzold, scoutmaster 1914–1916, and Reverend Hoover, scoutmaster 1942–1949. (Courtesy Williamsport Town Museum.)

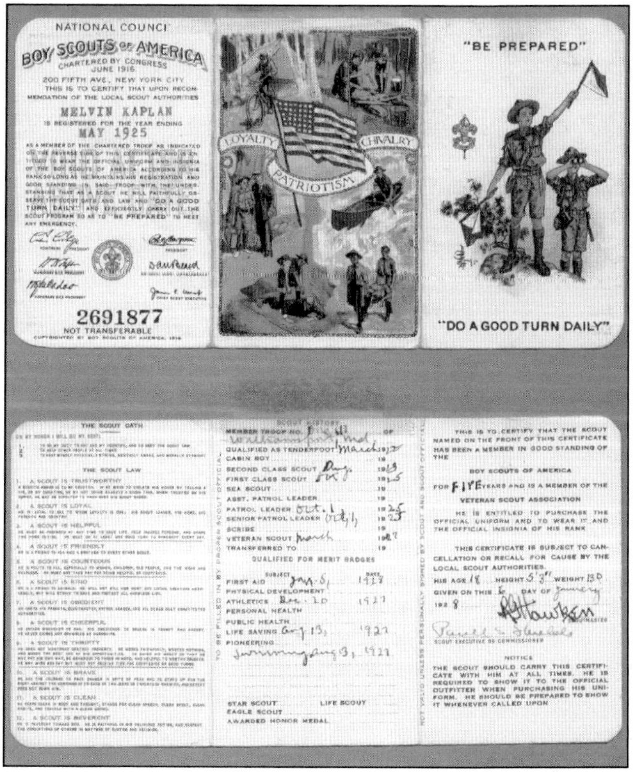

These cards from 1925 and 1928 belonged to a young Melvin Kaplan during his years as a Boy Scout. The Williamsport Troop is the oldest continuously chartered troop in the state of Maryland. Though begun in 1914, the troop did not become formally affiliated with a council until 1922, when it was chartered as Troop No. 1 by the Baltimore Council. When the Williamsport troop joined the newly formed Washington County Council in 1929, there was a troop renumbering that took place, and thus they became the current Troop No. 17. (Courtesy Williamsport Town Museum.)

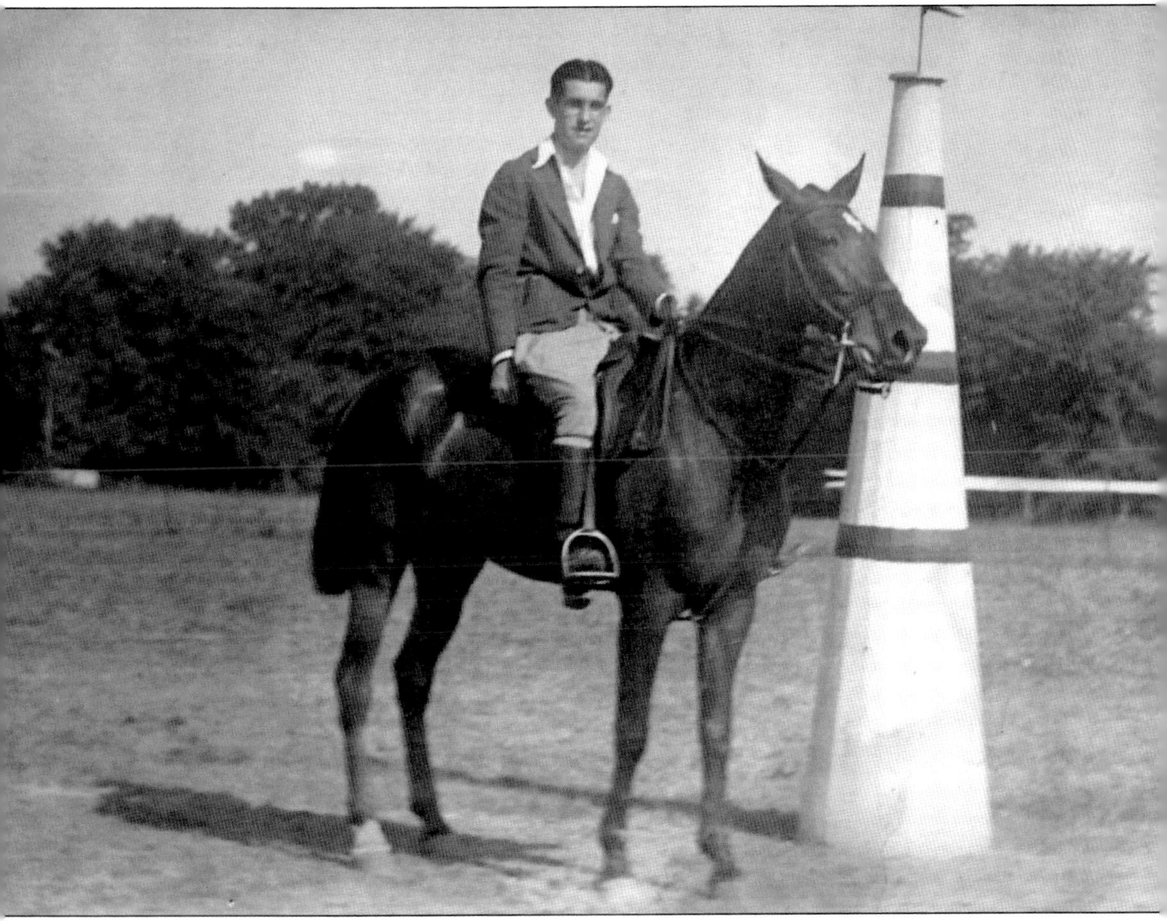

The Washington County Polo Association, founded in 1926, was headquartered in Williamsport, and the polo field was located in back of Byron's Tannery. The club played others from throughout the region including the U.S. Marine team from Quantico, Virginia, and the Greenbrier Club from White Sulphur Springs, West Virginia. Here we see one of the players mounted on his horse in 1933. William D. Byron and Bill Hurd were among the members of the club. Each club member maintained three or four ponies, sometimes buying cast-offs from quality teams from Long Island, New York. A pony could cost between $400 and $500, with a higher-end pony running to $1,200 or more. (Courtesy Western Maryland Room Washington County Free Library.)

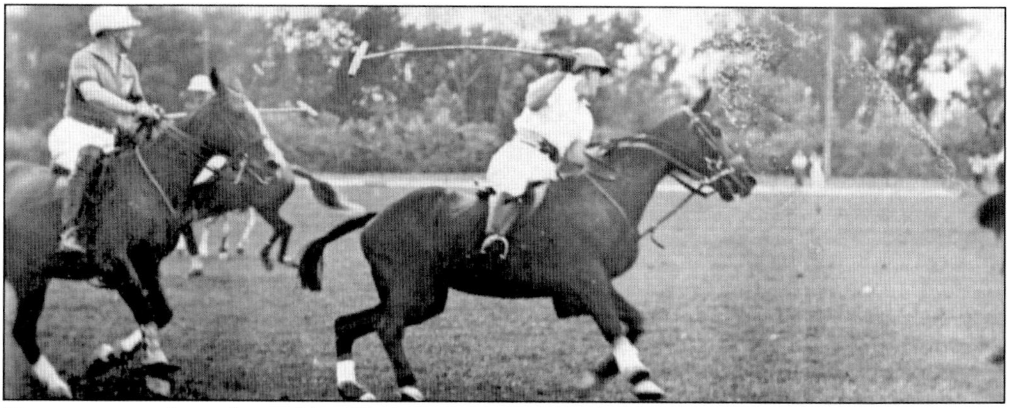

Here is a view of members of the Washington County Polo Club taking a shot at the ball during a polo match. World War II caused a rapid decline in the sport that had been all the rage just years earlier in the 1920s and 1930s. (Courtesy *Maryland Cracker Barrel*.)

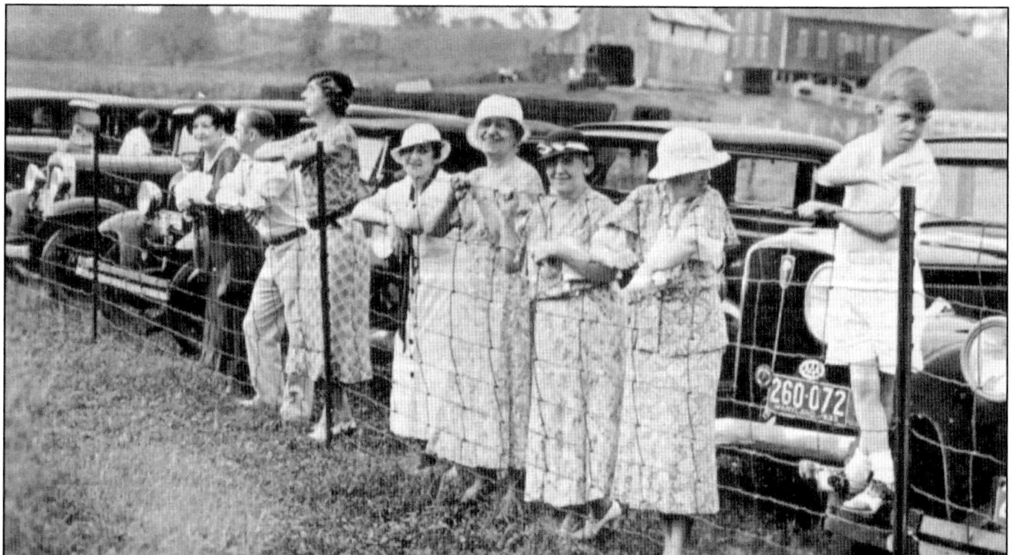

This 1933 photograph shows a group of spectators that had turned out to watch a polo match and lend support to the local team. (Courtesy *Maryland Cracker Barrel*.)

Here is just another example of one of the many community events held in Williamsport throughout the years. This program is from the First Annual Tournament and Ox-Roast held on September 8, 1934. Note that there were separate tables for "ladies and gentlemen" to try their hand at billiards and bowling. (Courtesy Williamsport Town Museum.)

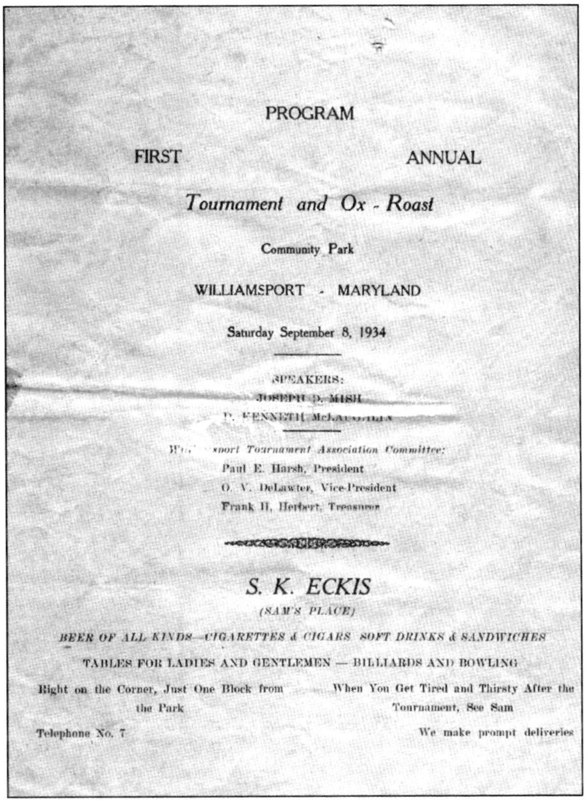

PROGRAM

FIRST ANNUAL

Tournament and Ox - Roast

Community Park

WILLIAMSPORT - MARYLAND

Saturday September 8, 1934

SPEAKERS:

JOSEPH D. MISH

D. KENNETH McLA[illegible]

W[illegible]sport Tournament Association Committee:

Paul E. Harsh, President

O. V. DeLawter, Vice-President

Frank H. Herbert, Treasurer

S. K. ECKIS

(SAM'S PLACE)

BEER OF ALL KINDS—CIGARETTES & CIGARS SOFT DRINKS & SANDWICHES

TABLES FOR LADIES AND GENTLEMEN — BILLIARDS AND BOWLING

Right on the Corner, Just One Block from the Park

When You Get Tired and Thirsty After the Tournament, See Sam

Telephone No. 7

We make prompt deliveries

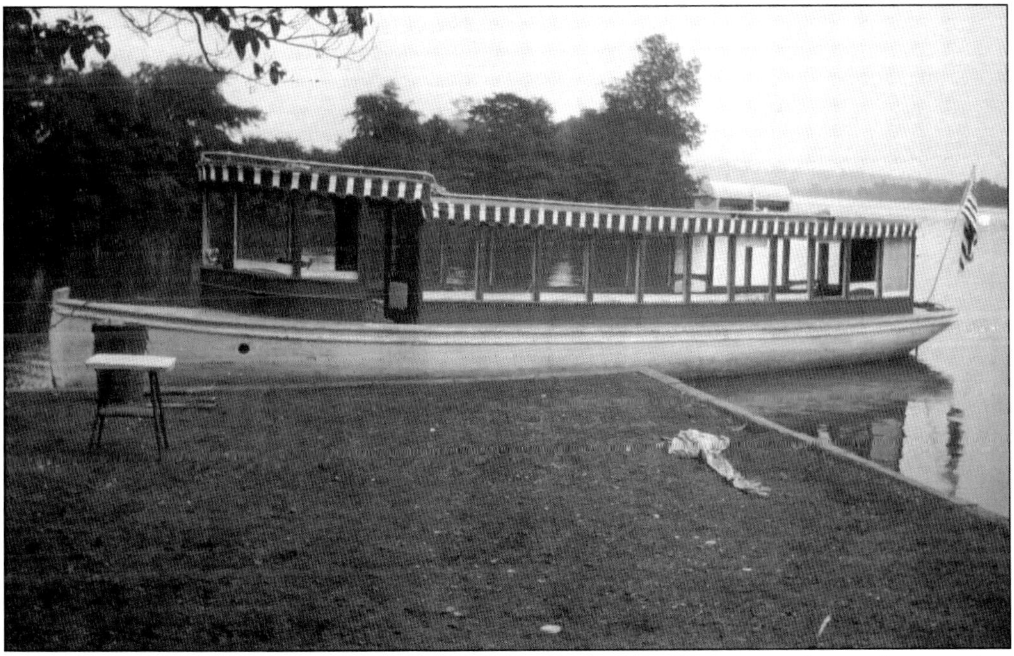

Here is a river pleasure boat in the vicinity of the canal. These boats were designed to travel in the canal. (Courtesy C&O Canal National Historical Park Headquarters.)

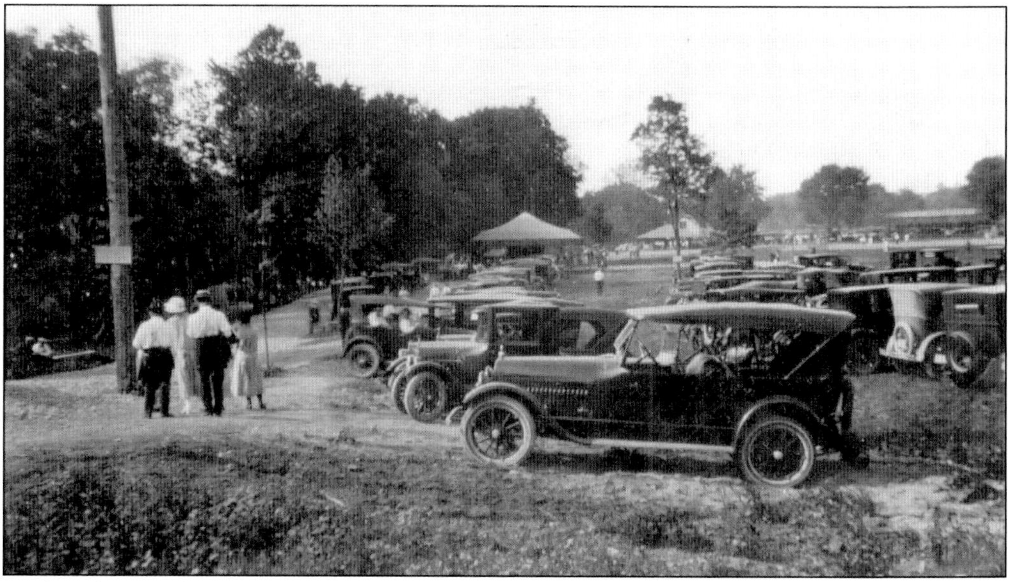

Look at the crowd of cars packing the parking area in this photograph from the 1920s at Conomac Park. The park was opened in 1924 along the eastern edge of the Conococheague Creek. Founded by Bess Lemen, the 22-acre park was named after the Conococheague Creek ("Cono") and the nearby Potomac River ("Mac"). (Courtesy Williamsport Town Museum.)

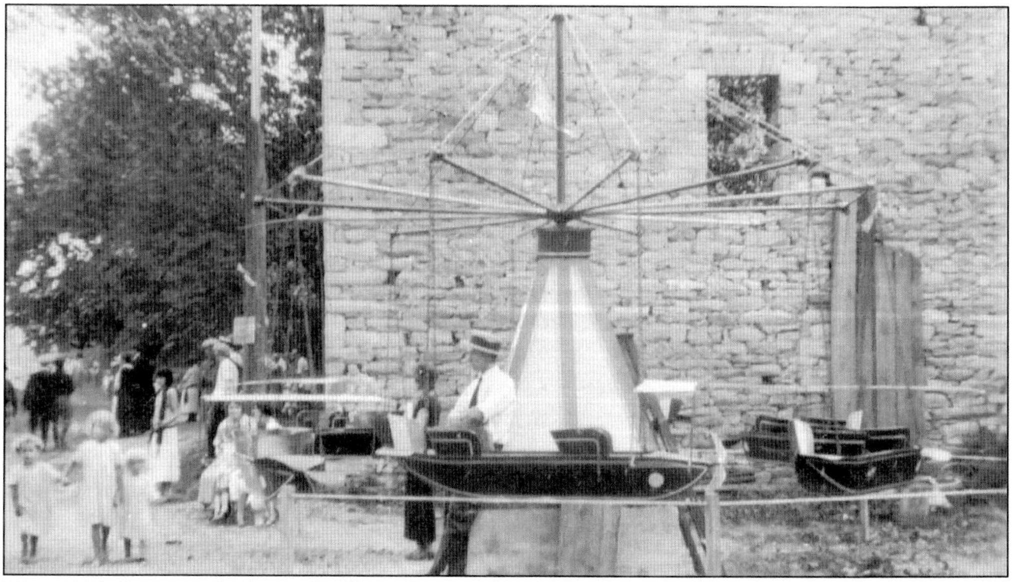

This 1925 photograph shows the flying boats ride at Conomac Park. Note the children dressed in light outfits and going barefoot on the left. During the park's short existence, it became well known, and many tourists visited during "touring" vacations. (Courtesy Williamsport Town Museum.)

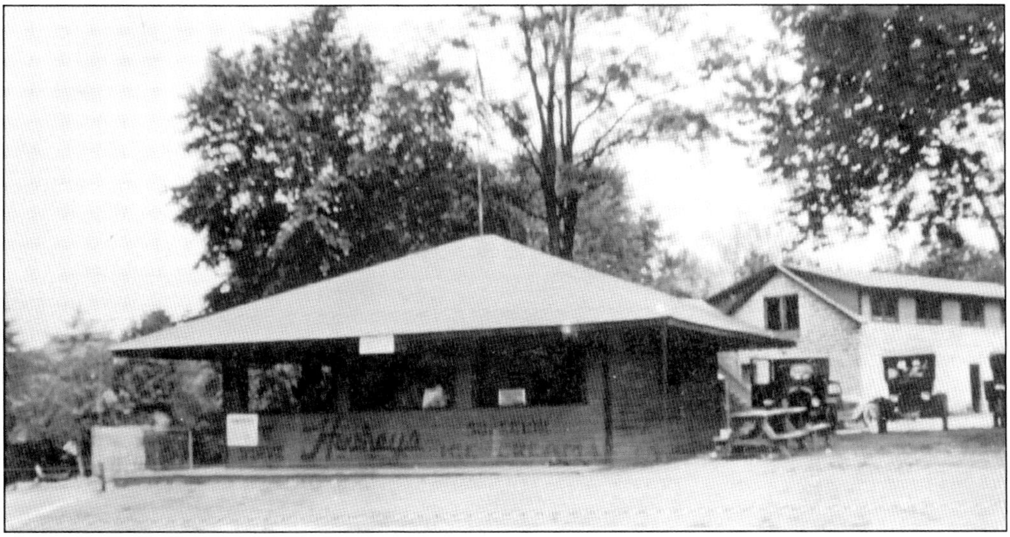

This shot of Conomac Park shows the concession stand and the boathouse. The park was well equipped with lifeguards, picnic tables, a grandstand, and more. The park closed in 1936 after that year's devastating flooding. (Courtesy Williamsport Town Museum.)

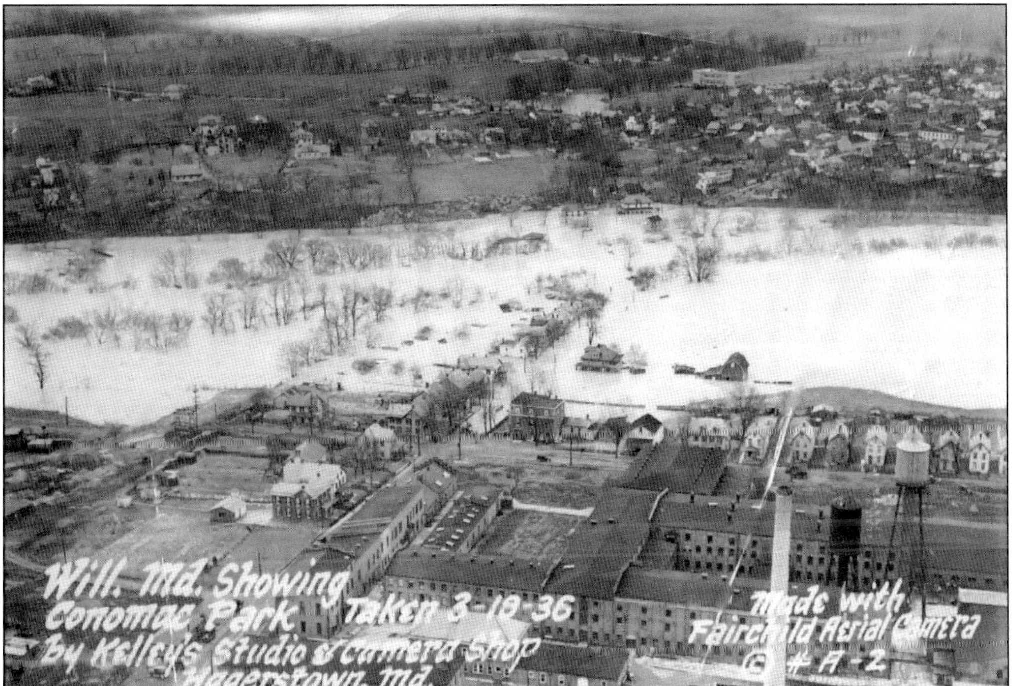

Taken on March 19, 1936, with a Fairchild aerial camera, this photograph shows Williamsport and Conomac Park in the aftermath of the flood of March 18, 1936. Floods of historic proportions have often plagued the town that sits on the banks of the Potomac River. The first documented flood (called a "freshet" in a 1933 Williamsport Chamber of Commerce town history) was in 1819. Other documented floods occurred on April 20, 1852, and November 25, 1877. The 1877 flood carried away a sawmill and a bridge from the Cumberland Valley Rail Road. (Courtesy Western Maryland Room Washington County Free Library.)

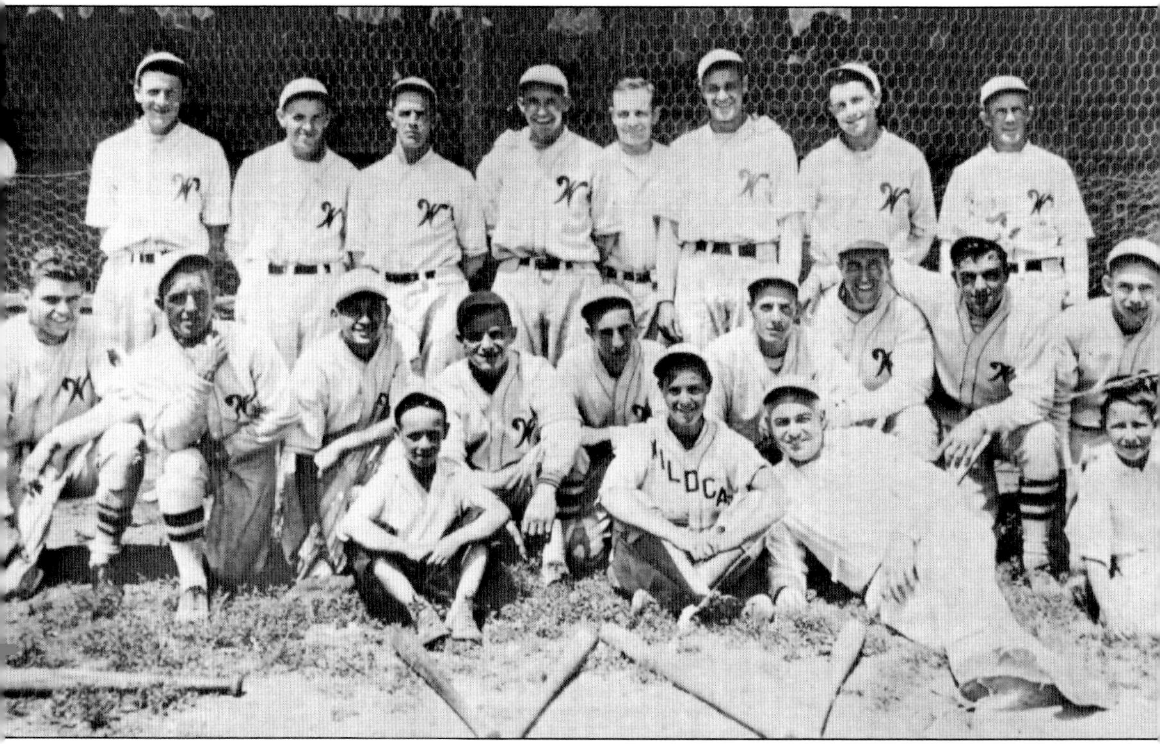

This photo, taken between 1928 and 1930, shows the Williamsport Wildcats. Baseball has long been popular in Williamsport, and teams used to play in Conomac Park before it was forced to close after the 1936 flood. Shown in the photograph from left to right are (first row) Andy Grimes, bat boy; Doris Chrisman; Howard Betts, business manager; and Roy Kreps, bat boy; (middle row) Shorty Knode; Jack Potts; Melvin Kaplan; Hudson Norman; Bee Secker, manager; Nathan Buharp; Tuck Robinson; Boots Poffenberger, later a player for the Detroit Tigers; and Billy Hammaker; (back row) Fritz Guessford; Russ Lowman; Bill Zimmerman; Jack Kreps; John Hetzer; Giggs Myers; Clyde Mauck; and Russ Zimmerman. (Courtesy *Maryland Cracker Barrel.*)

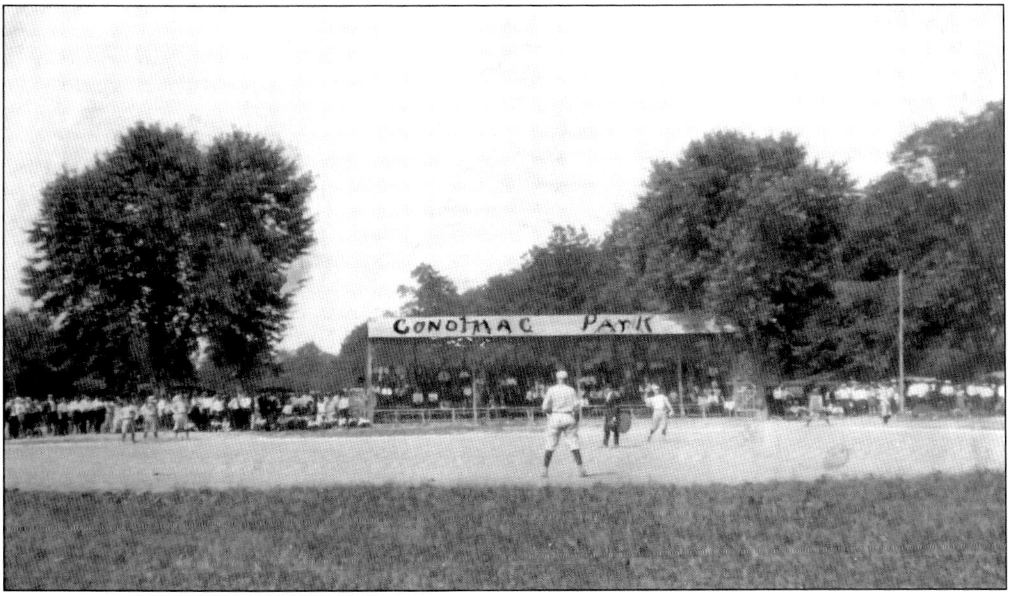

Baseball was definitely one of the favorite activities at Conomac Park. This photograph was taken on July 20, 1924, and features the Williamsport team playing against the team from Martinsburg, West Virginia. (Courtesy Williamsport Town Museum.)

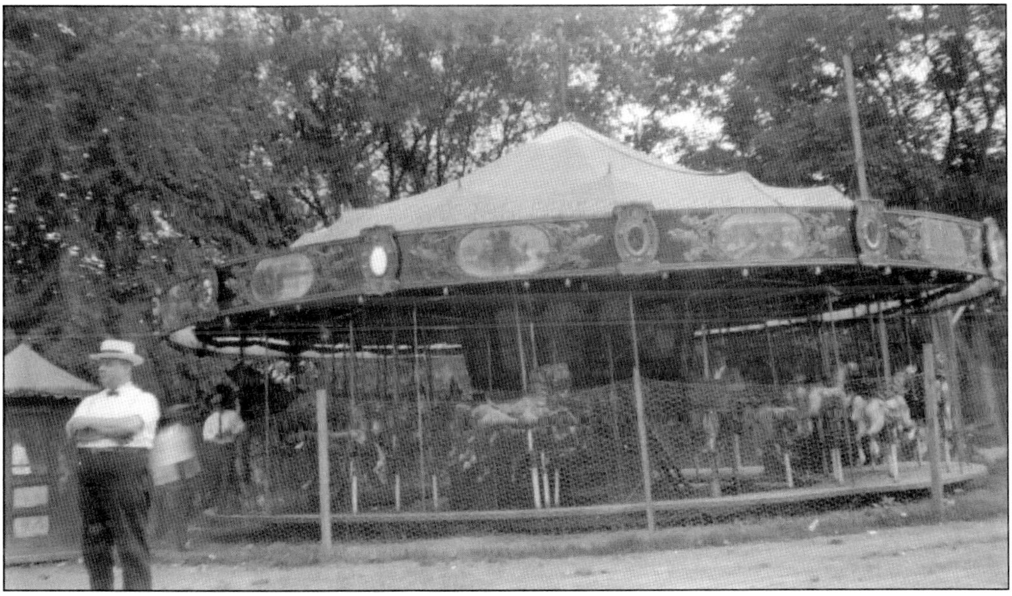

Here is the merry-go-round at Conomac Park. Note the man in the hat in the foreground. You can almost imagine he's drumming up business, calling out for you to come ride the painted horses. (Courtesy Williamsport Town Museum.)

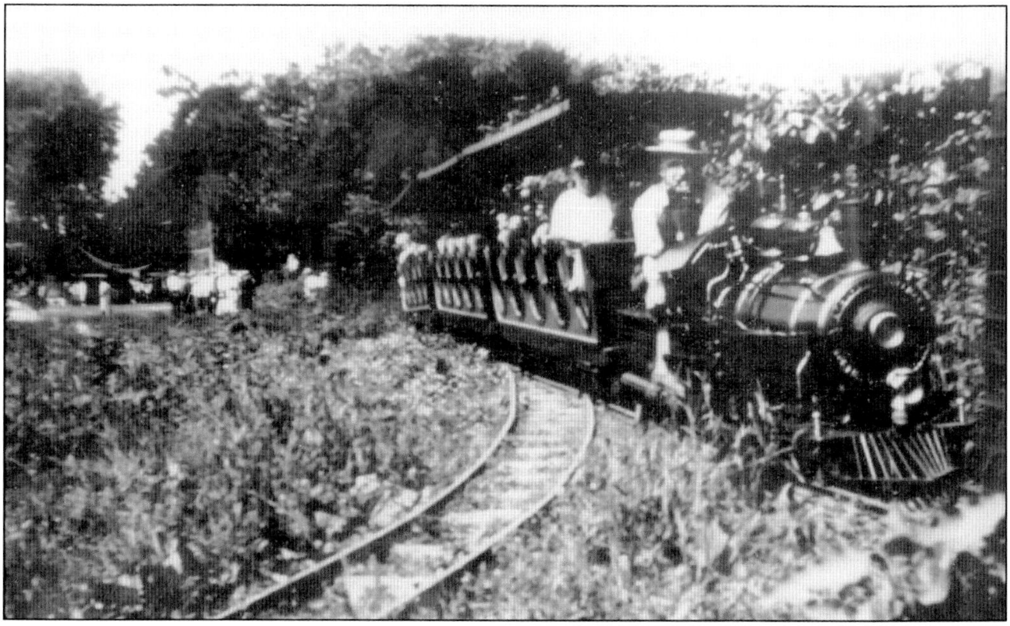

When local people think of trains at area parks, they often think of the one that used to ply the grounds of Pen Mar. This photograph, however, shows that Conomac Park in Williamsport had a miniature train as one of its popular attractions too. The train began near a spring and traveled on down into the park. Water from this spring was also used at the tannery. While Conomac Park didn't have the same breathtaking mountain views of Pen Mar, it was able to boast of something that Pen Mar couldn't—water for swimming and boating. (Courtesy Williamsport Town Museum.)

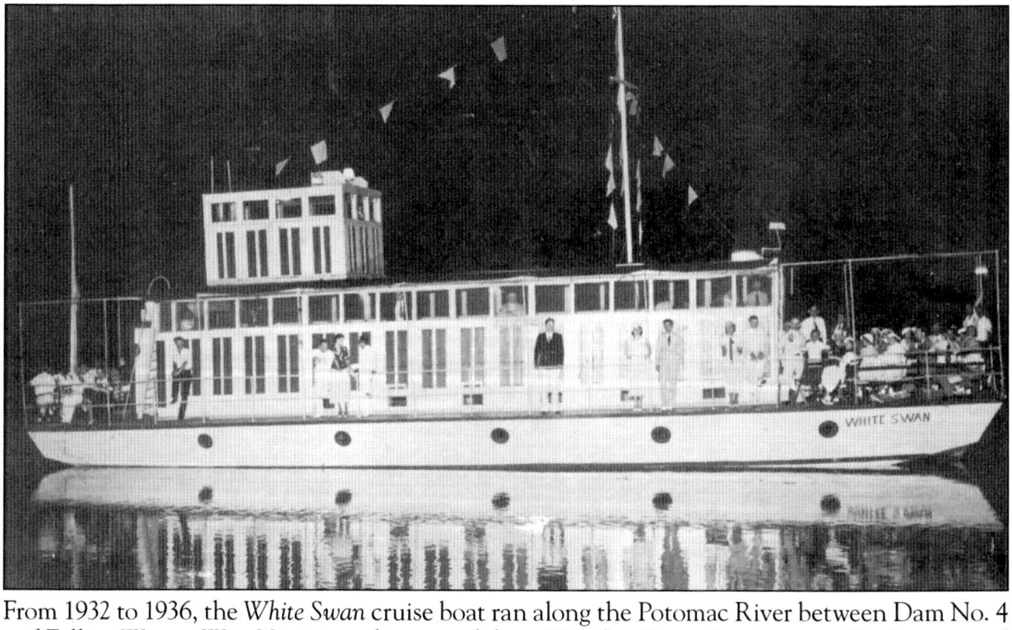

From 1932 to 1936, the *White Swan* cruise boat ran along the Potomac River between Dam No. 4 and Falling Waters, West Virginia, a distance of about 20 miles. Owned and operated by Preston and Leila Carl, it cost $6,000 and carried between 3,000 and 6,000 passengers a year. Accommodating 125 people per voyage, the boat had a 35-foot long dining room and a 40-foot long dance floor. The boat was destroyed in the 1936 flood. (Courtesy *Maryland Cracker Barrel.*)

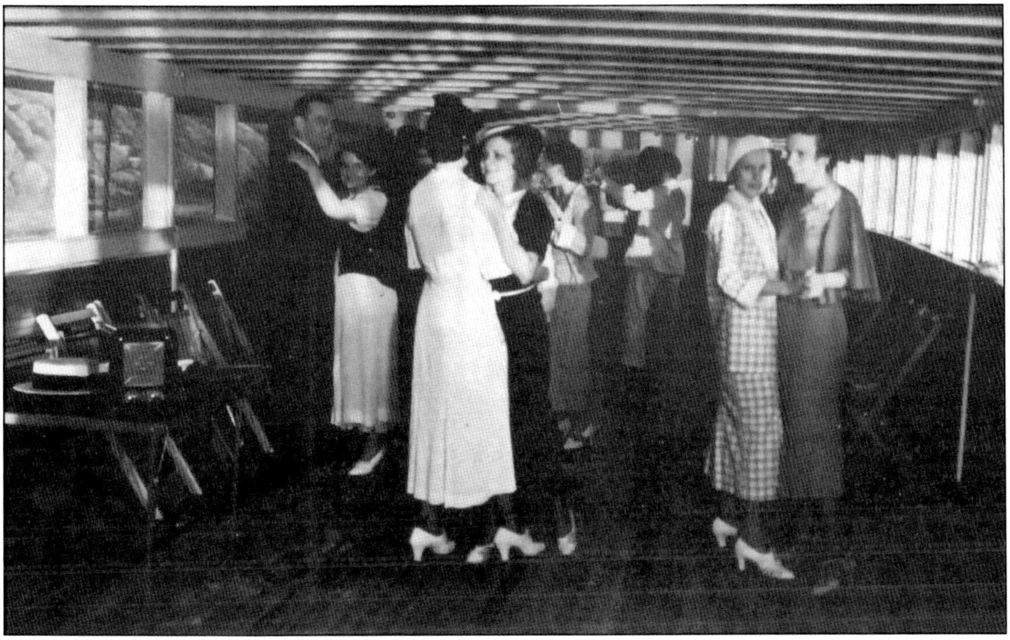

This photograph shows the large, 40-foot-long dance parlor on the *White Swan* excursion boat. In 1936, the boat was destroyed by that year's monumental flood. Pieces of the boat were washed down the river, and the piano was found lodged in a tree. (Courtesy *Maryland Cracker Barrel.*)

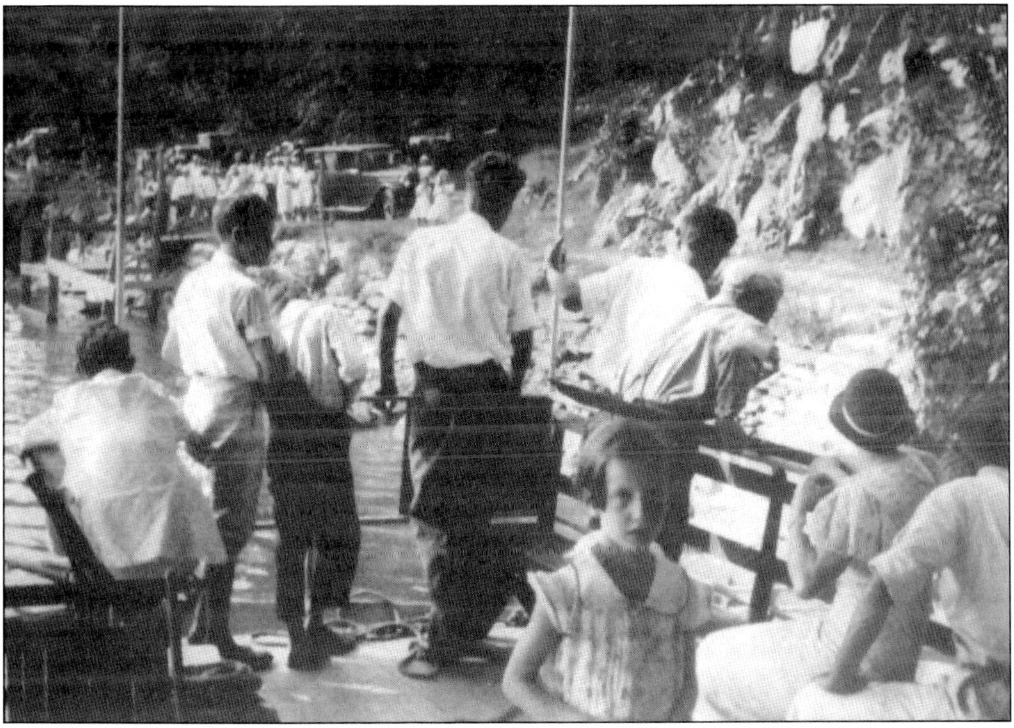

This view shows the *White Swan* coming into shore to dock in the 1930s. The boat was also known as *Carl's Pleasure Boat*, named after the owners Leila and Preston Carl. (Courtesy *Maryland Cracker Barrel.*)

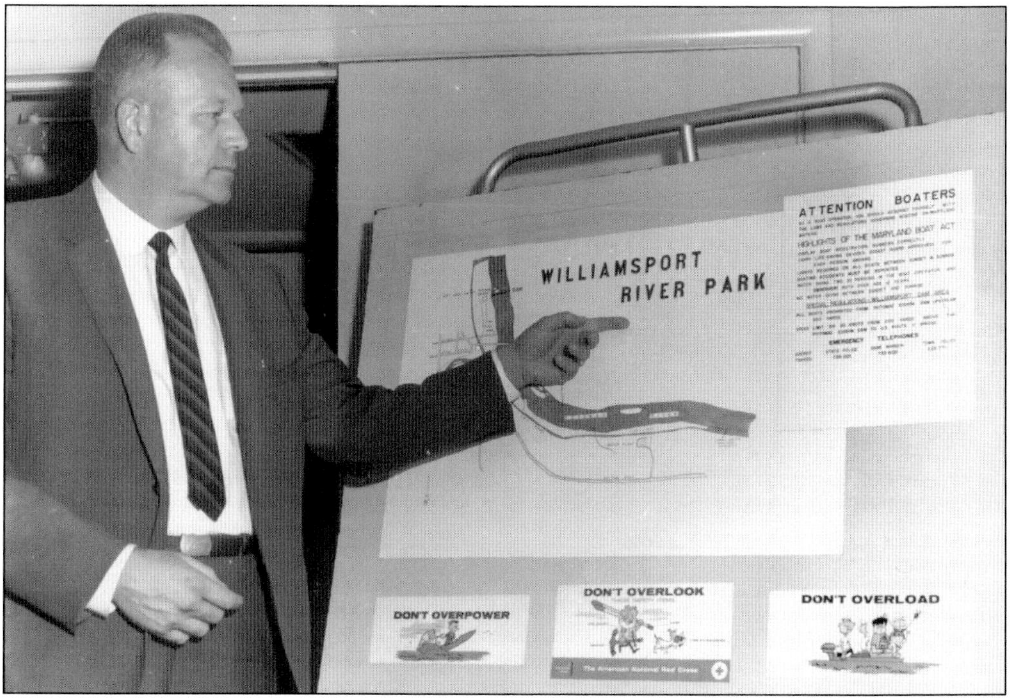

This photograph was taken during a presentation about the Potomac River and Williamsport's River Park. Note all the safety instructions for boaters about not overloading their boats or using excess power. Each year, rescue services are called out to rescue boaters who have gotten in trouble on the river. (Courtesy C&O Canal National Historical Park Headquarters.)

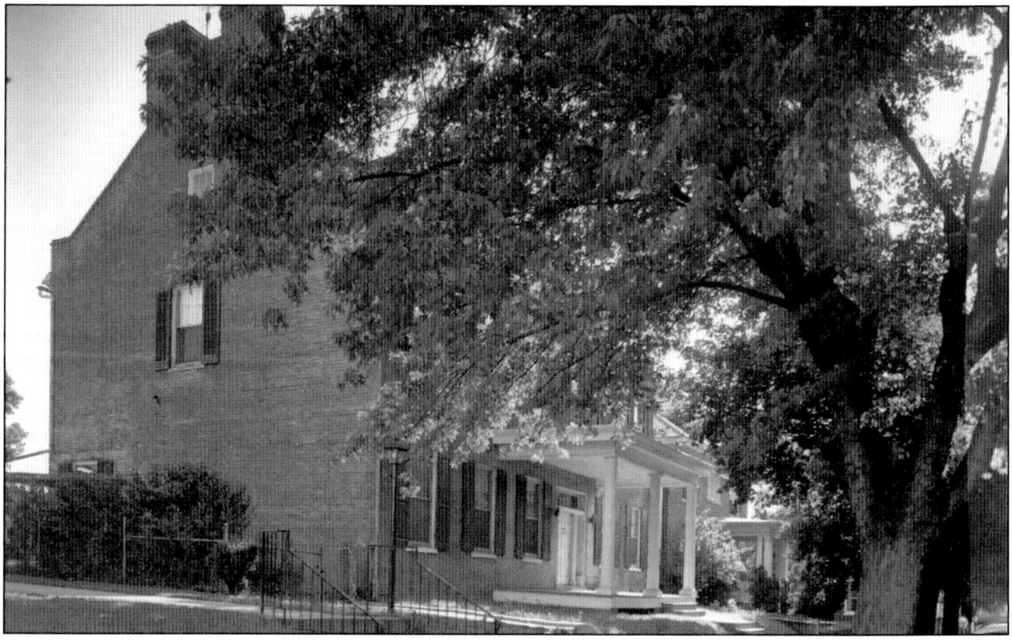

Located at 26 E. Salisbury Street in Williamsport is the Steffey House, built in 1804. The brick house was originally designed as a bank and, in the custom of the day, a residence for the banker's family. (Courtesy Western Maryland Room Washington County Free Library.)

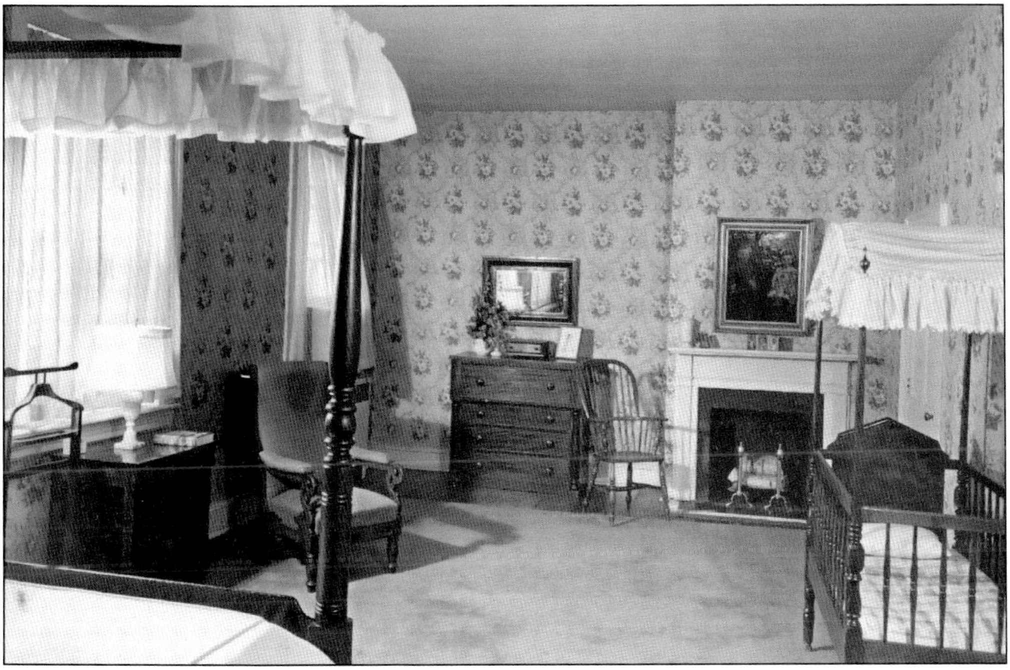

This interior view of the Steffey House shows the master bedroom, just one of five bedrooms, three with fireplaces. Note some of the period furnishings such as the infant's crib and four-poster master bed. (Courtesy Western Maryland Room Washington County Free Library.)

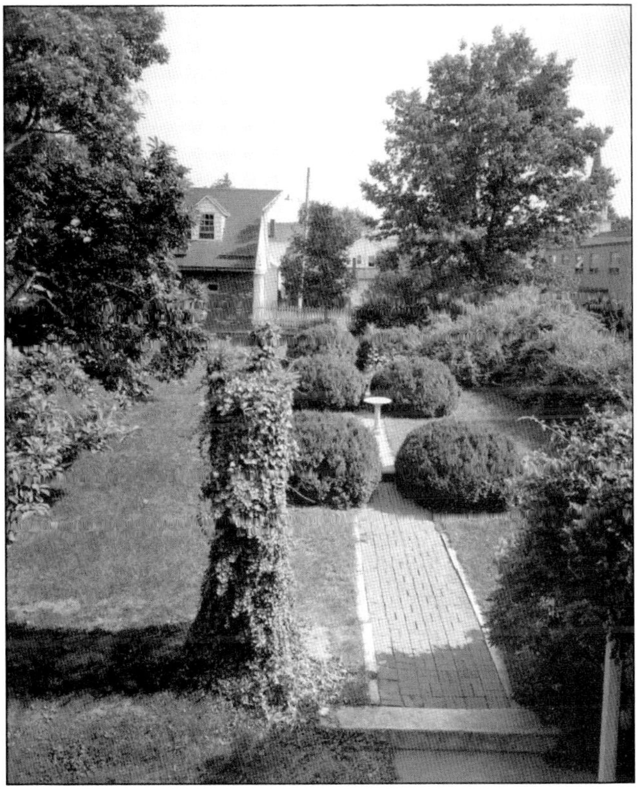

Here is another view of the Old Steffey House, this time showing the gardens in the back of the property. (Courtesy Western Maryland Room Washington County Free Library.)

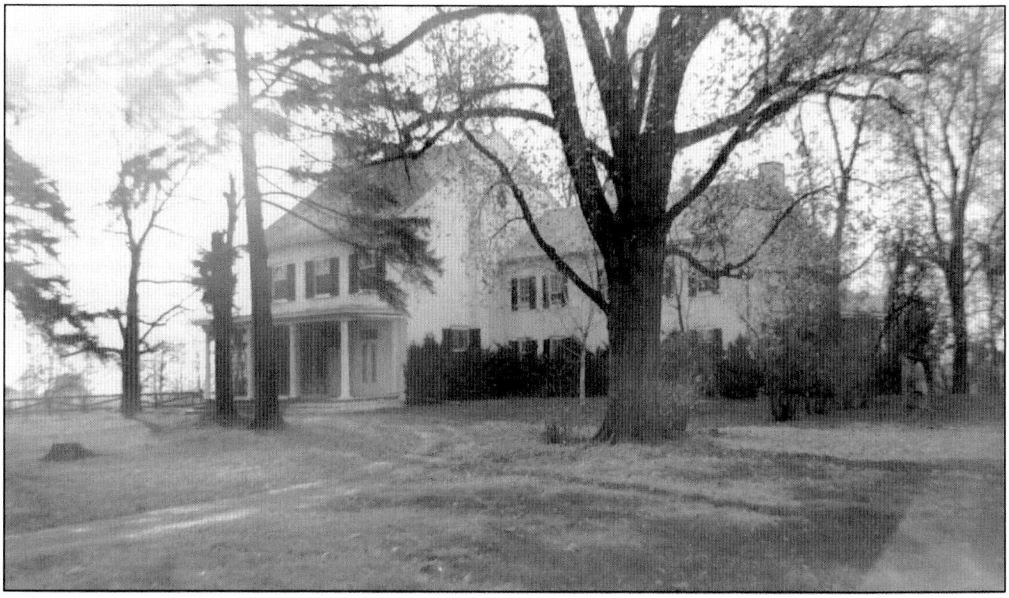

Taken in November 1956, this photograph shows Tammany Manor (also known as Mount Tammany) not far from downtown Williamsport. Built after the Revolutionary War by Matthew Van Lear, the home was named Tammany after the chief of the Delaware Indians. Related by marriage to the Van Lears, William Henry Harrison, the ninth U.S. president, dined at Tammany on his way to Washington, D.C., to be inaugurated in 1841. (Courtesy Washington County Historical Society.)

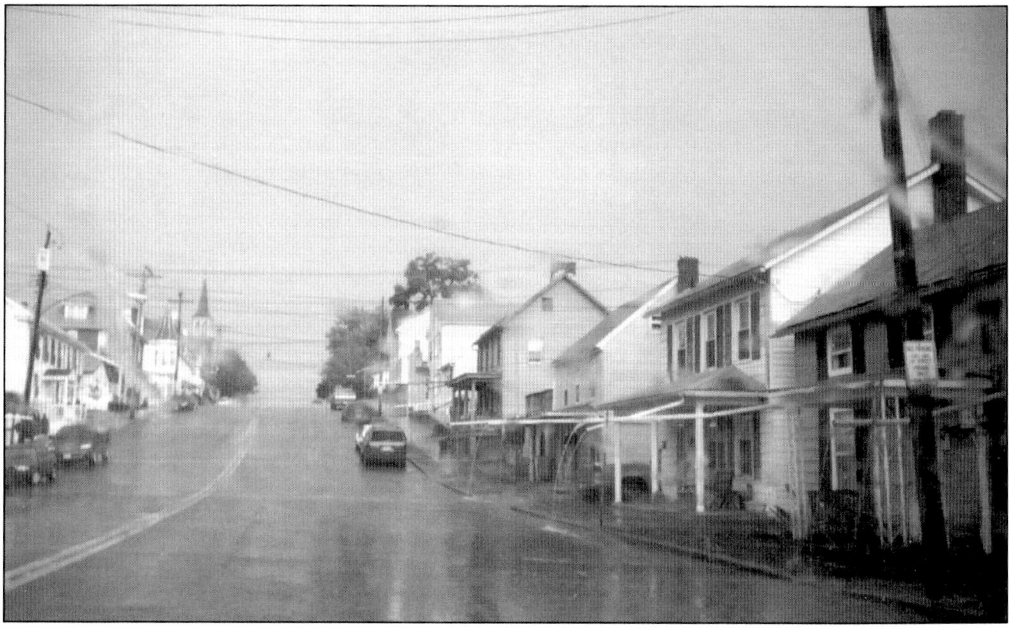

This photo, taken during a late spring storm, shows Church Street. The most interesting aspect of this photograph is all the drainpipes sticking straight out from the houses into the street. The water is pouring out of the pipes, and you are guaranteed a good drenching if you walk underneath. This style of rain gutter is common throughout downtown Williamsport and attracts comments from visitors seeing this for the first time. (Courtesy Mary H. Rubin.)

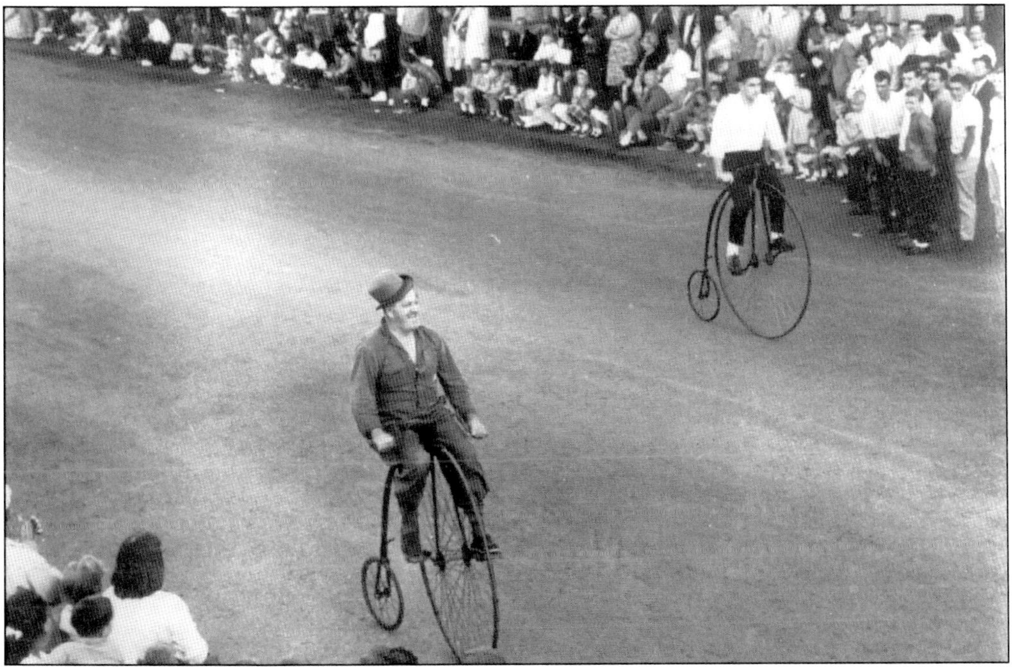

Here is a photograph of Lloyd "Leggs" Lemen and Jim Baker riding their big-wheelers during a town parade. Note how the handlebars come down across their laps. Quite a crowd had turned out to line the streets for the parade. Leggs is just one of the many nicknames given to Williamsport residents over the years. Others include Chow Wow, Porky Wine, Windy Zimmerman, Gumps Knode, Wimpy Ardinger, Bassey Harsh, Turkey Bird Anderson, Mutt Robinson, and Moonbeam Guessford. (Courtesy Williamsport Town Museum.)

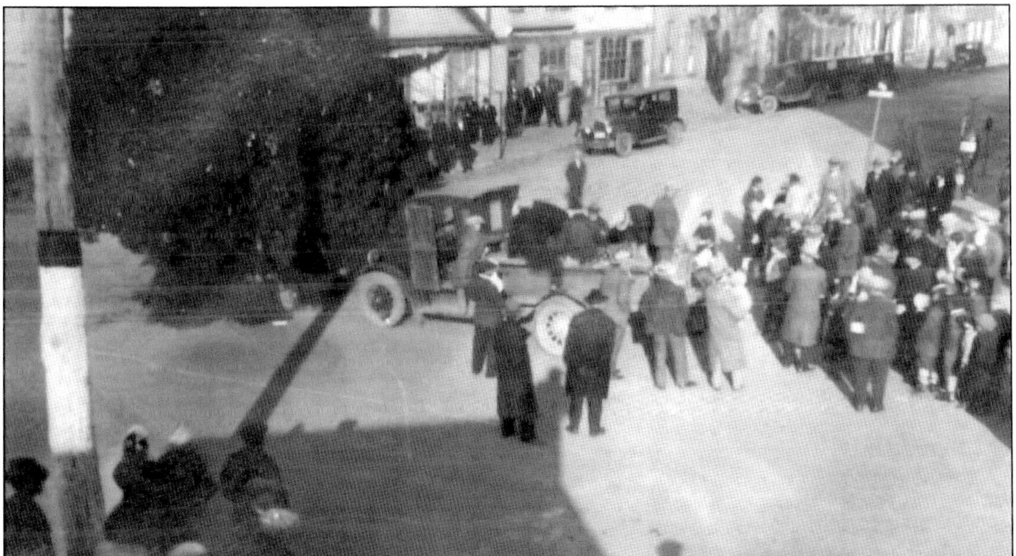

Every year, citizens of Williamsport watched the town tree erected for the holidays. In this 1920s photograph, lines formed as everyone waited eagerly for their turn to collect some of the treats being distributed from the back of the truck. (Courtesy Williamsport Town Museum.)

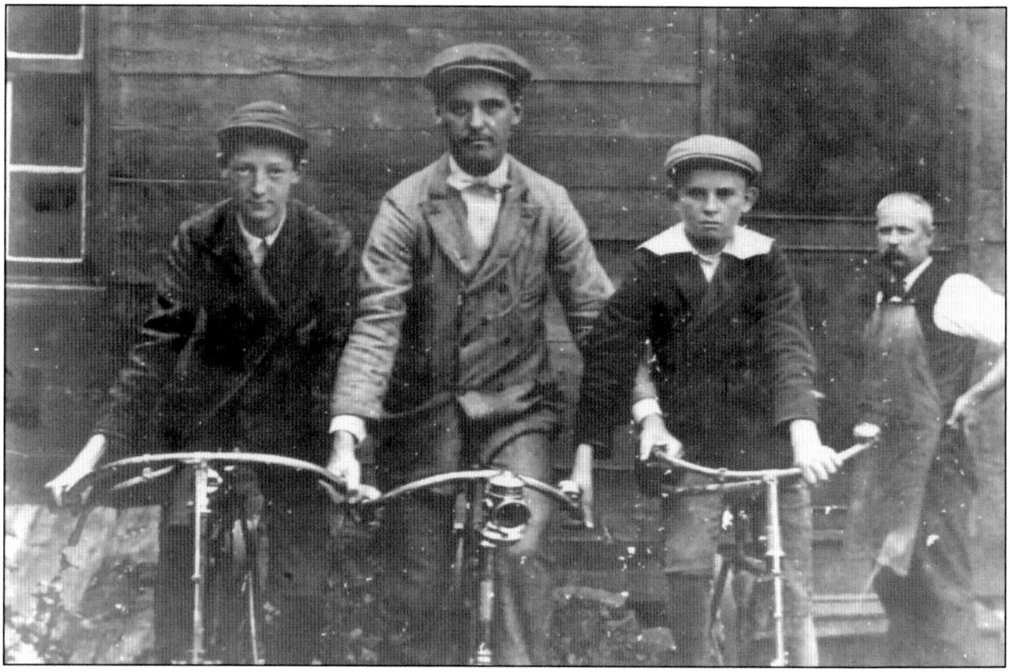

Here is a group of local citizens posing for the camera before taking off for some fun on their bicycles. Pictured from left to right are Charles Goodrich Jr., J. D. Grove, Eldrige Dorns, and Theo Reeder. (Courtesy Williamsport Town Museum.)

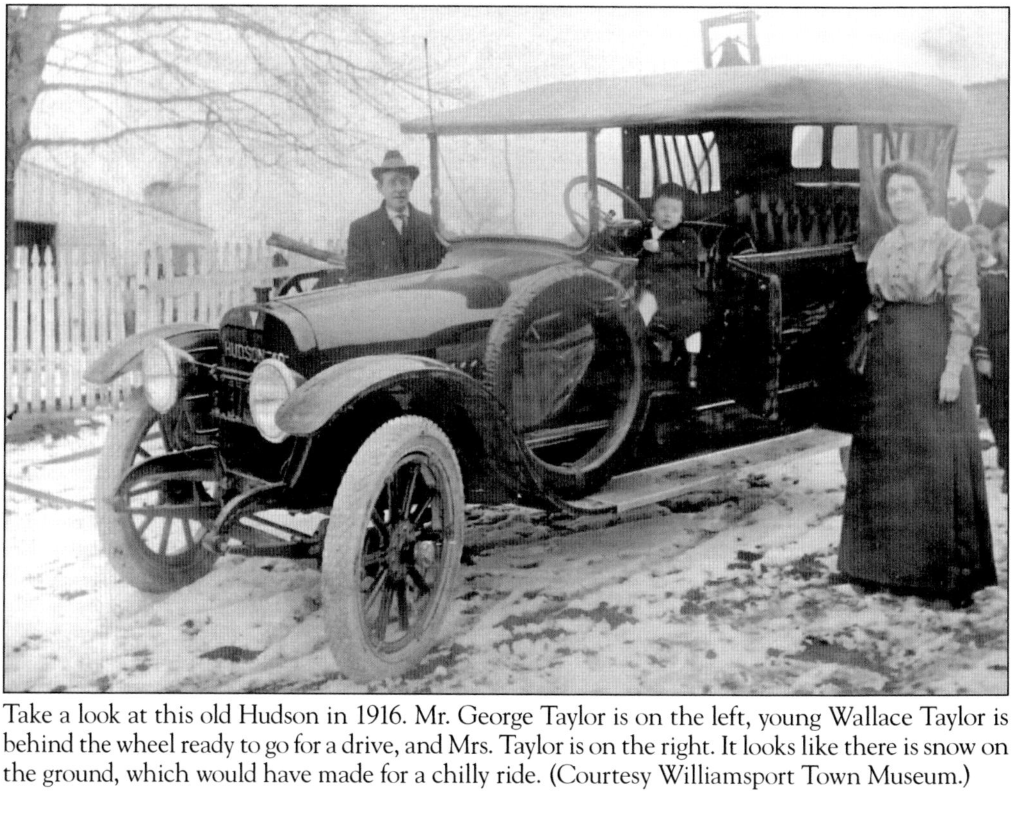

Take a look at this old Hudson in 1916. Mr. George Taylor is on the left, young Wallace Taylor is behind the wheel ready to go for a drive, and Mrs. Taylor is on the right. It looks like there is snow on the ground, which would have made for a chilly ride. (Courtesy Williamsport Town Museum.)

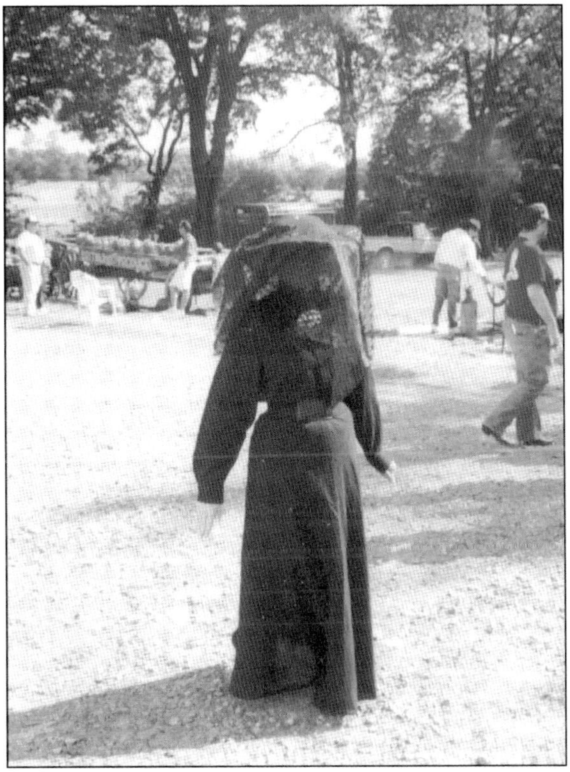

Here is Williamsport's famed Veiled Lady in her shadowy outfit. Stories about sightings of her creeping through Williamsport's dark alleys have passed into legend, many firm in their belief she existed, others equally determined she is no more than a myth. Legend has it that she was the ghost of a dead woman who could not rest in her grave or a woman seeking to catch her husband in an illicit affair. True or not, all legends are said to have some basis in truth, and it is certainly true that in years before bright street lights made an appearance in Williamsport, children came in before dark, and even adults would glance behind them in the night. (Courtesy Williamsport Town Museum.)

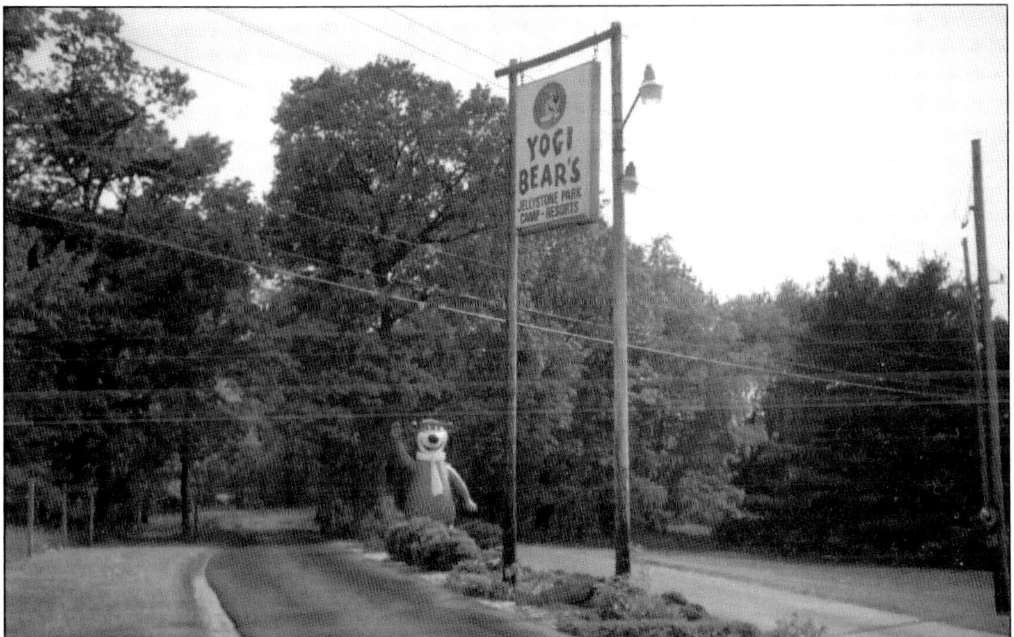

Just outside Williamsport, past Hippity-Hop Lane, is the Yogi Bear Jellystone Park Campsite. Many visitors to the area make their home base here while exploring the natural and historic sites in and around Williamsport. (Courtesy Mary H. Rubin.)

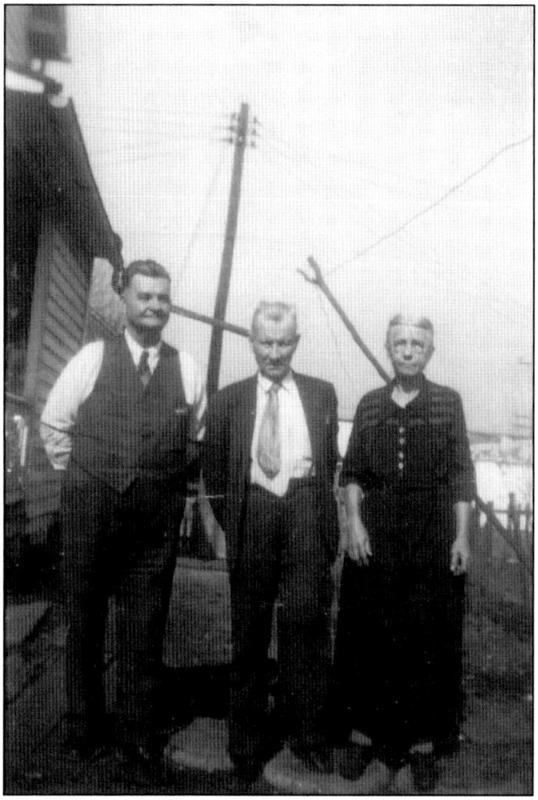

This photograph shows another group of Williamsport residents posing for the camera. Pictured from left to right are Charlie Nave, Joseph Nave, and Laura Nave. Note what appears to be a forked pole to hoist up a clothes line in the background. (Courtesy Williamsport Town Museum.)

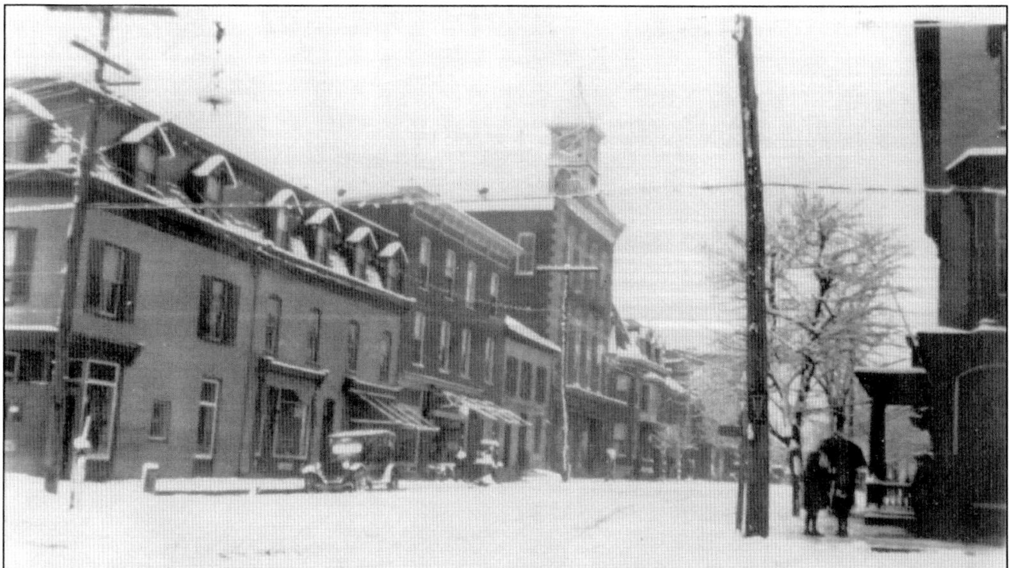

This winter scene from the early 20th century shows Conococheague Street. It looks like the snow was still falling as this photograph was taken. Note the vintage automobile parked across the street. (Courtesy Williamsport Town Museum.)

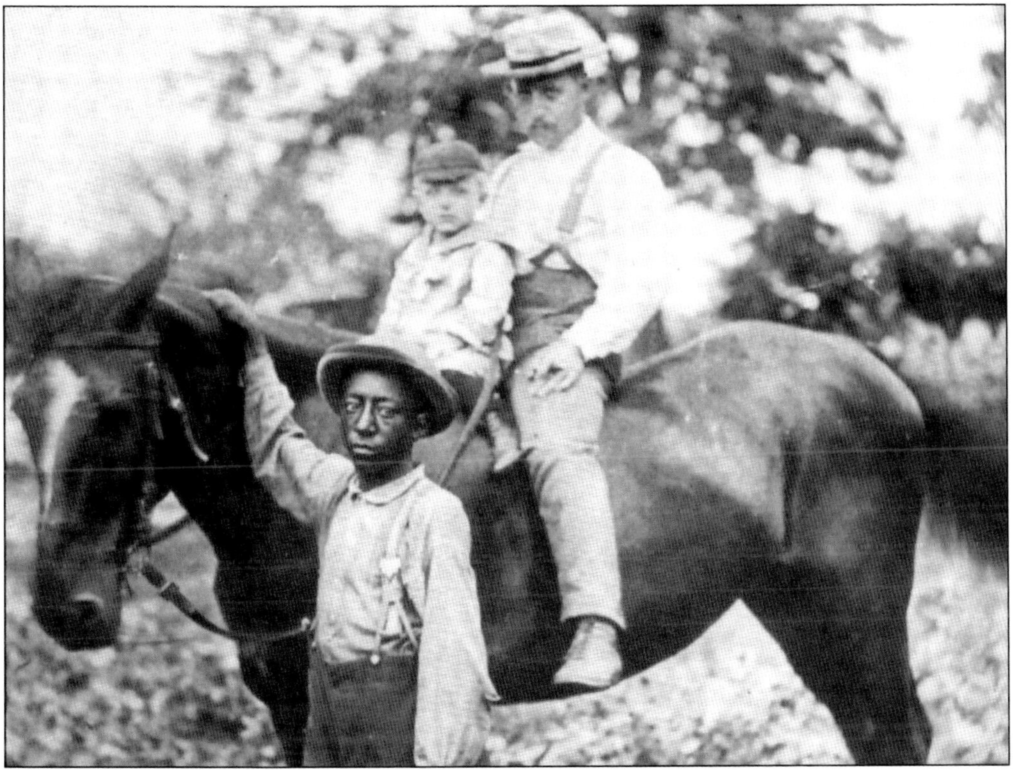

This photograph shows Albert S. Harsh sitting on a horse with his son Ike. Albert was the founder of Harsh's Meat Market. Jerry Smith is assisting him with the horse. (Courtesy *Maryland Cracker Barrel*.)

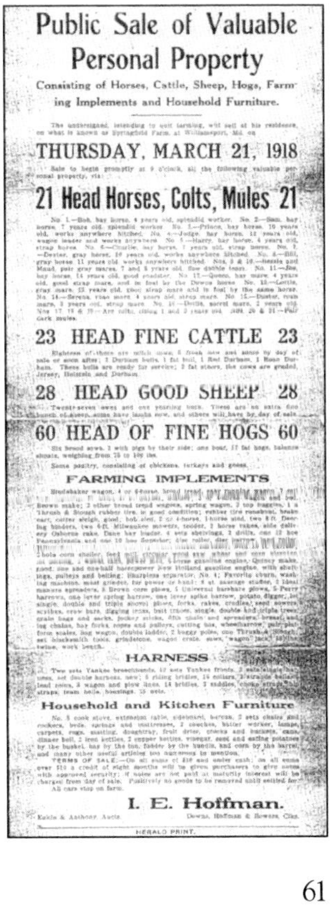

Public Sale of Valuable Personal Property

Consisting of Horses, Cattle, Sheep, Hogs, Farming Implements and Household Furniture.

THURSDAY, MARCH 21, 1918

21 Head Horses, Colts, Mules 21

23 HEAD FINE CATTLE 23

28 HEAD GOOD SHEEP 28

60 HEAD OF FINE HOGS 60

FARMING IMPLEMENTS

HARNESS

Household and Kitchen Furniture

I. E. Hoffman.

HERALD PRINT.

This image is from a notice of a public sale held at Springfield Farm on March 21, 1918. The Isaac Hoffman family farmed the property from 1897 to 1918. The long list of items for sale provides a unique glimpse back to the items in use in that era. Anyone for a cutter sleigh or a butter worker? (Courtesy Williamsport Town Museum.)

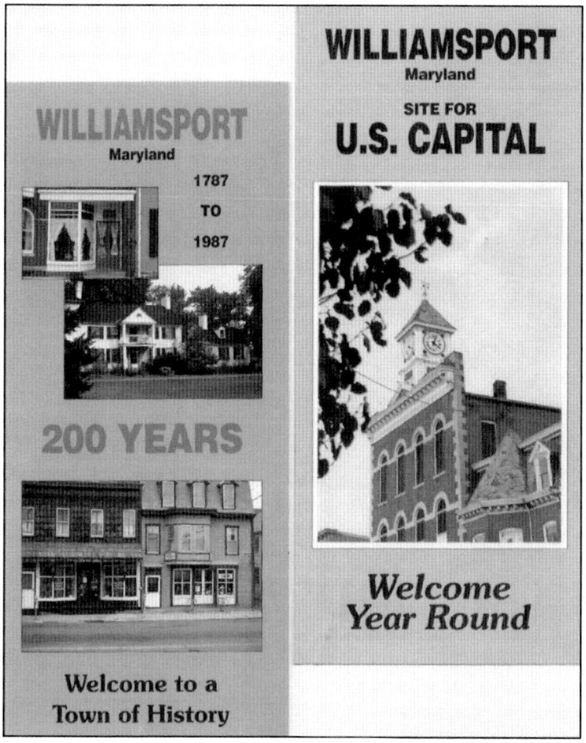

Here the old and new are next to each other. The town brochure on the left was released during the town's bicentennial in 1987, while the brochure on the right is the one currently in use. (Courtesy Williamsport Town Museum.)

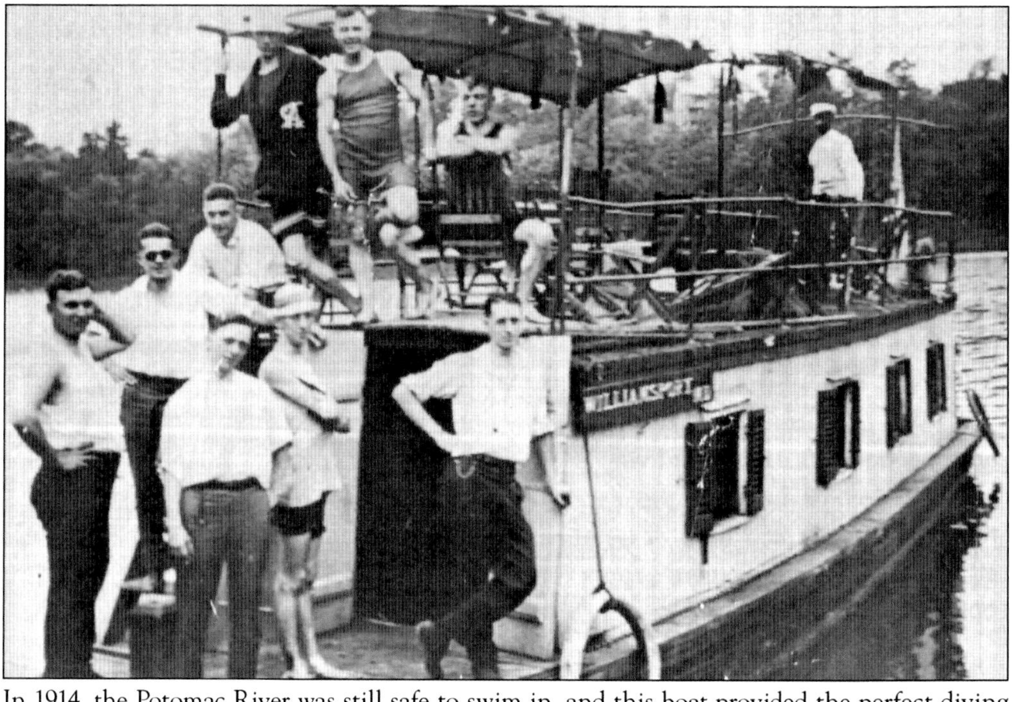

In 1914, the Potomac River was still safe to swim in, and this boat provided the perfect diving platform. In this photo, shown clockwise from the main deck, are: W. Geary Porter, John J. Firey, Hugh Troxell, Walter Hudson, Frank Elliott, Hubert Stottlemyer, Ned Ridenour, Bob Tenney, and Butch Firey. (Courtesy *Maryland Cracker Barrel.*)

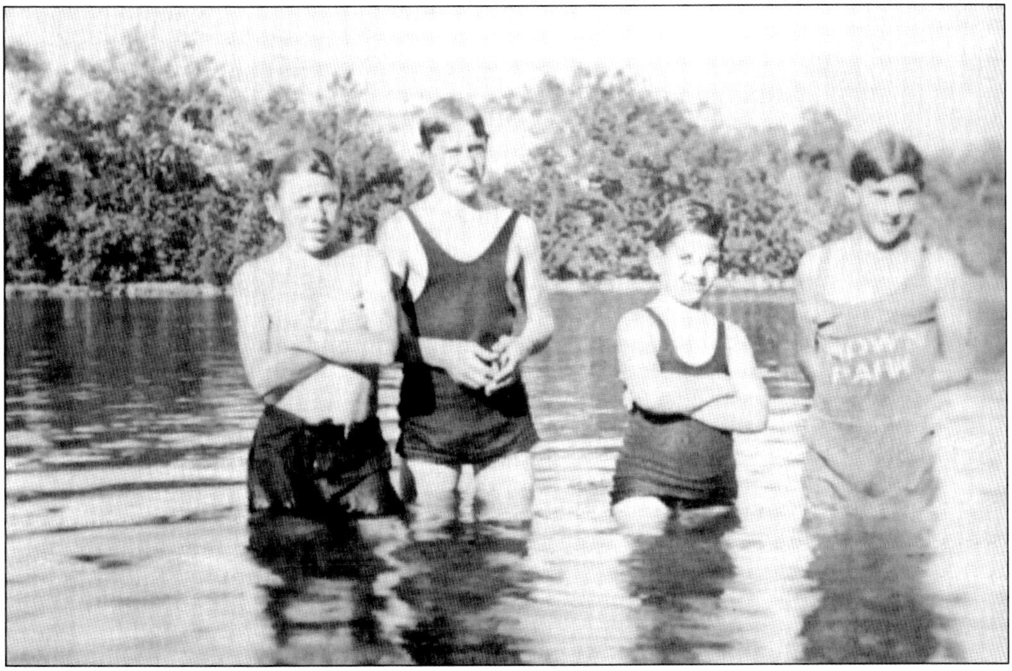

The river was one of the best places to be on a hot summer's day. This photograph from around 1930 shows a group of friends enjoying the cool waters of the Potomac River. (Courtesy *Maryland Cracker Barrel.*)

When the Union army camped near the site of John Brown's fort in Harpers Ferry, West Virginia, in 1861, they sought something of value to take with them as a souvenir of the historic site. They chose the bell from the Engine House, but arrangements were made for William Ensminger of Williamsport to care for the bell until funds could be raised to get the bell home. After his death, it remained in the care of his wife Elizabeth, shown in the photograph at right. It was often used in town for election celebrations such as President Cleveland's election in 1884. In 1892, the bell was finally retrieved and taken to Massachusetts. (Courtesy *Maryland Cracker Barrel.*)

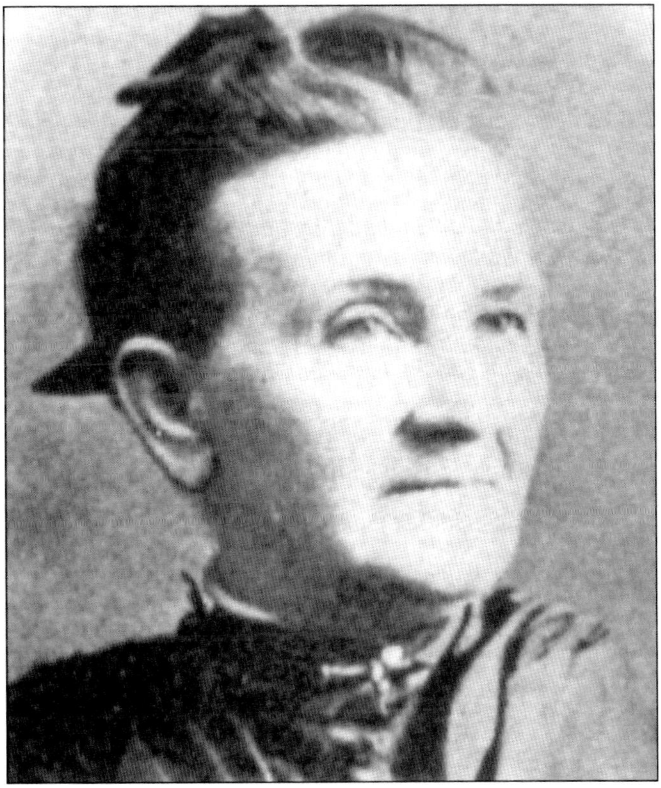

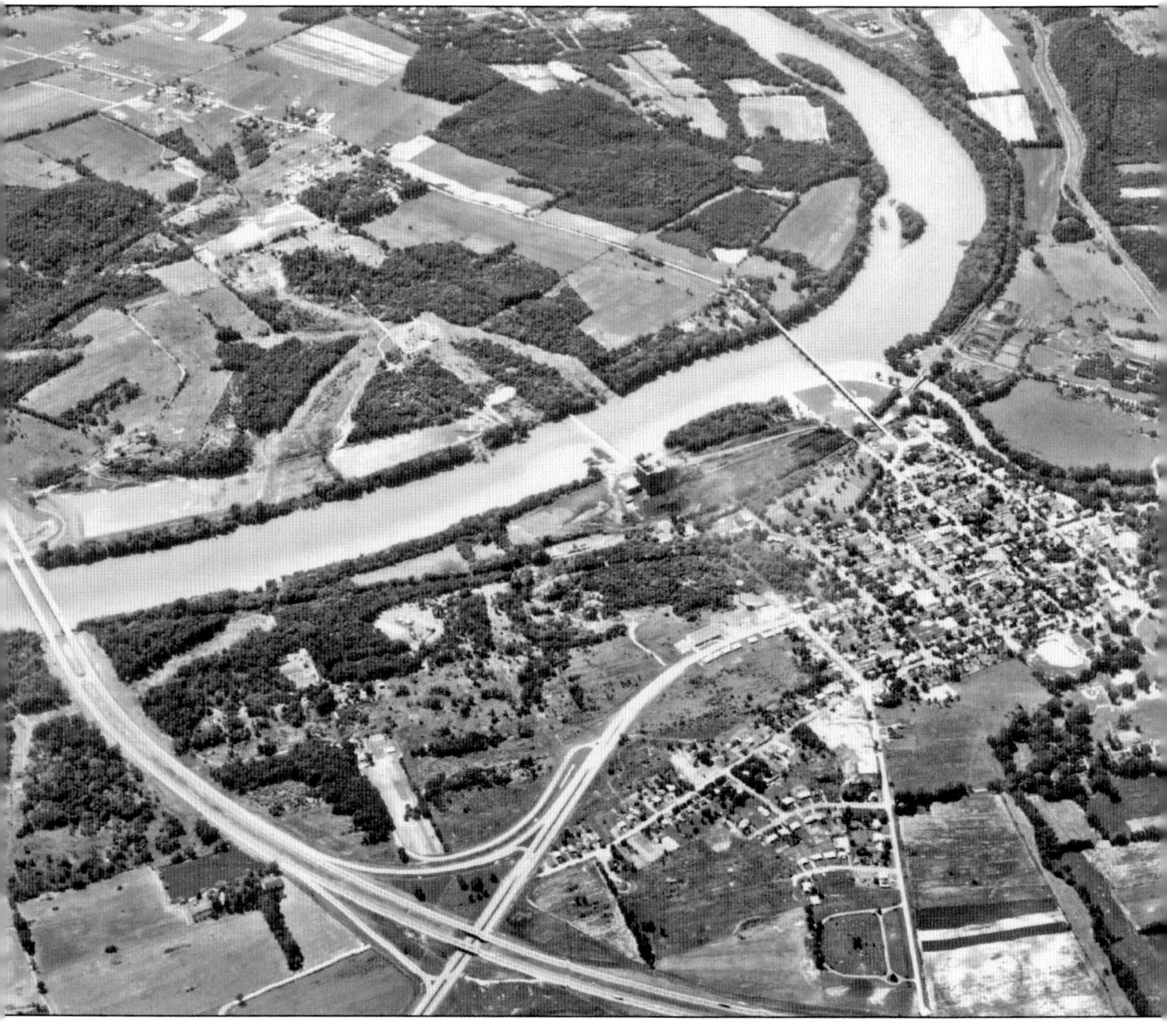

Here is a more modern-day aerial view of Williamsport taken by the Park Service during a survey of the C&O Canal. The U.S. Route 11 bridge crosses into West Virginia on the right-hand side of the photograph, while the two-span bridge of Interstate 81 by-passes the downtown area in the far left of the photo. The Potomac Edison plant can be seen on the banks of the Potomac near the center of the photo. (Courtesy C&O Canal National Historical Park Headquarters.)

Three

Commerce and Industry

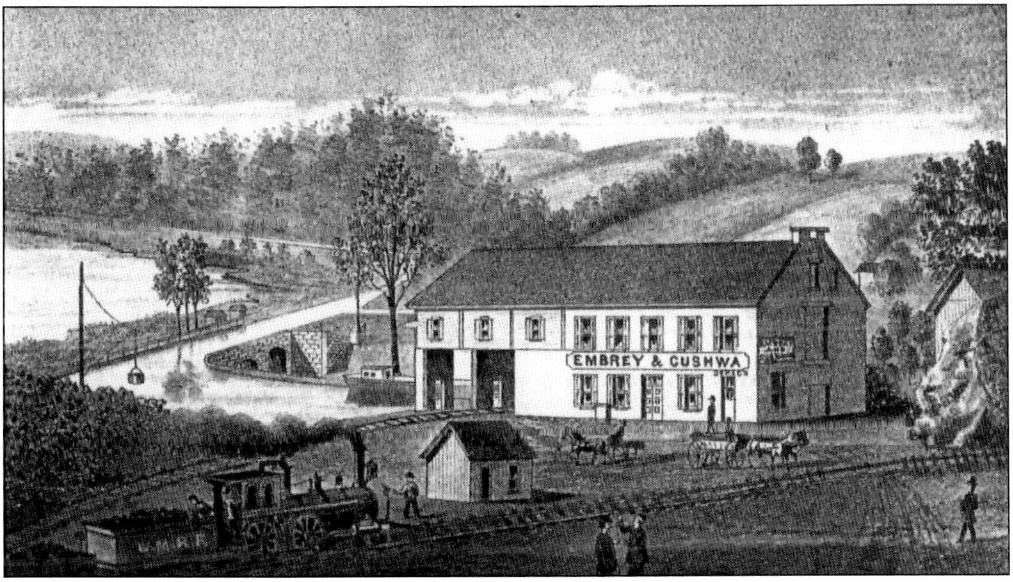

This drawing shows Williamsport during the early days of both the canal and the railroad. At this time, Cushwa's was known as Embrey and Cushwa. A Western Maryland engine is in the forefront, and a canal boat is pulled up in the basin behind the building. The aqueduct leads off to the left. (Courtesy Williamsport Town Museum.)

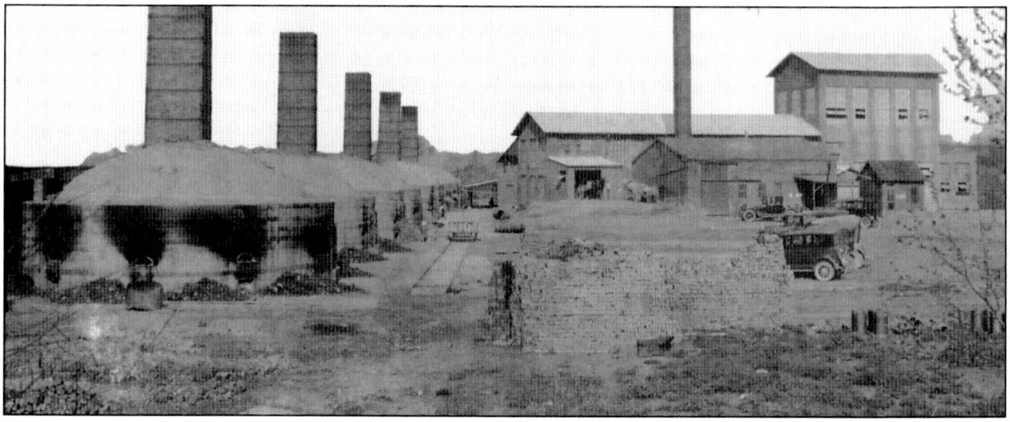

This photograph shows the Victor Cushwa and Sons brick-making plant in Williamsport, Maryland, as it appeared in 1924. Victor Cushwa purchased the Conococheague Brick and Earthenware Company in 1897 to supplement his coal business along the banks of the C&O Canal. Bricks from the company have been used in historic restorations in places such as Williamsburg, Virginia, and Independence Square in Philadelphia, Pennsylvania. (Courtesy *Maryland Cracker Barrel.*)

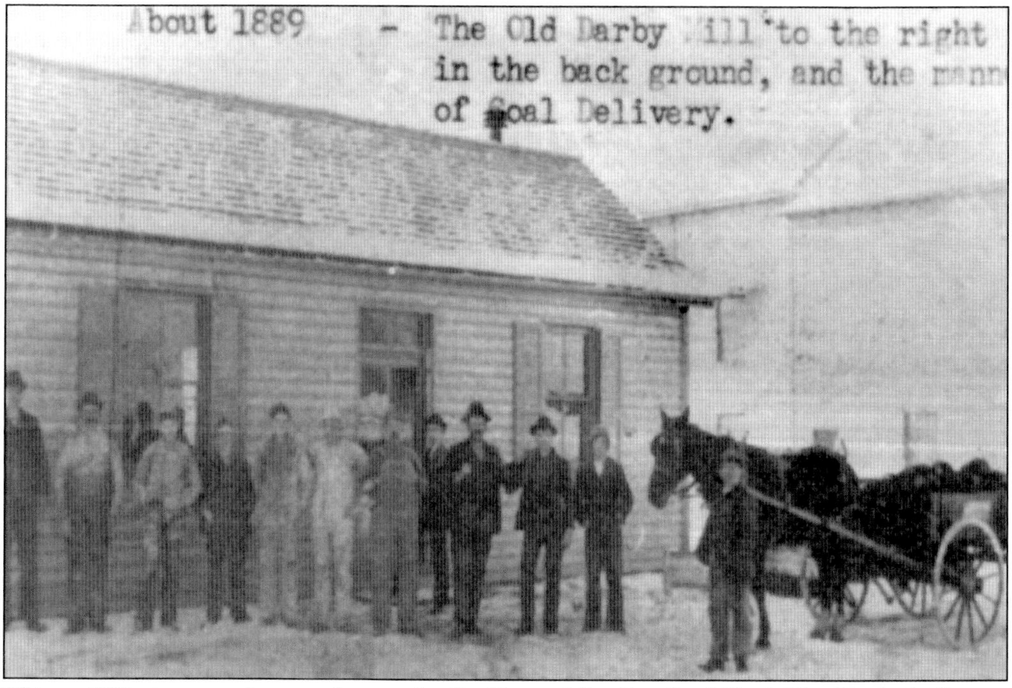

This c. 1889 photograph was taken at the Steffey and Findlay Coal Yard. The Darby Mill is in the background. Note the horse-drawn wagon full of coal waiting to be delivered. The Darby Mill suffered a loss of about $5,000 from damage in the 1889 flood. (Courtesy Williamsport Town Museum.)

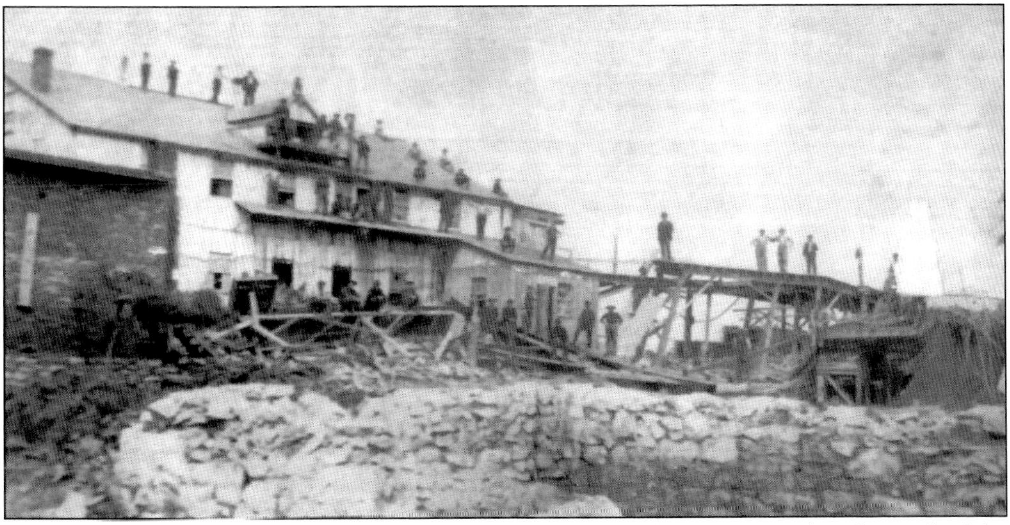

This is another 1889 flood photograph, this time showing the destruction in the aftermath of the flood at the DeFrehn Chair Factory. Located just beyond the Conococheague Aqueduct, the mill was powered by water from the canal. The factory and its storage building were washed away by the surging floodwater, causing between $7,000 and $9,000 in losses. The company relocated in Johnstown, Pennsylvania, after it was unable to raise the needed funds to start the business up again after the machinery was damaged and the finished stock was lost. (Courtesy Williamsport Town Museum.)

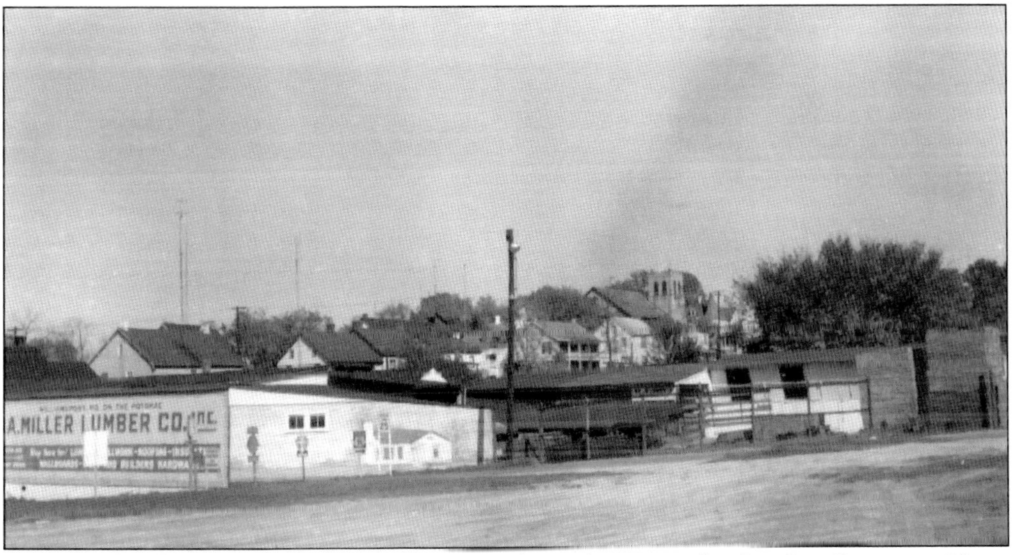

This October 21, 1958, photograph shows the plant of G. A. Miller Lumber Company. Three generations of the Miller family have served the company since George A. Miller began selling lumber in 1887. The flood of 1889 destroyed the original mill located near the C&O aqueduct in Williamsport. Moved to higher ground, the company office was located in an old stone building that was reportedly used as a hospital for wounded soldiers during the Civil War skirmishes in the area. The 1936 flood brought more damage, and the main office was moved again. The lumberyard is still in Williamsport today and can be seen from the back when you come around the corner onto Commerce Street. (Courtesy Western Maryland Room Washington County Free Library.)

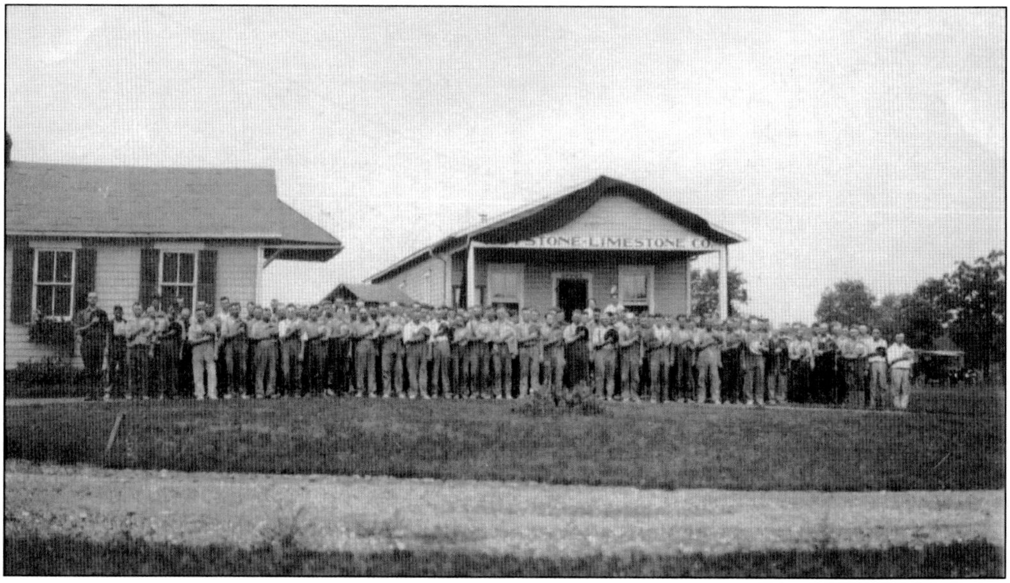

This early-1930s photograph shows the workers at the Keystone Lime Company. Prior to the 1936 flood, which destroyed the Nessle quarry in West Virginia, limestone from the Nessle quarry was sent on to the quarry in Williamsport and from there by rail to Pittsburgh. Both quarries were owned at that time by U.S. Steel. The Keystone Lime Company, now known as the Pinesburg Quarry, is owned by Martin Marietta Aggregates as part of their stone, gravel, and sand division. (Courtesy Western Maryland Room Washington County Free Library.)

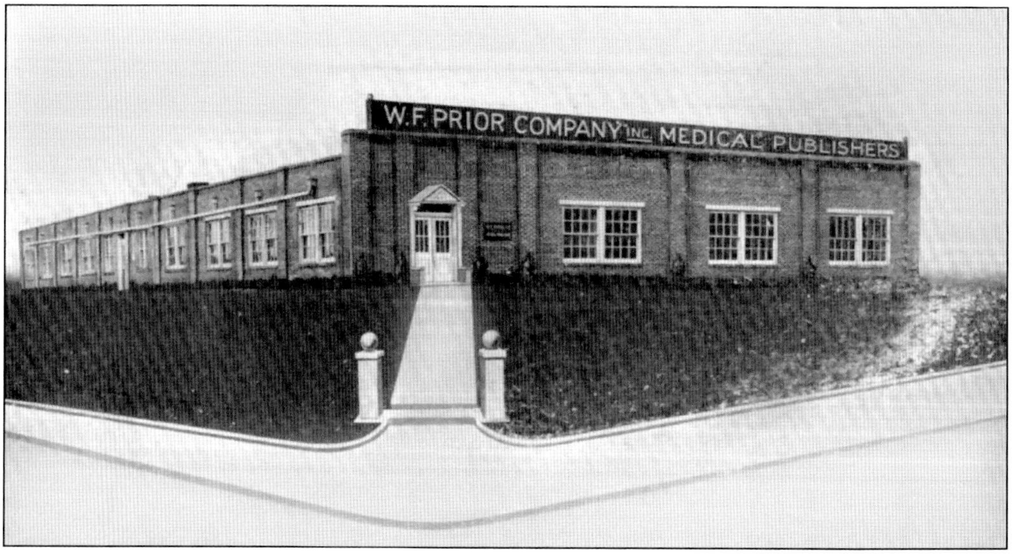

An advertising brochure for Williamsport included this photograph of another one of the town's business enterprises. While no longer in business in town today, the W. F. Prior Medical Publishing business was once on the corner of Bower Avenue, the current site of an antique shop. (Courtesy Williamsport Town Museum.)

This image is of a 1944 calendar ribbon made of silk from the Federal Silk Mills prior to the 1959 fire that closed the plant. Fire companies from Williamsport, Halfway, Hagerstown, and Funkstown all responded in an attempt to contain the blaze that was listed as the largest structural fire loss in the state of Maryland for the year. (Courtesy Williamsport Town Museum.)

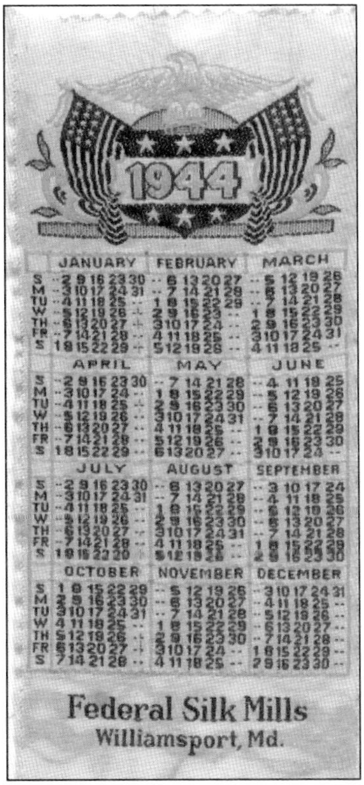

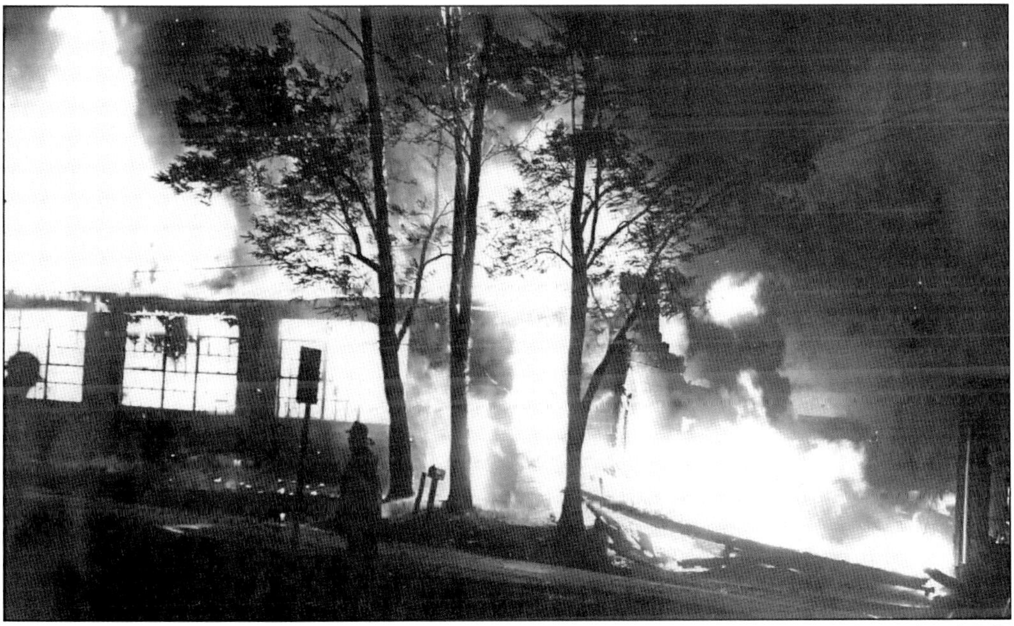

This photograph was taken during the October 13, 1959, blaze that destroyed the Federal Silk Mills during the early morning hours. A newspaper article blamed the total destruction on a lack of sprinkler systems and firewalls, which allowed the fire to spread. Other companies damaged were the Holland Woven Label Company, the A. T. Pony Express Company, and the California Spray Chemical Corporation. (Courtesy Williamsport Town Museum.)

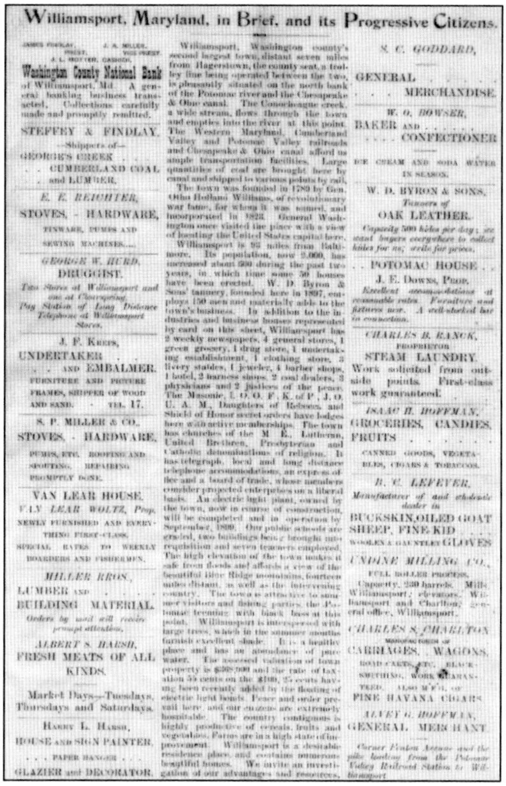

Williamsport, Maryland, in Brief, and its Progressive Citizens.

Washington County National Bank
of Williamsport, Md. A general banking business transacted. Collections carefully made and promptly remitted.

STEFFEY & FINDLAY.
—Shippers of—
GEORGE'S CREEK . . . CUMBERLAND COAL . . and LUMBER.

E. E. REICHTER,
STOVES, - HARDWARE,
TINWARE, PUMPS AND SEWING MACHINES....

GEORGE W. HURD,
DRUGGIST.
Two Stores at Williamsport and one at Clearspring. Pay Station of Long Distance Telephone at Williamsport Stores.

J. F. Kreps,
UNDERTAKER . . . . AND EMBALMER.
FURNITURE AND PICTURE FRAMES, SHIPPER OF WOOD AND SAND. · TEL. 17.

S. P. MILLER & CO.,
STOVES, - HARDWARE,
PUMPS, ETC. ROOFING AND SPOUTING. REPAIRING PROMPTLY DONE.

VAN LEAR HOUSE.
VAN LEAR WOLTZ, Prop.
NEWLY FURNISHED AND EVERYTHING FIRST-CLASS.
SPECIAL RATES TO WEEKLY BOARDERS AND FISHERMEN.

MILLER BROS.,
LUMBER AND . . . . BUILDING MATERIAL.
Orders by mail will receive prompt attention.

ALBERT S. HARSH,
FRESH MEATS OF ALL KINDS.

Market Days—Tuesdays, Thursdays and Saturdays.

Harry L. Harsh,
HOUSE AND SIGN PAINTER,
. . . PAPER HANGER . . .
GLAZIER and DECORATOR.

Williamsport, Washington county's second largest town, distant seven miles from Hagerstown, the county seat, a trolley line being operated between the two, is pleasantly situated on the north bank of the Potomac river and the Chesapeake & Ohio canal. The Conococheague creek, a wide stream, flows through the town and empties into the river at this point. The Western Maryland, Cumberland Valley and Potomac Valley railroads and Chesapeake & Ohio canal afford us ample transportation facilities. Large quantities of coal are brought here by canal and shipped to various points by rail.

The town was founded in 1789 by Gen. Otho Holland Williams, of revolutionary war fame, for whom it was named, and incorporated in 1823. General Washington once visited the place with a view of locating the United States capital here.

Williamsport is 93 miles from Baltimore. Its population, now 2,000, has increased about 500 during the past two years, in which time some 50 houses have been erected. W. D. Byron & Sons' tannery, founded here in 1897, employs 150 men and materially adds to the town's business. In addition to the industries and business houses represented by card on this sheet, Williamsport has 2 weekly newspapers, 4 general stores, 1 green grocery, 1 drug store, 1 undertaking establishment, 1 clothing store, 3 livery stables, 1 jeweler, 4 barber shops, 1 hotel, 2 harness shops, 2 coal dealers, 3 physicians and 2 justices of the peace. The Masonic, I. O. O. F., K. of P., J. O. U. A. M., Daughters of Rebecca, and Shield of Honor secret orders have lodges here with active memberships. The town has churches of the M. E., Lutheran, United Brethren, Presbyterian and Catholic denominations of religion. It has telegraph, local and long distance telephone accommodations, an express office and a board of trade, whose members consider projected enterprises on a liberal basis. An electric light plant, owned by the town, now in course of construction, will be completed and in operation by September, 1899. Our public schools are graded, two buildings being brought into requisition and seven teachers employed. The high elevation of the town makes it safe from floods and affords a view of the beautiful Blue Ridge mountains, fourteen miles distant, as well as the intervening country. The town is attractive to summer visitors and fishing parties, the Potomac teeming with black bass at this point. Williamsport is interspersed with large trees, which in the summer months furnish excellent shade. It is a healthy place and has an abundance of pure water. The assessed valuation of town property is $508,000 and the rate of taxation 55 cents on the $100, 25 cents having been recently added by the floating of electric light bonds. Peace and order prevail here, and our citizens are extremely hospitable. The country contiguous is highly productive of cereals, fruits and vegetables. Farms are in a high state of improvement. Williamsport is a desirable residence place, and contains numerous beautiful homes. We invite an investigation of our advantages and resources.

S. C. GODDARD,
GENERAL . . . . MERCHANDISE.

W. O. BOWSER,
BAKER AND . . . . CONFECTIONER
ICE CREAM AND SODA WATER IN SEASON.

W. D. BYRON & SONS,
Tanners of
OAK LEATHER.
Capacity 500 hides per day; we want buyers everywhere to collect hides for us; write for prices.

. . POTOMAC HOUSE . .
J. E. Downs, Prop.
Excellent accommodations at reasonable rates. Furniture and fixtures new. A well-stocked bar in connection.

CHARLES B. RANCK,
PROPRIETOR
STEAM LAUNDRY.
Work solicited from outside points. First-class work guaranteed.

ISAAC H. HOFFMAN,
GROCERIES, CANDIES, FRUITS . . . . . .
CANNED GOODS, VEGETABLES, CIGARS & TOBACCOS.

B. C. LEFEVER,
Manufacturer of and wholesale dealer in
BUCKSKIN, OILED GOAT SHEEP, FINE KID . . . WOOLEN & GAUNTLET GLOVES

UNDINE MILLING CO.,
FULL ROLLER PROCESS.
Capacity, 230 barrels. Mills, Williamsport; elevators, Williamsport and Charlton; general office, Williamsport.

CHARLES S. CHARLTON
MANUFACTURER OF
CARRIAGES, WAGONS,
ROAD CARTS, ETC. BLACKSMITHING. WORK GUARANTEED. ALSO M'F'R. OF
FINE HAVANA CIGARS

ALVEY G. HOFFMAN,
GENERAL MERCHANT
Corner Fenton Avenue and the pike leading from the Potomac Valley Railroad Station to Williamsport

This Williamsport briefing gives a host of information about the town and the various services offered by local citizens. There are ads telling us that the furniture and fixtures at the Potomac House are new and that rates to stay are reasonable, Harry Harsh is available to paint both signs and houses, the Van Lear House offers special rates to fishermen, and Charles Charlton provides Havana cigars in addition to manufacturing carriages and wagons. (Courtesy Williamsport Town Museum.)

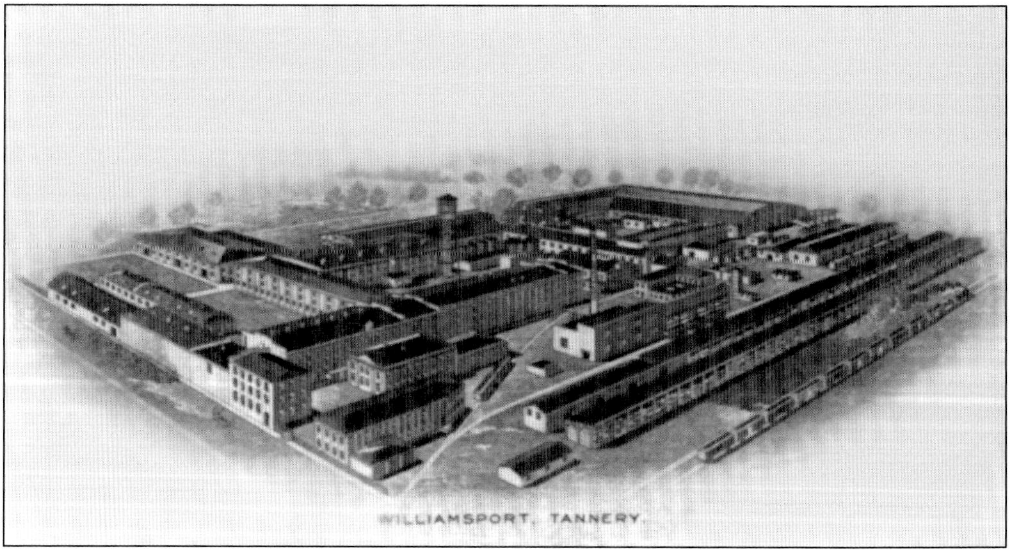

This aerial view shows the Byron Tannery, Williamsport's largest industry at the time of this brochure and still one of the county's largest employers, operating under the name Garden State Tanning. Constructed in 1897, the "Oak Tanned" leather produced by the tannery was used for suitcases, shoes, harnesses, furniture, and much more. At one time, the company published an informative booklet for the public about the tanning process titled *The Story of Real Leather and the Journey of a Hide Through One of the Byron Tanneries*. Note the train puffing away on the tracks to the right. (Courtesy Williamsport Town Museum.)

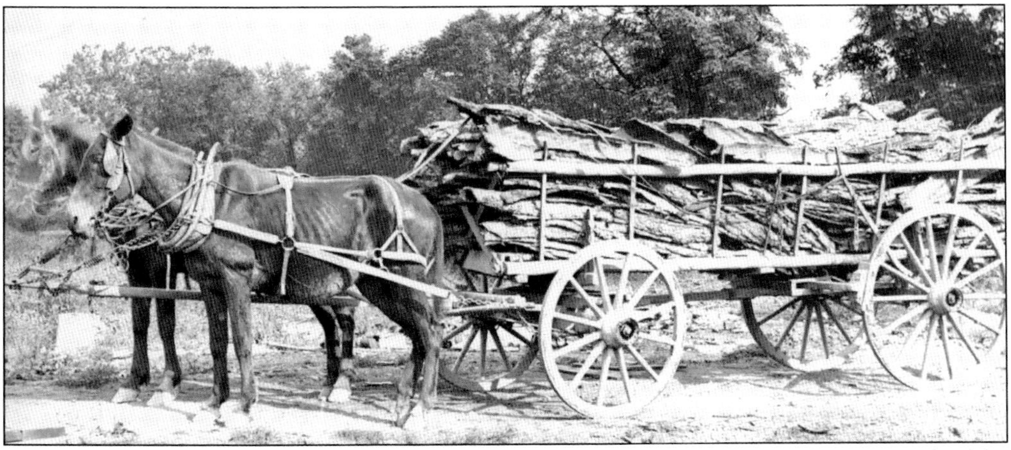

Here is a mule-drawn wagon hauling bark for use at the Byron Tannery in Williamsport. A booklet issued by the company states that approximately 10,000 tons of oak bark were gathered during bark season for use in the factory to tan the hides. Still in business today as the Garden State Tannery, the tannery turns hides into finished leather for use in the automotive industry. Byron once had factories operating in Mercersburg, Pennsylvania; Hanover, Pennsylvania; Williamsport; and three factories in Hagerstown. (Courtesy Washington County Historical Society.)

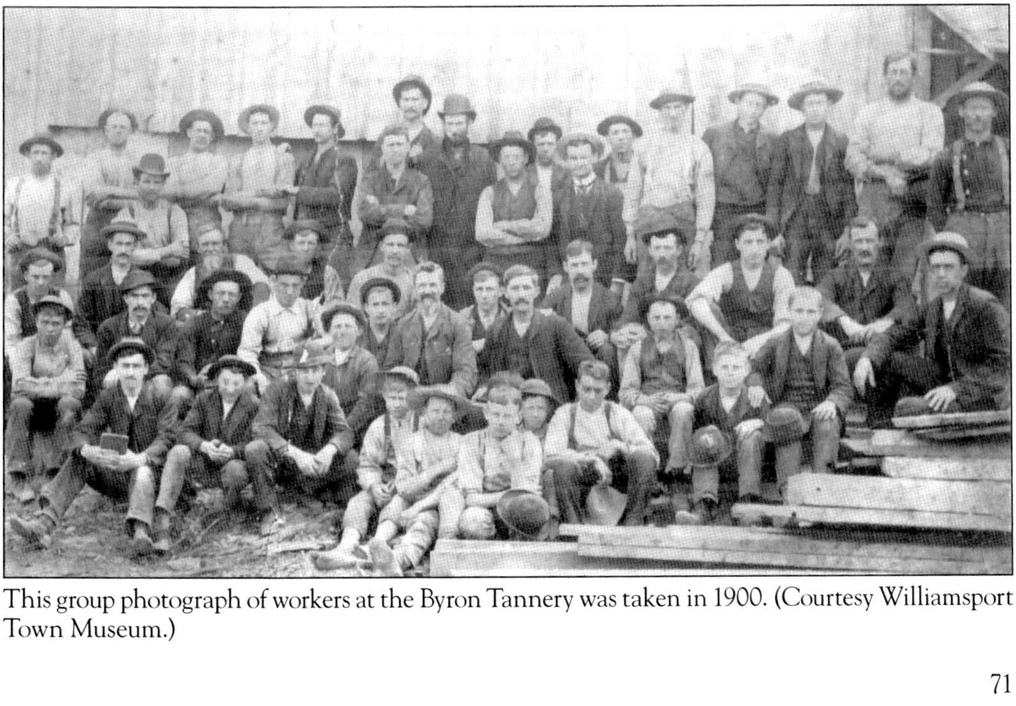

This group photograph of workers at the Byron Tannery was taken in 1900. (Courtesy Williamsport Town Museum.)

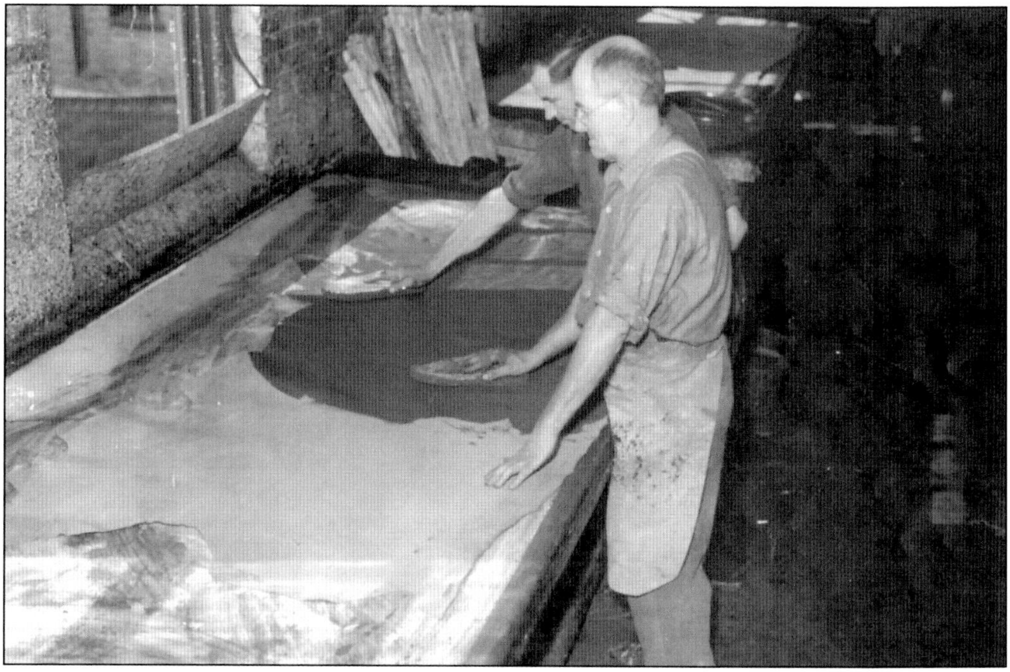

Here is a view of two employees working on a hide inside the Byron Tannery. Byron touted their leather as made "to outlast any automobile, carriage, or furniture." (Courtesy Williamsport Town Museum.)

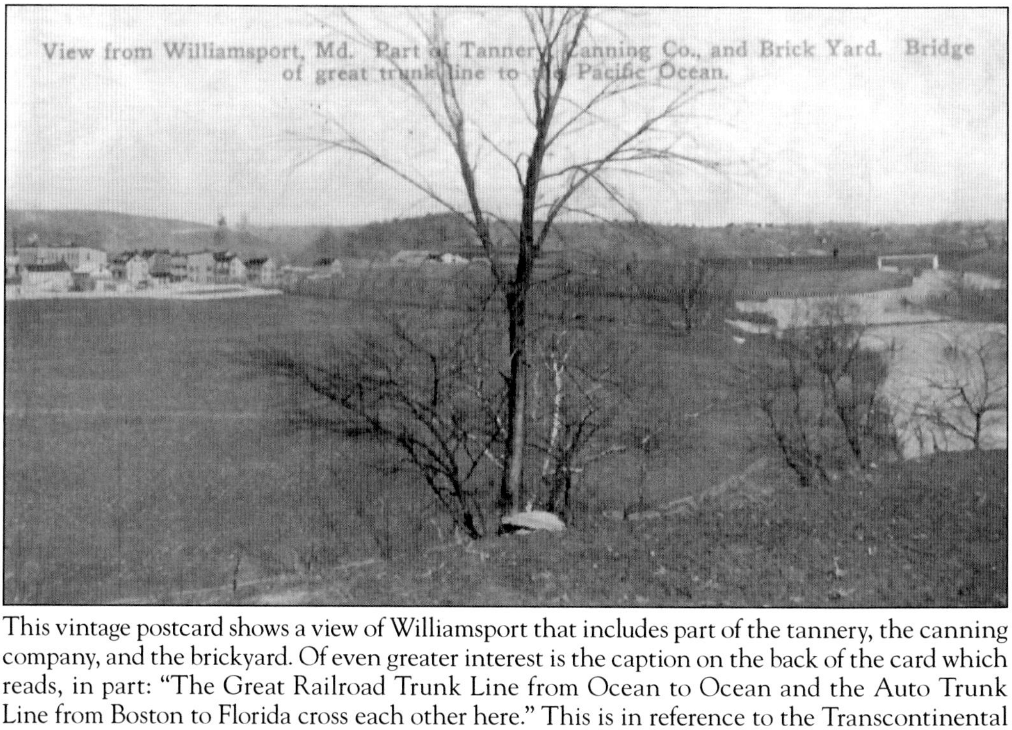

This vintage postcard shows a view of Williamsport that includes part of the tannery, the canning company, and the brickyard. Of even greater interest is the caption on the back of the card which reads, in part: "The Great Railroad Trunk Line from Ocean to Ocean and the Auto Trunk Line from Boston to Florida cross each other here." This is in reference to the Transcontinental Railroad running east and west and U.S. Route 11 running north and south. (Courtesy Western Maryland Room Washington County Free Library.)

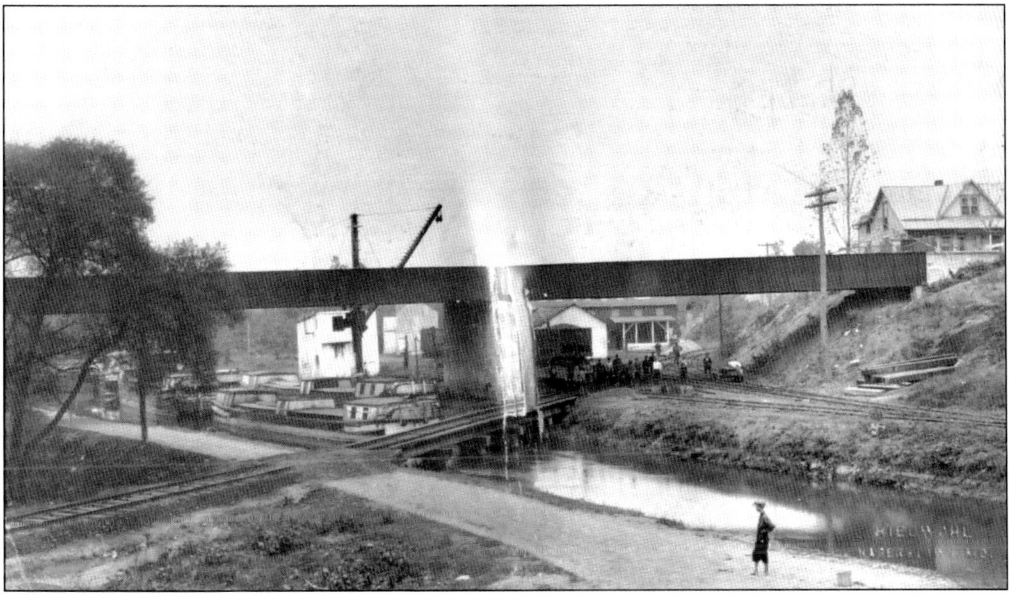

This interesting 1920 photograph of the C&O Canal at Williamsport shows something of a conundrum; how were the canal boats supposed to get past the railroad tracks that were laid at ground-level across the canal? It turns out that the tracks were only a temporary installation to allow trains to deliver equipment for the construction of the Potomac Edison Power Plant. (Courtesy C&O Canal National Historical Park Headquarters.)

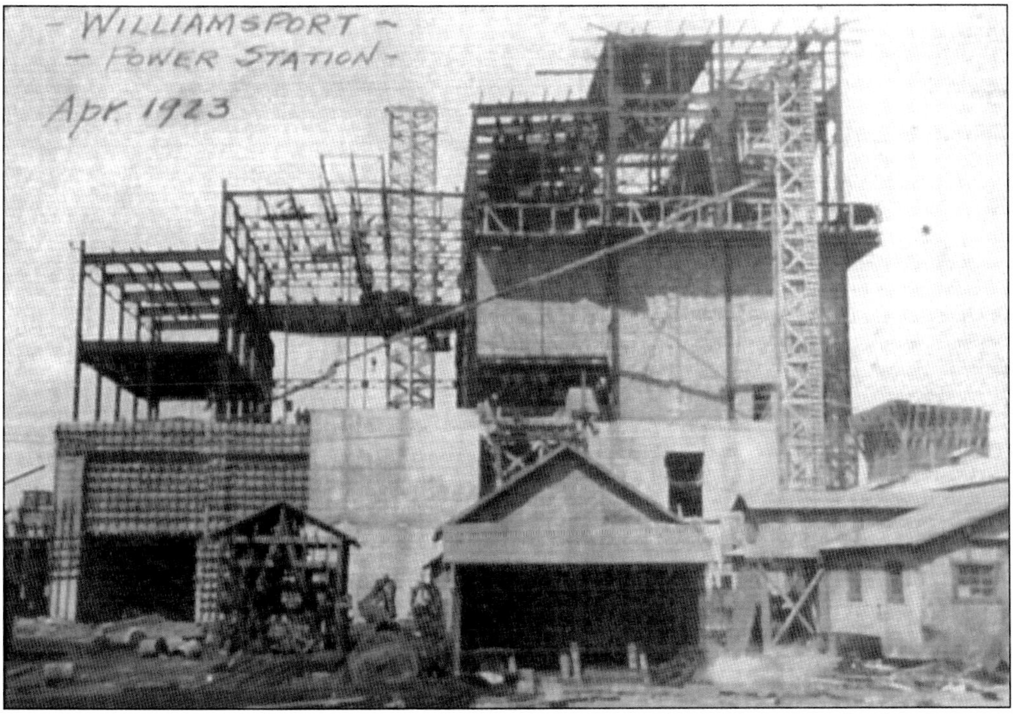

This 1923 photograph was taken when the power station was being constructed. The plant is a coal-fired electric plant, which uses coal brought in via rail and water from the river. (Courtesy Williamsport Town Museum.)

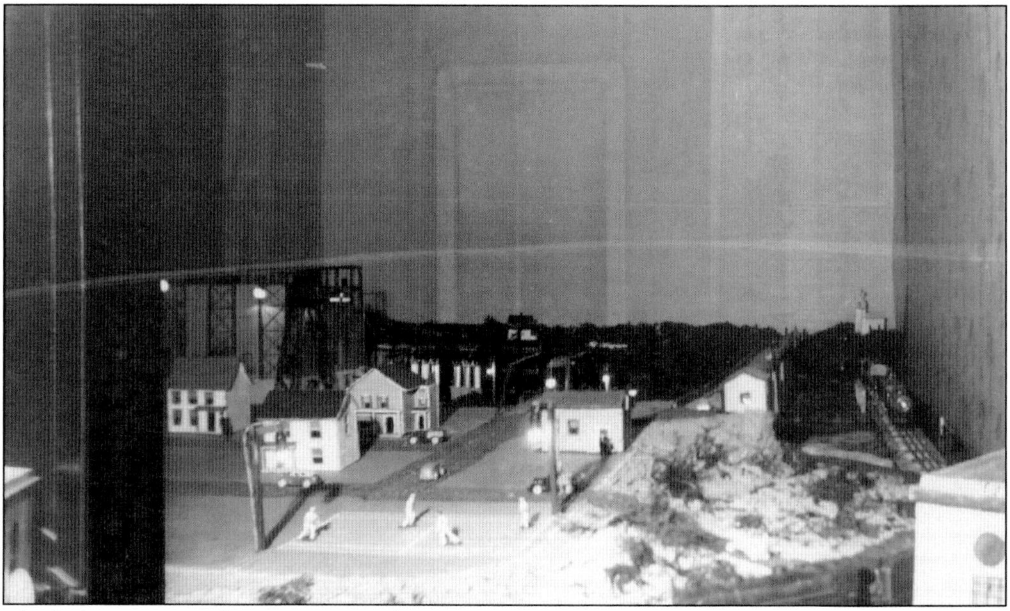

The kid in everyone loves a train, and Williamsport residents are no different. This photograph shows a Christmas 1940 model train layout at the Potomac Edison Plant. The headlight on the train is shining as the train comes down the track on the right. The R. Paul Smith Station of the Potomac Edison Company was constructed in 1923. Today, the plant is part of Allegheny Power. (Courtesy Williamsport Town Museum.)

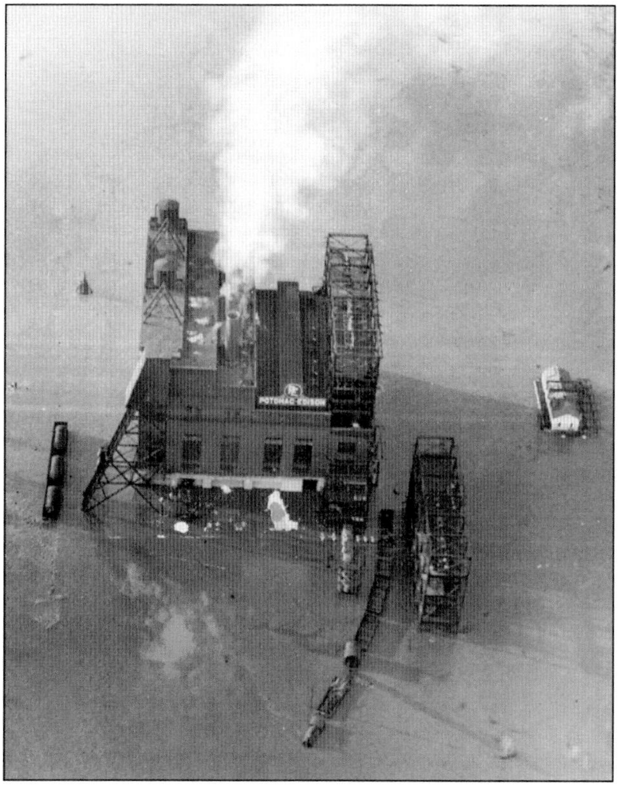

Here is the Potomac Edison Power Plant under water during the 1936 flood. Note the rail cars on tracks that are well under water as well as the smoke coming from the plant as workers try to get back on track. (Courtesy Western Maryland Room Washington County Free Library.)

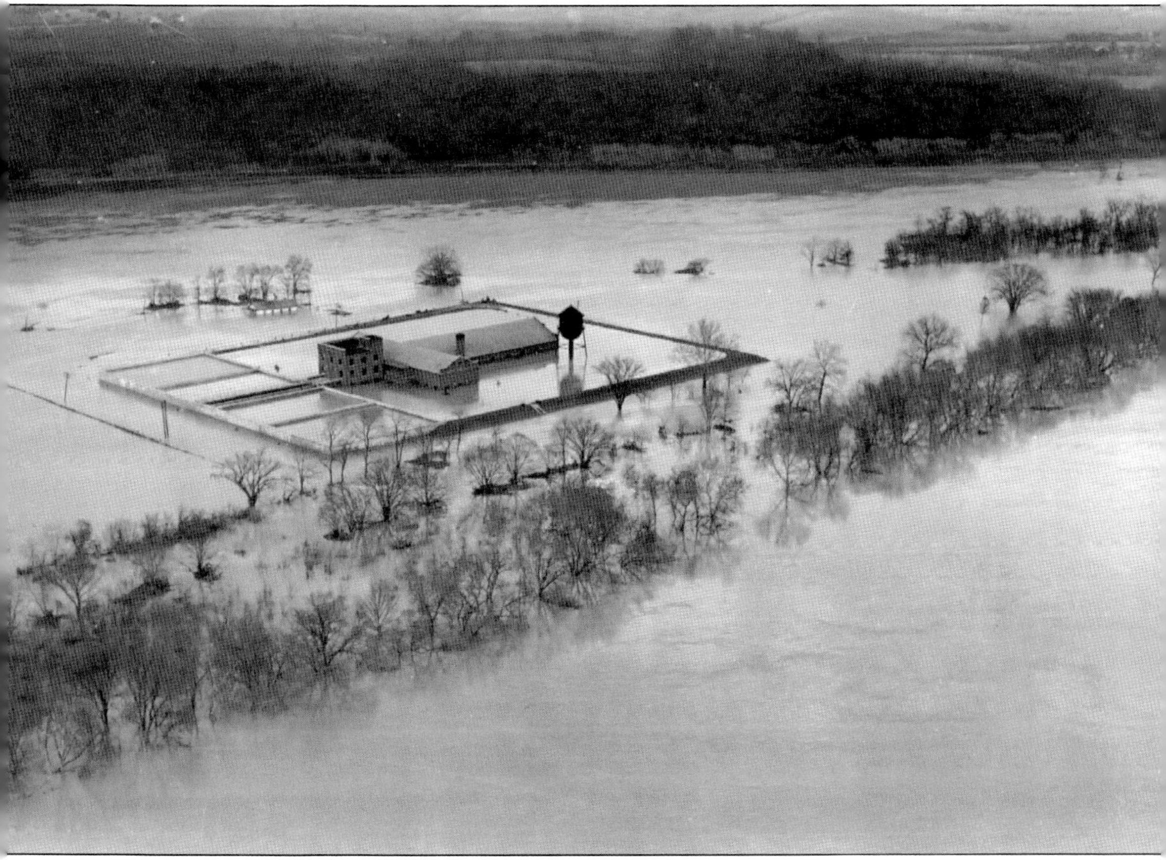

This photograph shows the Hagerstown Water Filtration Plant on March 18, 1936. Located just a mile west of Williamsport, the plant was constructed in 1928 to finally provide a reliable supply of water. Prior to the construction of the plant, residents relied on reservoirs in Smithsburg and Edgemont that were subject to seasonal water shortages. The 61-foot high embankments constructed around the plant shielded it from view of the Potomac River and were intended to protect the plant from flooding. Even these high embankments were not enough to prevent the devastation that put the plant out of service for 17 days when the Potomac crested 47 feet and 9 inches above normal during the 1936 flood. Though difficult to distinguish, the small objects in the center background on the dyke are horses and cows that remained there during the flood. The plant was renamed in later years the R. C. Willson Water Treatment Facility in honor of Richard Willson, a chemist and superintendent who worked at the plant for almost 30 years. (Courtesy Western Maryland Room Washington County Free Library.)

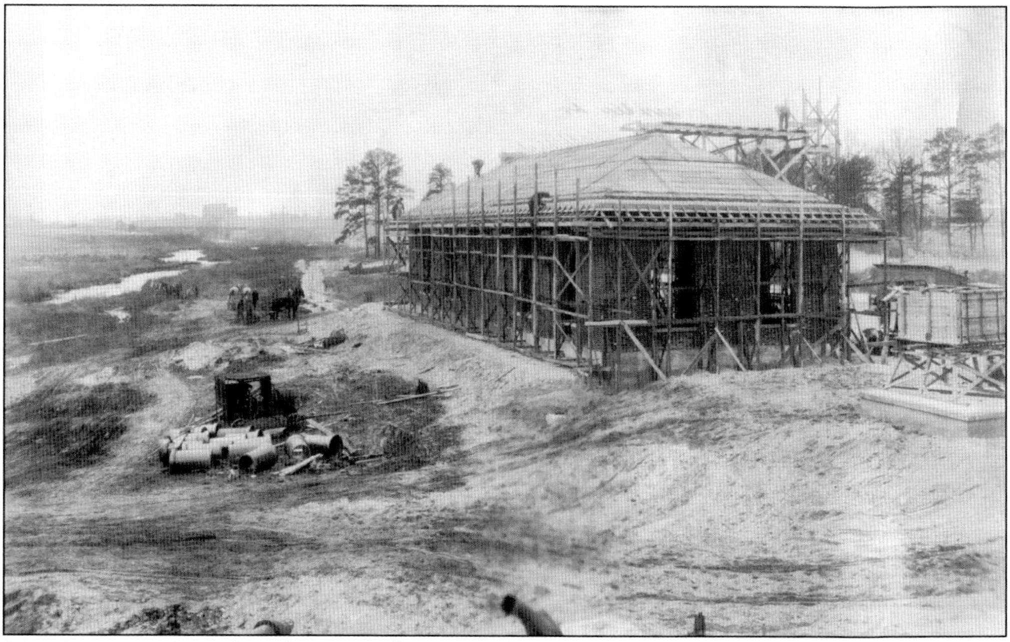

This shot was taken when the water plant in Williamsport was being constructed. Note the man standing on top of the scaffolding on the top right. Cisterns and wells had provided water for over 100 years when Williamsport finally installed its first water system in 1928 and 1929, entering into an agreement with Hagerstown to purchase water from the new plant they had recently constructed on the Potomac just outside of Williamsport. (Courtesy Williamsport Town Museum.)

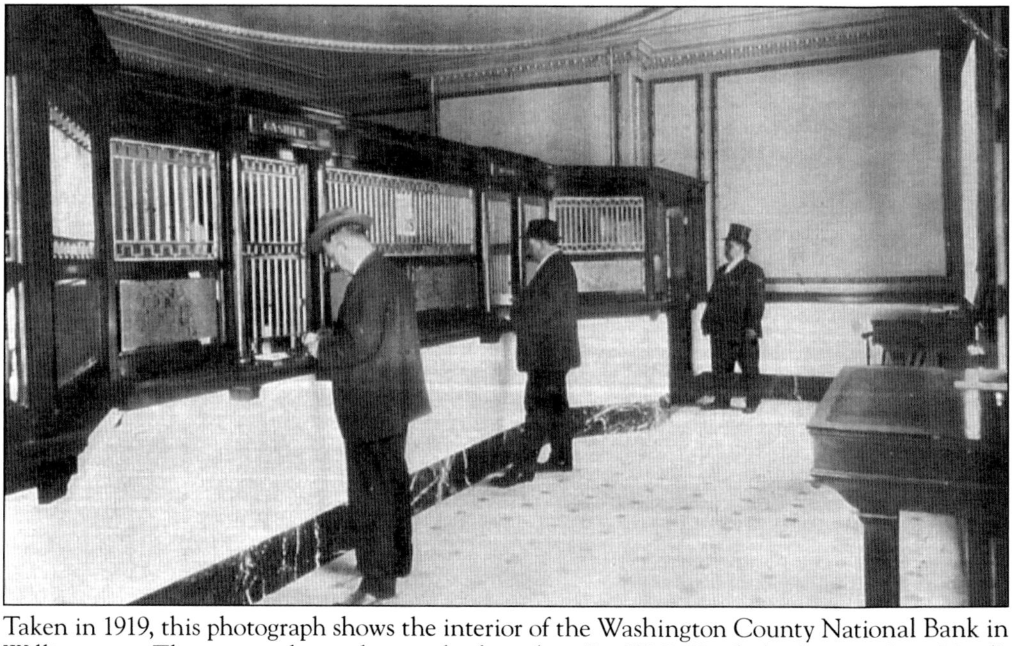

Taken in 1919, this photograph shows the interior of the Washington County National Bank in Williamsport. The man in the top hat on the far right is Dr. W. S. Hurd, the druggist from Hurd's store. Originally founded as the Williamsport Bank in 1827, three years after the closing of the Conococheague Bank, the bank became a national bank under the name Washington County National Bank in 1865. (Courtesy Western Maryland Room Washington County Free Library.)

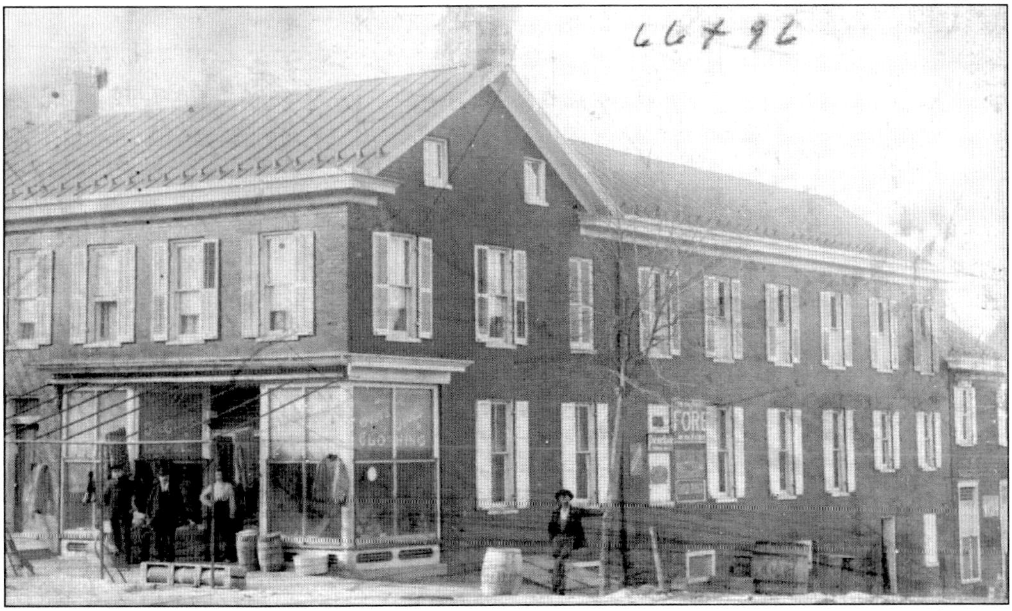

Here is an old photograph from 1900 showing Frank Goddard's general store on Conococheague Street. Leaning against the tree on the right is Joe Nave. Dr. Richardson and Miss Rena Corby are in front of the store. (Courtesy Williamsport Town Museum.)

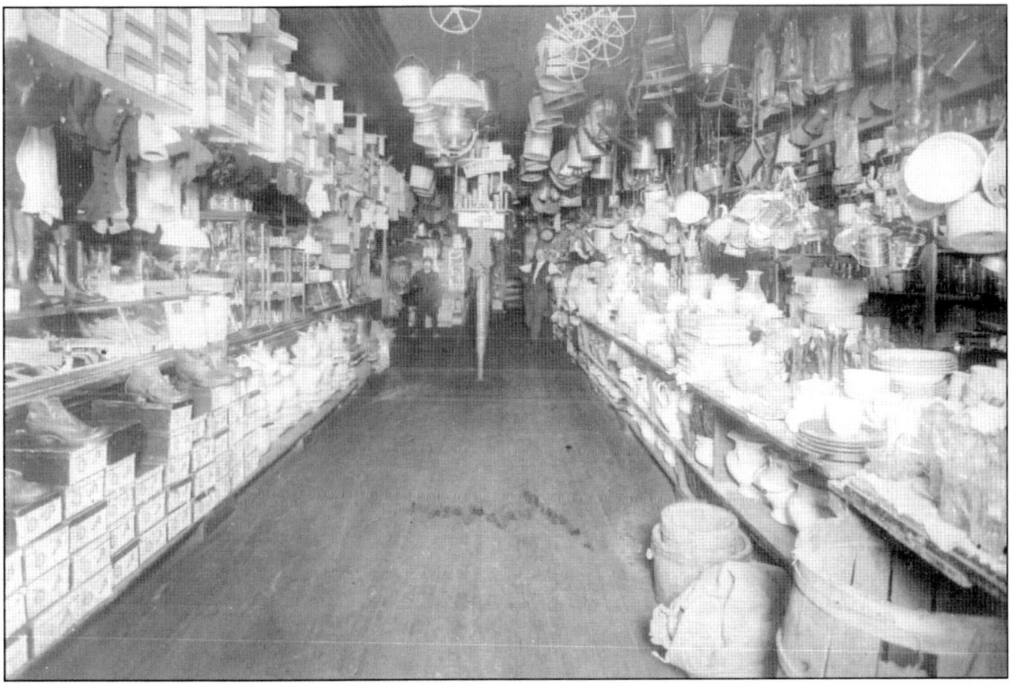

Here is an interior view of John Goddard's store taken in 1920. He sold general merchandise, and the store does indeed seem packed with all manner of items such as shoes, dishes, flour sifters, and much more. There are even items hanging from the ceiling. (Courtesy Williamsport Town Museum.)

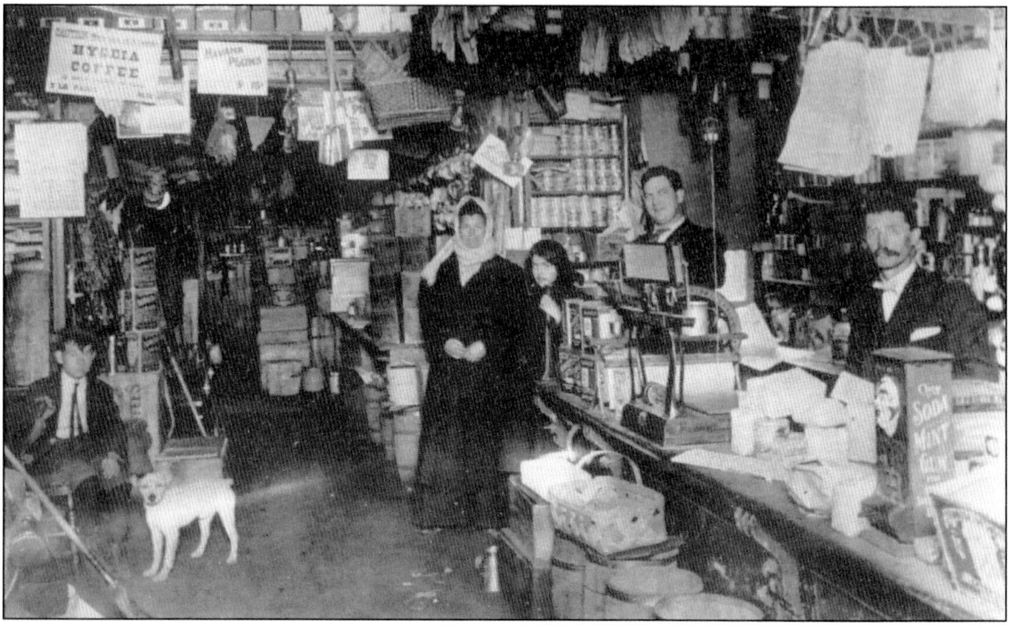

This photograph shows the interior of another general merchandise store, this one belonging to Charles Davis on N. Conococheague Street. Here too, the shop is packed to the brim with all sorts of items. Havana plums are going at the rate of nine for 15¢, and a countertop display asks everyone to chew Soda Mint Gum. The photograph shows that even a small local dog was welcome to shop here. (Courtesy Williamsport Town Museum.)

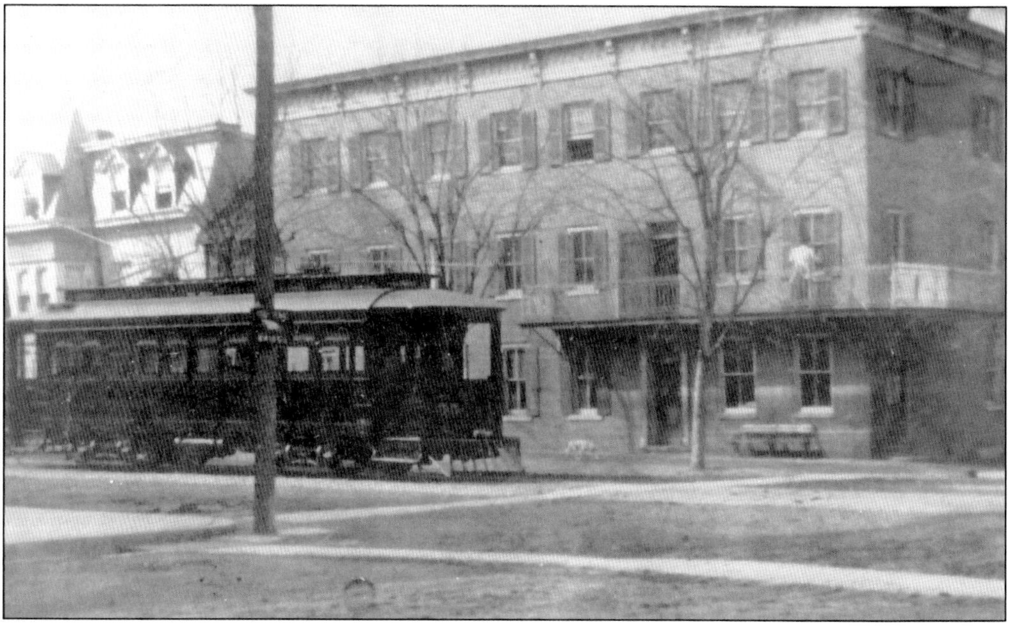

After the retreat from Gettysburg, Gen. Robert E. Lee came into Williamsport and stopped at the Taylor Hotel, where he was called upon by local citizens inquiring about the state of the war. General Lee sat upon a sandstone two and a half feet above the ground and spoke with the group. That same stone can still be seen today in what is now Wolfe's On The Square. (Courtesy Williamsport Town Museum.)

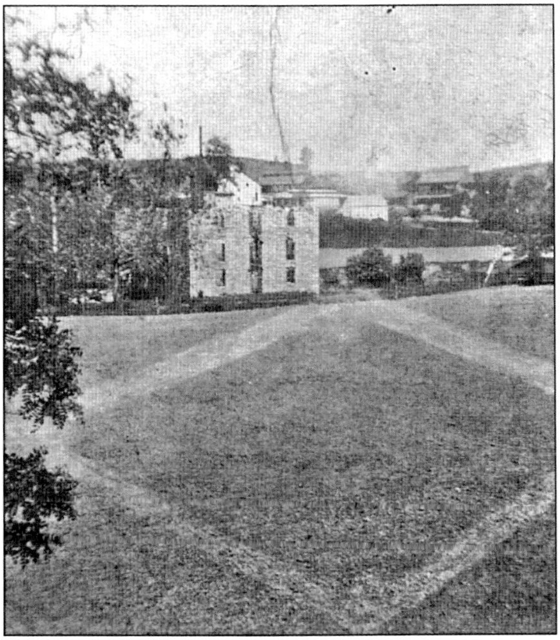

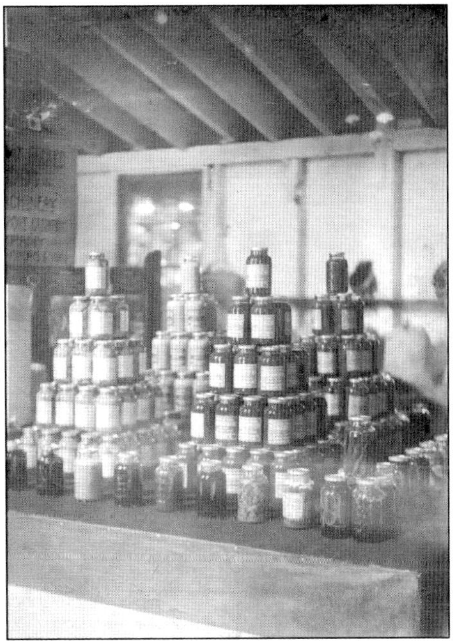

Here is a view of the Williamsport Canning Factory along with a store display of items canned at the factory. The factory was located across the tracks from the tannery to the west of the tannery and the brickyard. (Courtesy Williamsport Town Museum.)

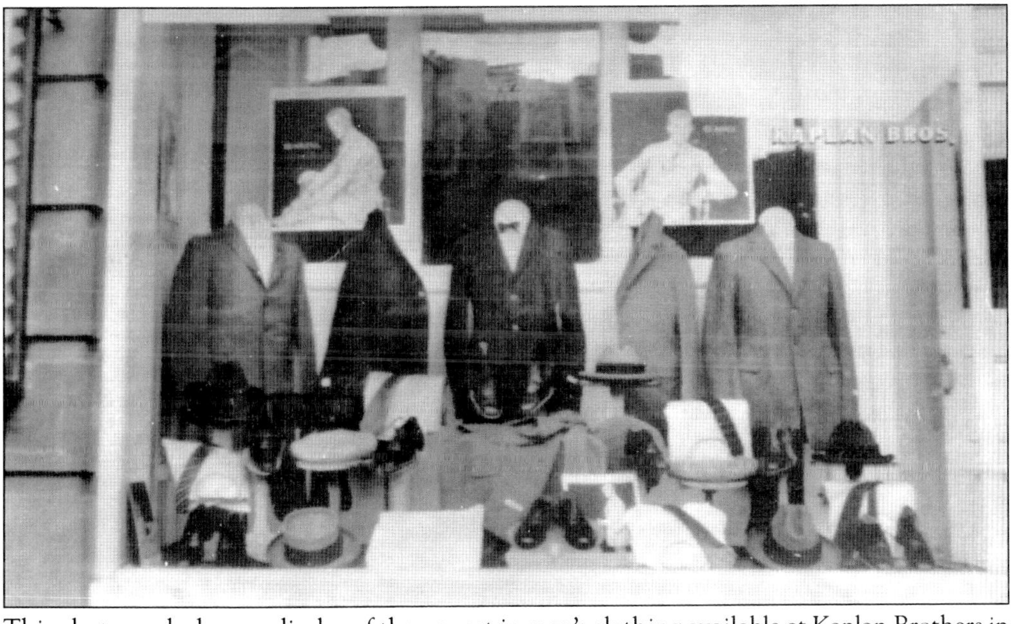

This photograph shows a display of the newest in men's clothing available at Kaplan Brothers in the fall of 1919. The store, owned by Melvin Kaplan's father, was located on N. Conococheague Street in the first floor of the clock tower building, also known as the Pythian Castle. (Courtesy Williamsport Town Museum.)

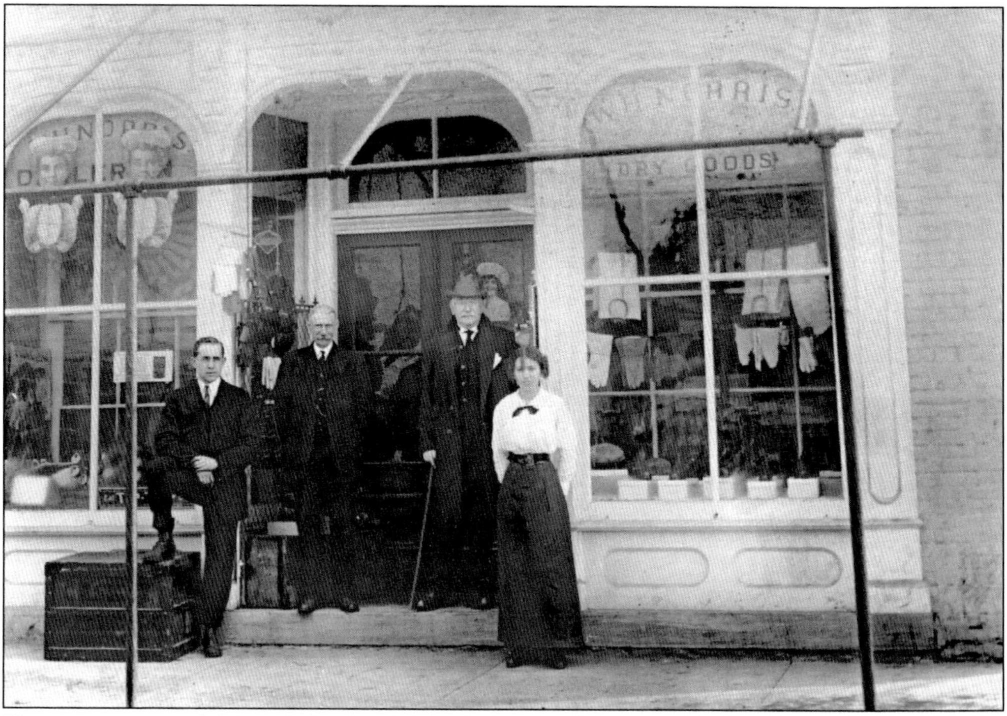

Here is a group of shop clerks posing outside yet another one of Williamsport's dry goods establishments in the early years of the 20th century. (Courtesy Williamsport Town Museum.)

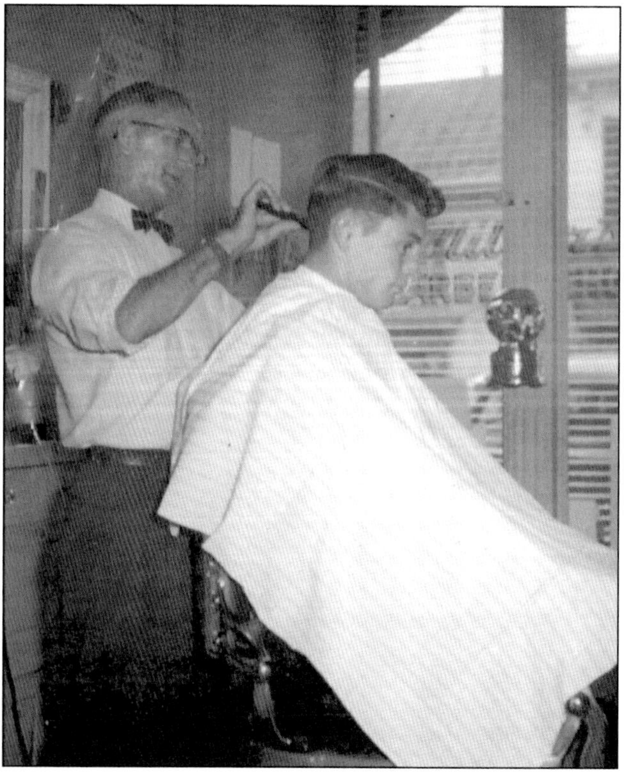

The barbershop was another fixture in town. In fact, there were several. Here is Maurice Miller giving a trim to a customer in his shop on Conococheague Street. (Courtesy Williamsport Town Museum.)

A. O. Murray had one of several eating establishments in town, and here he has not just the restaurant but the entire building on N. Conococheague decked out for celebrations on July 4, 1923. He was one of the first in town to begin selling beer after Prohibition ended, when he offered Piels beer for 10¢ a glass. (Courtesy Williamsport Town Museum.)

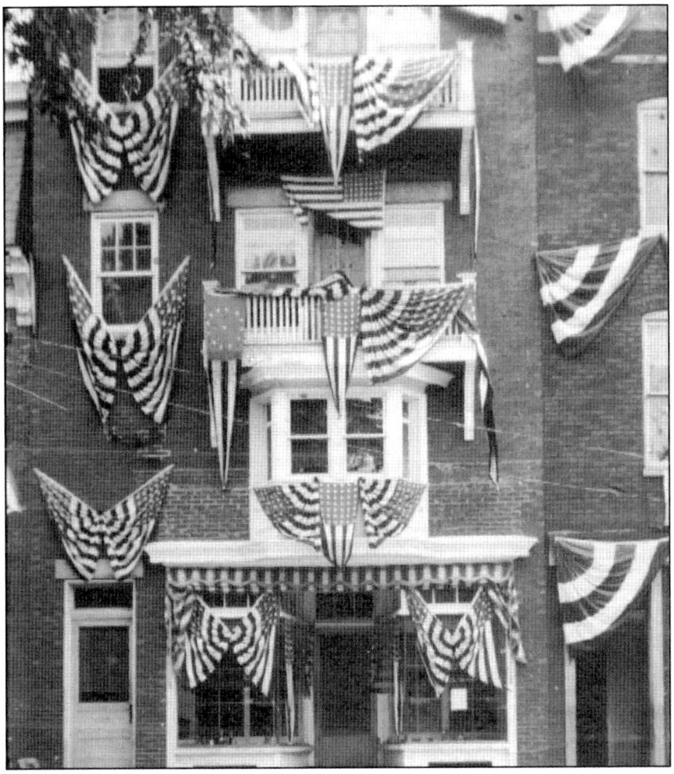

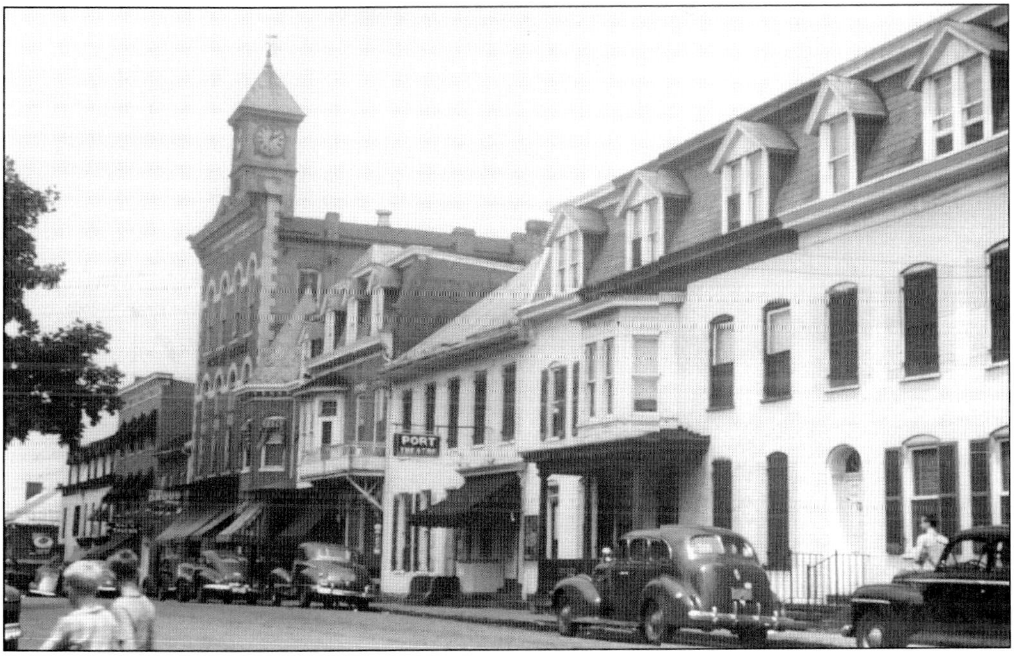

Here is a view of downtown Williamsport in the days when the Port Theatre was still in operation on Conococheague Street. The clock tower building (the Knights of Pythian Hall) was built in 1900, and the clock was donated to the town by W. D. Byron. The theater closed some time in the 1950s. (Courtesy Williamsport Town Museum.)

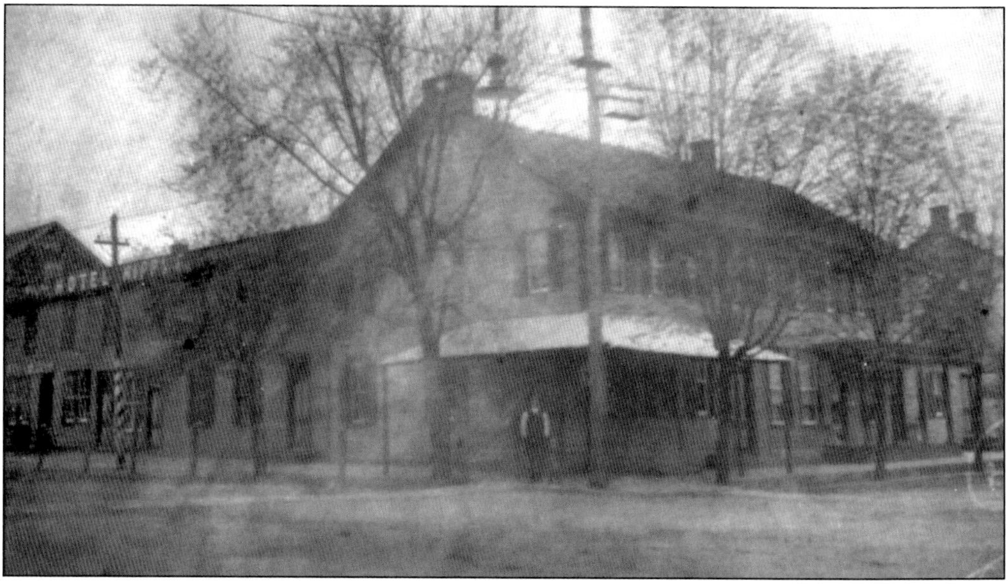

This photograph from the early 20th century is of the Hotel Ripple located on the corner of Conococheague and Salisbury Streets, where Tony's Pizza is located today. (Courtesy Williamsport Town Museum.)

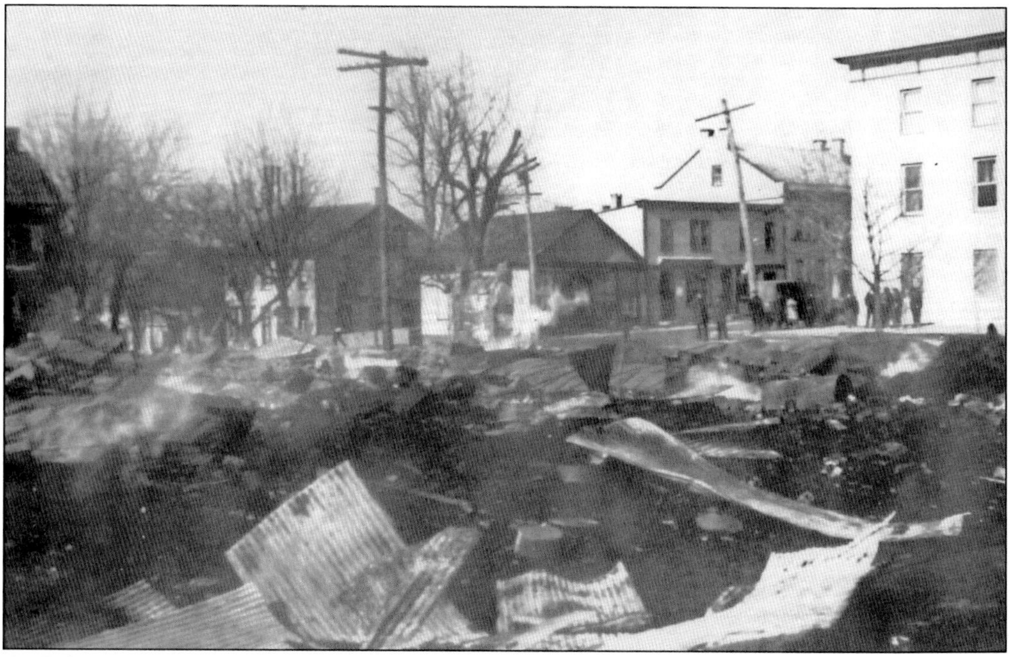

On February 12, 1923, tragedy struck in the form of a fire that demolished the Hotel Ripple. This photograph was taken from the vantage point of the destroyed hotel and looks across the street to the corner where the town hall now stands. (Courtesy Williamsport Town Museum.)

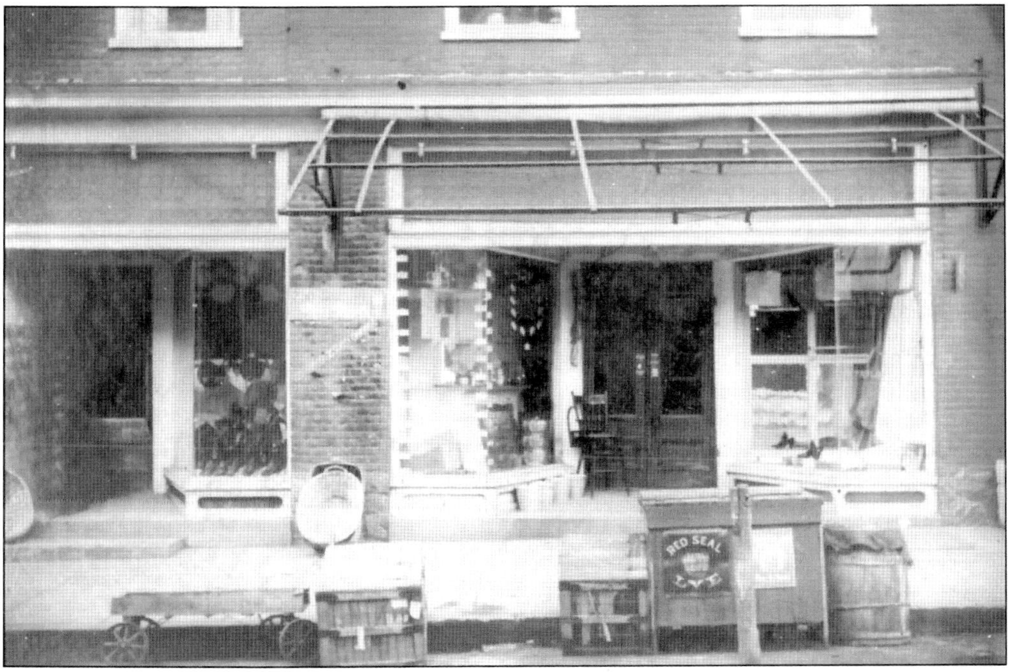

This 1916 photograph shows the outside of George Taylor's general merchandise store on Conococheague Street. Note the bin on the curb advertising Red Seal Lye. (Courtesy Williamsport Town Museum.)

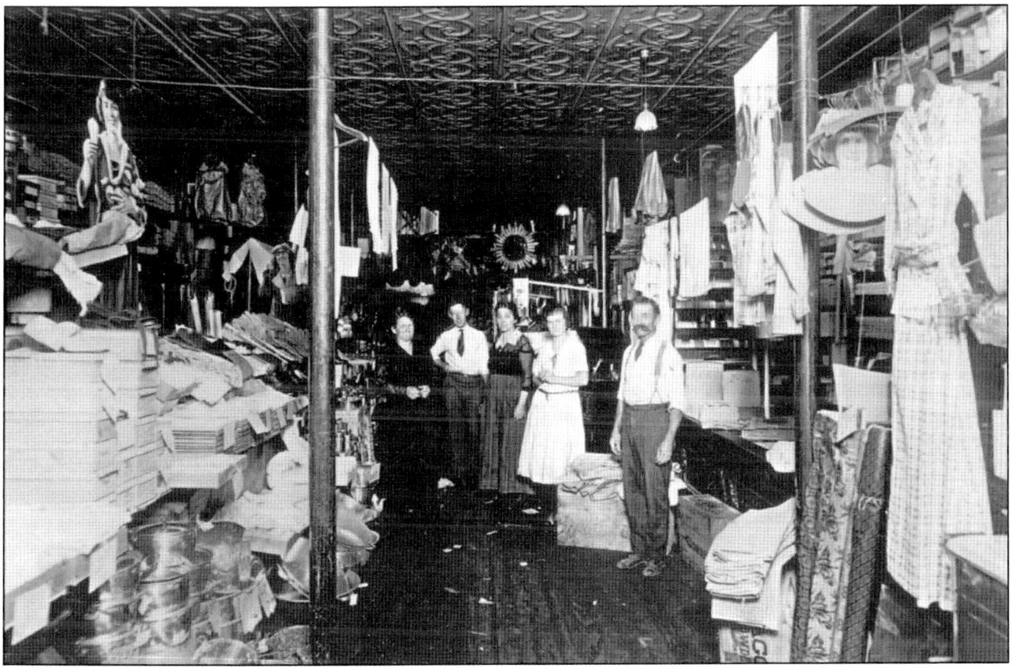

Here is an interior view, also from 1916, of George Taylor's store. Pictured from left to right are an unidentified employee, George Taylor, Mrs. Taylor, another unidentified employee, and Jim Madison. The fashions of the day are illustrated in the dress hanging in the foreground. (Courtesy Williamsport Town Museum.)

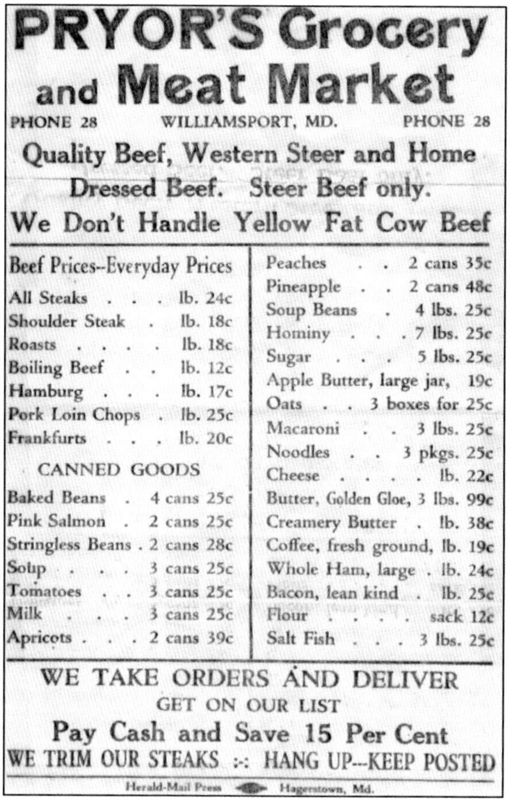

PRYOR'S Grocery and Meat Market

PHONE 28 WILLIAMSPORT, MD. PHONE 28

Quality Beef, Western Steer and Home Dressed Beef. Steer Beef only.

We Don't Handle Yellow Fat Cow Beef

Beef Prices--Everyday Prices			
All Steaks	lb. 24c	Peaches	2 cans 35c
Shoulder Steak	lb. 18c	Pineapple	2 cans 48c
Roasts	lb. 18c	Soup Beans	4 lbs. 25c
Boiling Beef	lb. 12c	Hominy	7 lbs. 25c
Hamburg	lb. 17c	Sugar	5 lbs. 25c
Pork Loin Chops	lb. 25c	Apple Butter, large jar,	19c
Frankfurts	lb. 20c	Oats	3 boxes for 25c
CANNED GOODS		Macaroni	3 lbs. 25c
		Noodles	3 pkgs. 25c
		Cheese	lb. 22c
Baked Beans	4 cans 25c	Butter, Golden Gloe,	3 lbs. 99c
Pink Salmon	2 cans 25c	Creamery Butter	lb. 38c
Stringless Beans	2 cans 28c	Coffee, fresh ground,	lb. 19c
Soup	3 cans 25c	Whole Ham, large	lb. 24c
Tomatoes	3 cans 25c	Bacon, lean kind	lb. 25c
Milk	3 cans 25c	Flour	sack 12c
Apricots	2 cans 39c	Salt Fish	3 lbs. 25c

WE TAKE ORDERS AND DELIVER

GET ON OUR LIST

Pay Cash and Save 15 Per Cent

WE TRIM OUR STEAKS :-: HANG UP--KEEP POSTED

Herald-Mail Press Hagerstown, Md.

This interesting piece of memorabilia is a price list from Pryor's Grocery and Meat Market. While not dated, we can tell this is an early piece from the phone number, just two digits long, and the prices. When was the last time you saw a roast for 18¢ a pound or got 3 cans of soup for 25¢? Notice that "hamburg," not "hamburger," is also for sale. (Courtesy Williamsport Town Museum.)

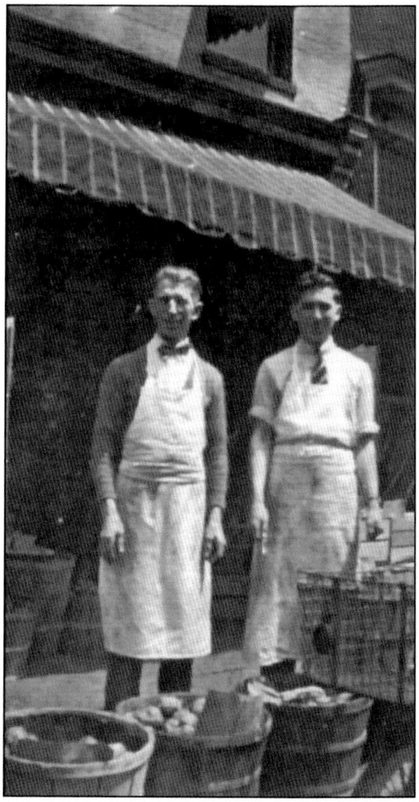

Another grocery store in town was Kesselring's on Conococheague Street. Here is Arthur F. Kesselring with his son, Richard, setting up produce outside their family store. (Courtesy Williamsport Town Museum.)

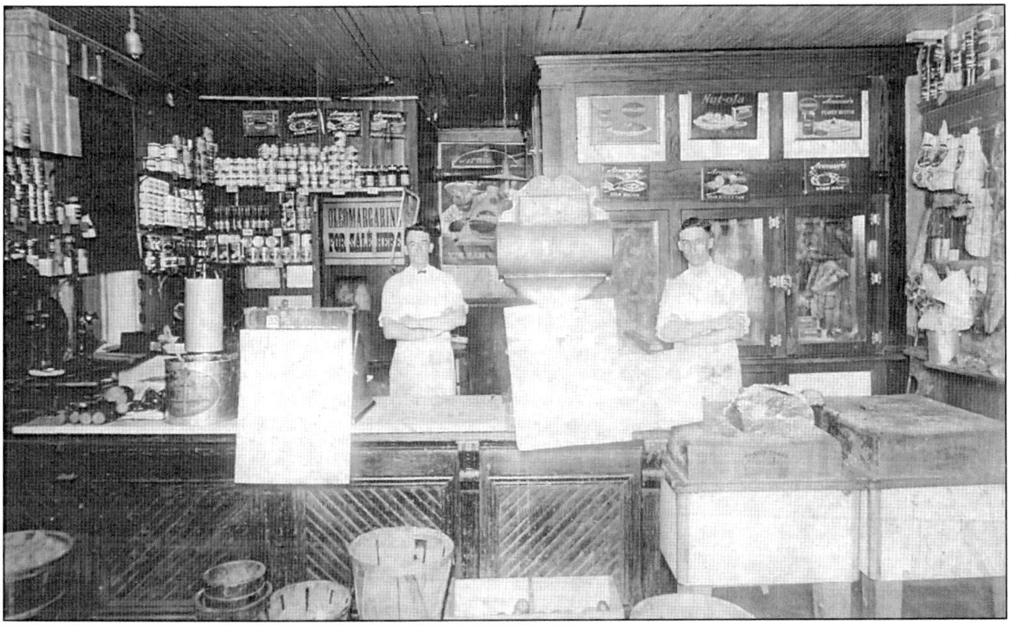

Here is a view of Middlekauff's Butcher Store on East Potomac. Roscoe Grove Middlekauff is on the right. Just a few of the items for sale include Armour's (of Armour-brand ham fame), peanut butter, and Nut-Ola Margarine. The man on the left is an employee, Jack Sterling. (Courtesy Williamsport Town Museum.)

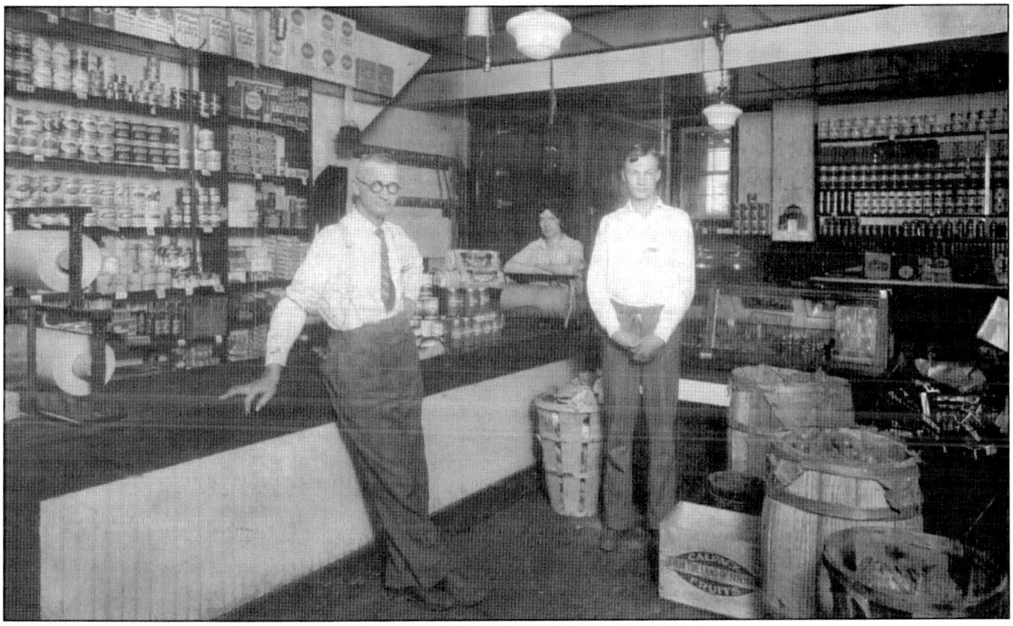

Here is another one of those great store interior photos that give such an informative glimpse back in time. Inside Pryor's Grocery on N. Conococheague Street, they had Corn Flakes, Duz, and Super Suds for sale, amongst many other items. Since Kellogg's Corn Flakes first became widely available to consumers in 1906, we know this photograph dates to some time after that. Note the large rolls of butcher paper on the left for wrapping items. Mr. Pryor is on the left, Irene Davis in the middle, and Mr. Pryor's son on the right. (Courtesy Williamsport Town Museum.)

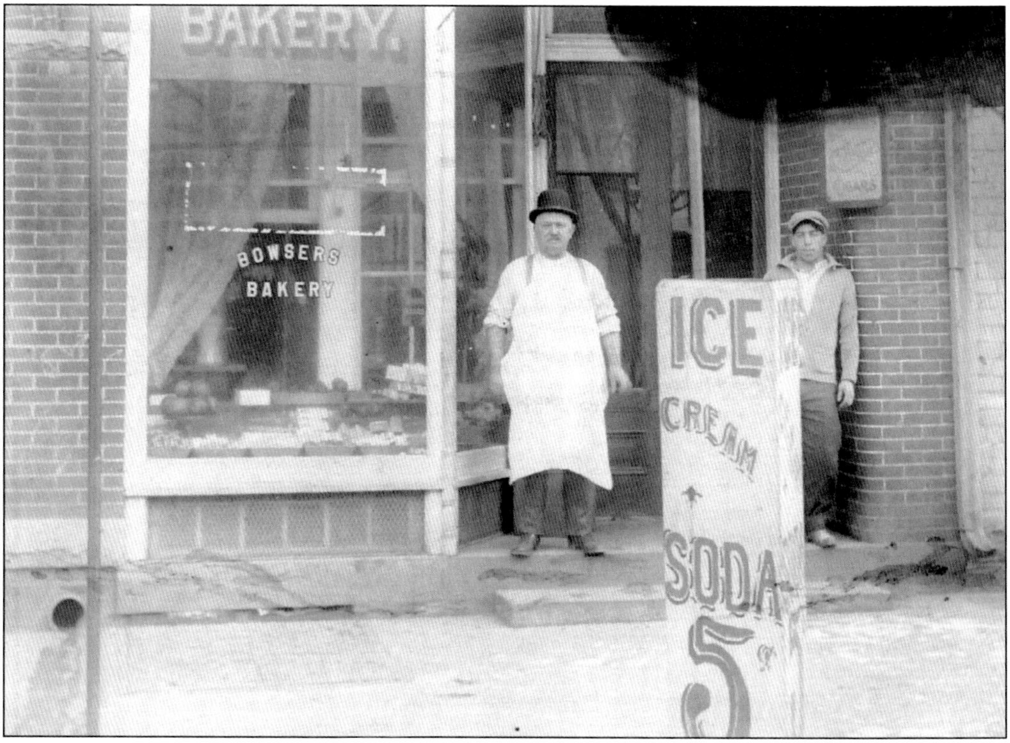

Here is Pop Bowser on the left and Frank Winters outside of Bowser's Bakery. (Courtesy Williamsport Town Museum.)

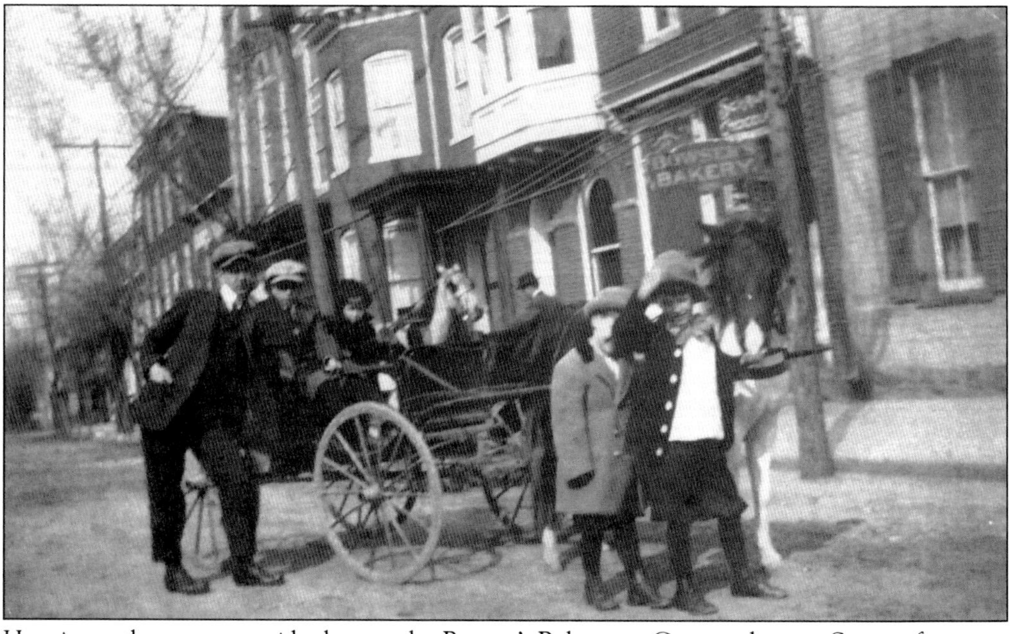

Here is another scene outside the popular Bowser's Bakery on Conococheague Street of a group posing with their pony-drawn cart. (Courtesy Williamsport Town Museum.)

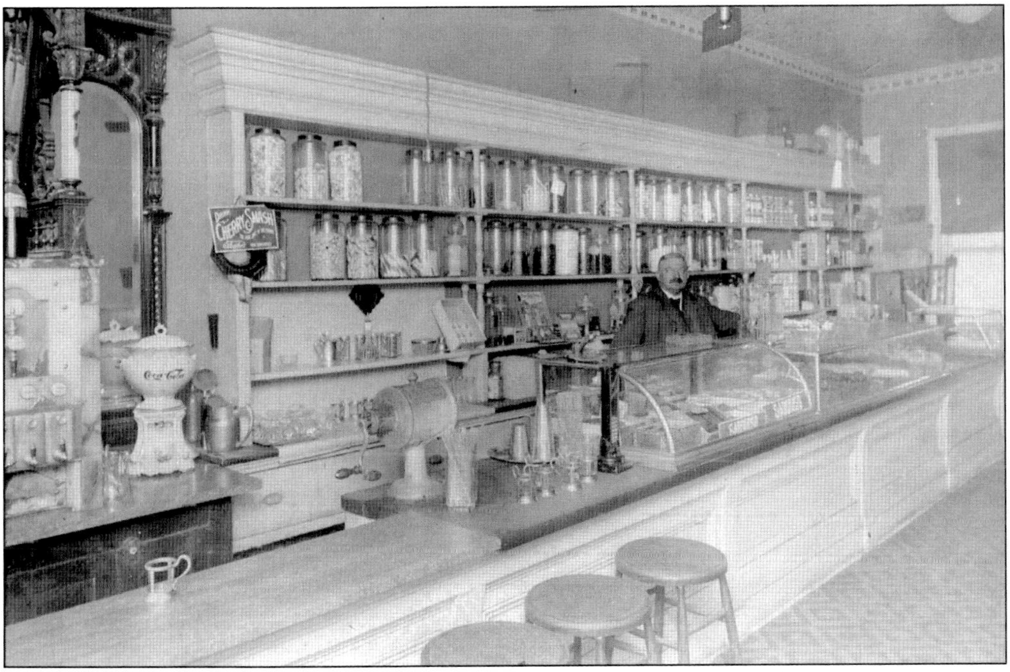

This 1900 photograph shows John Bowser's grandfather inside Bowser's shop. Note the old fashioned ceramic Coca-Cola dispenser on the counter to the left near the mirror. Today you can find pinkish-colored replicas of this same item for sale in places like Cracker Barrel restaurants and other "old time" places. (Courtesy Williamsport Town Museum.)

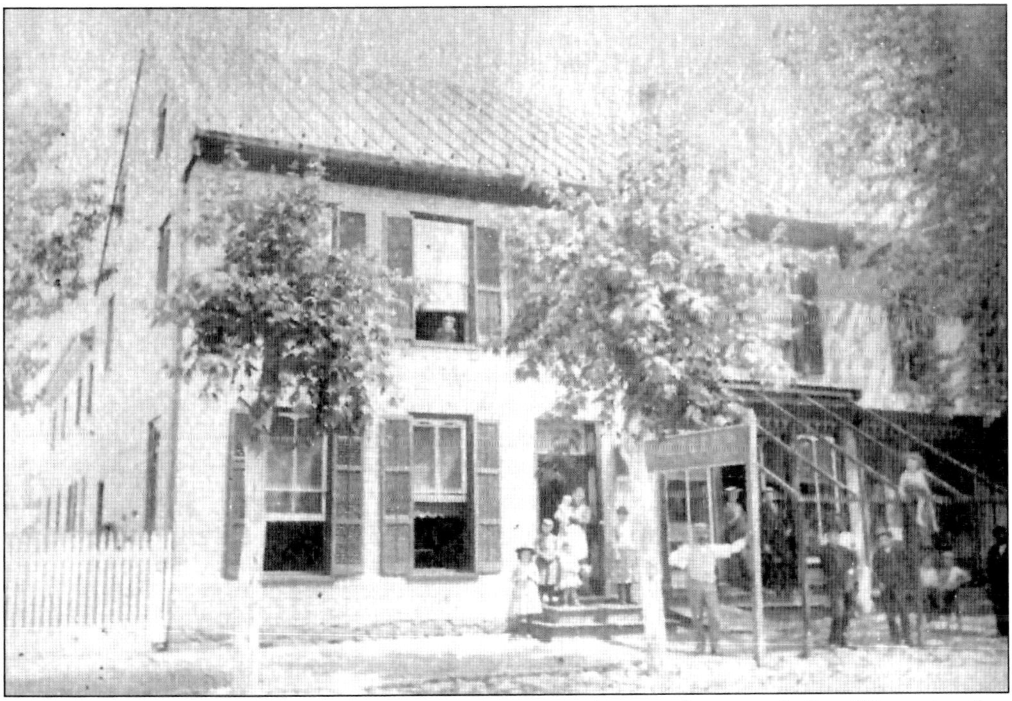

Here is an outside view of Bowser's Bakery on Conococheague Street with Doc Weaver's office next door. (Courtesy Williamsport Town Museum.)

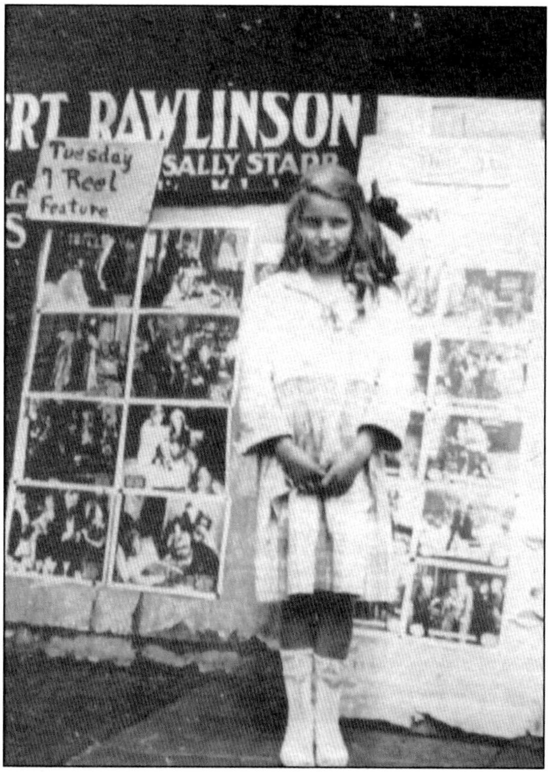

This young lady is standing outside Bowser's store after the bakery had moved to another location. The Bowsers operated this store as a nickelodeon, and the sign out front advertises a seven-reel feature on Tuesday. (Courtesy Williamsport Town Museum.)

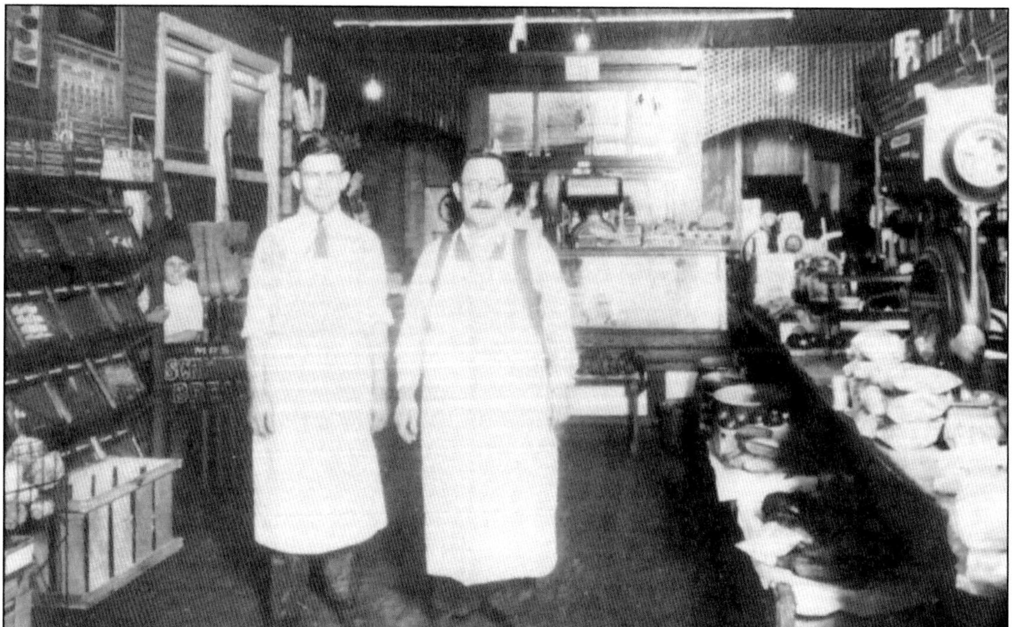

This photograph shows the interior of Harsh's Meat Market in 1927, when the market was at 5 E. Potomac Street in Williamsport, Maryland. The store later moved to Artizan Street. In the photo, store founder Albert S. Harsh (right) stands with his son, Martin D. Harsh Sr. (Courtesy *Maryland Cracker Barrel.*)

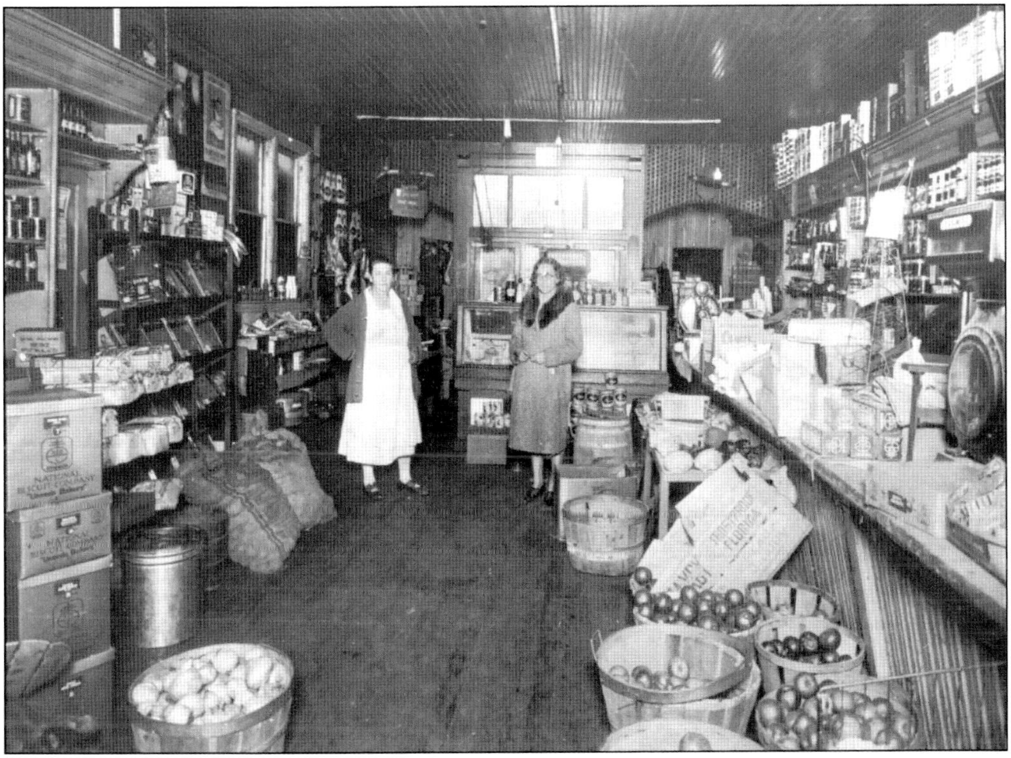

Here is another great photograph of a store interior. On the left in Harsh's Butcher Shop on E. Potomac Street is Carrie Harsh, and to the right is Edna Reichter. Note all the fresh produce, large sacks of potatoes, and containers perhaps full of crackers from the National Biscuit Company for sale. (Courtesy Williamsport Town Museum.)

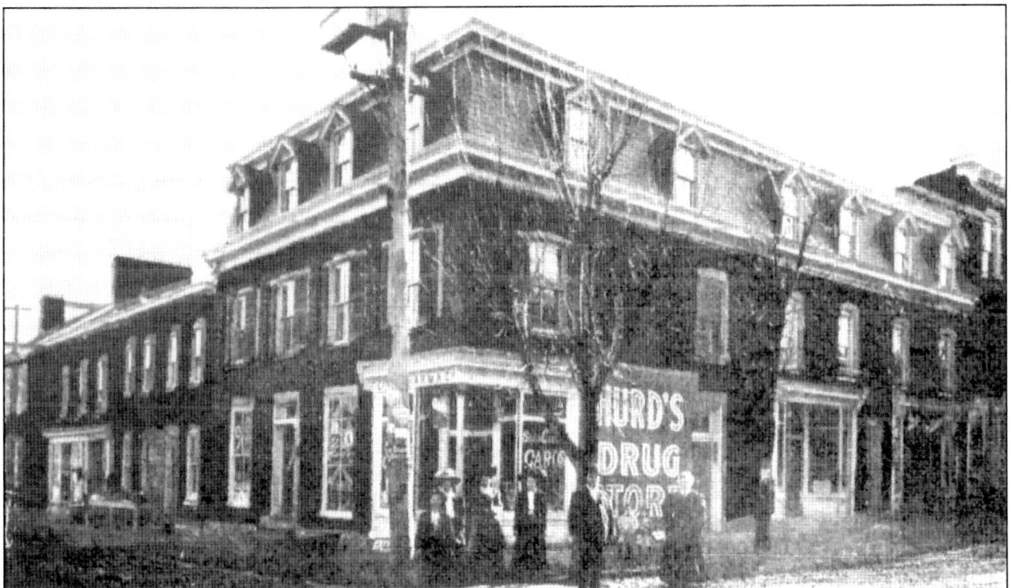

This photograph from the early 20th century shows the Hurd drugstore on the southeast corner of N. Conococheague Street. (Courtesy *Maryland Cracker Barrel.*)

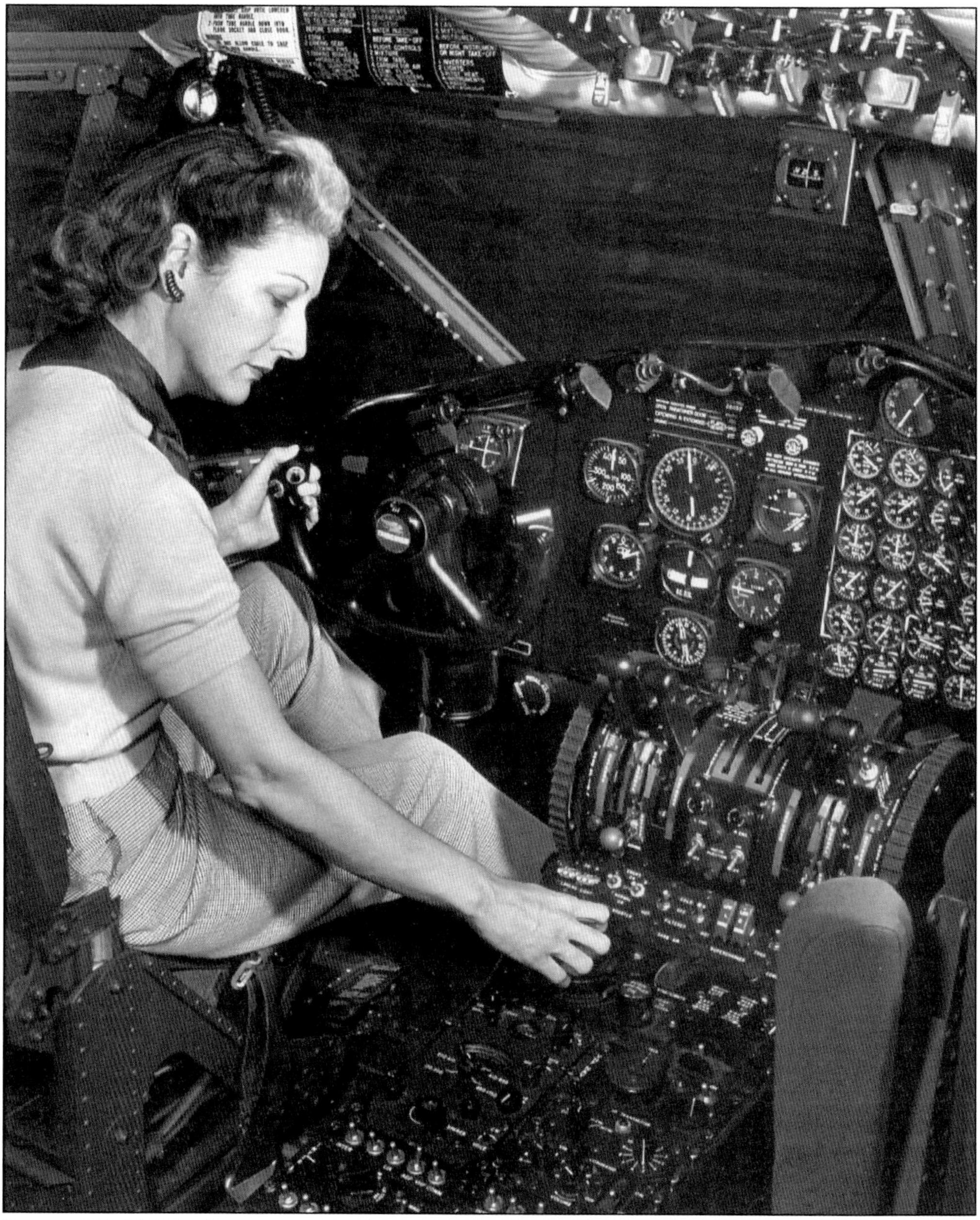

During World War II, women played a very important and vital role in the war effort. "Rosie the Riveter" was born in a 1942 song, when women in overalls or wielding industrial tools became a common sight as women took over factory jobs previously held by men to free them up for military service. Katherine Hanna Knode-Poffenberger was one such "Rosie" who worked at Fairchild Aircraft as a final assembly inspector for aircraft. In this photograph inside a C-123, Katherine is doing the final checkout before flight. Women also took flight lessons and earned their pilots' licenses to allow them to actually ferry the planes from factories to Europe. (Courtesy Williamsport Town Museum.)

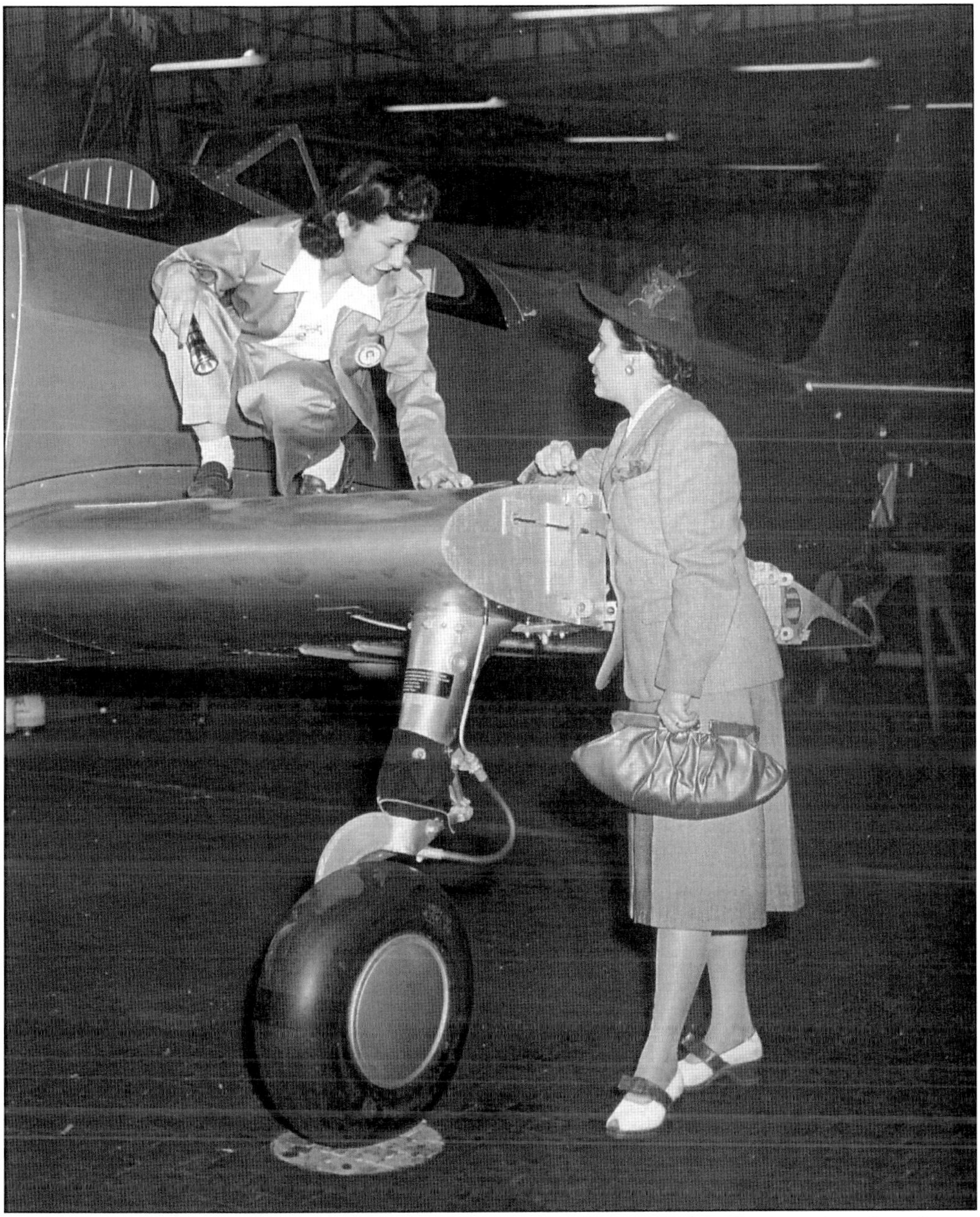

Here is Katherine Knode-Poffenberger on the wing of a Fairchild PT-19 at the plant being interviewed by Stella Monteiro, the head of the Women's Division of the Labor Department from the state of Minas Gerias, Brazil. Ms. Monteiro was studying the health, safety, training, and wages of women war workers and had a perfect opportunity at Fairchild, where over 30 percent of the employees were women. (Courtesy Williamsport Town Museum.)

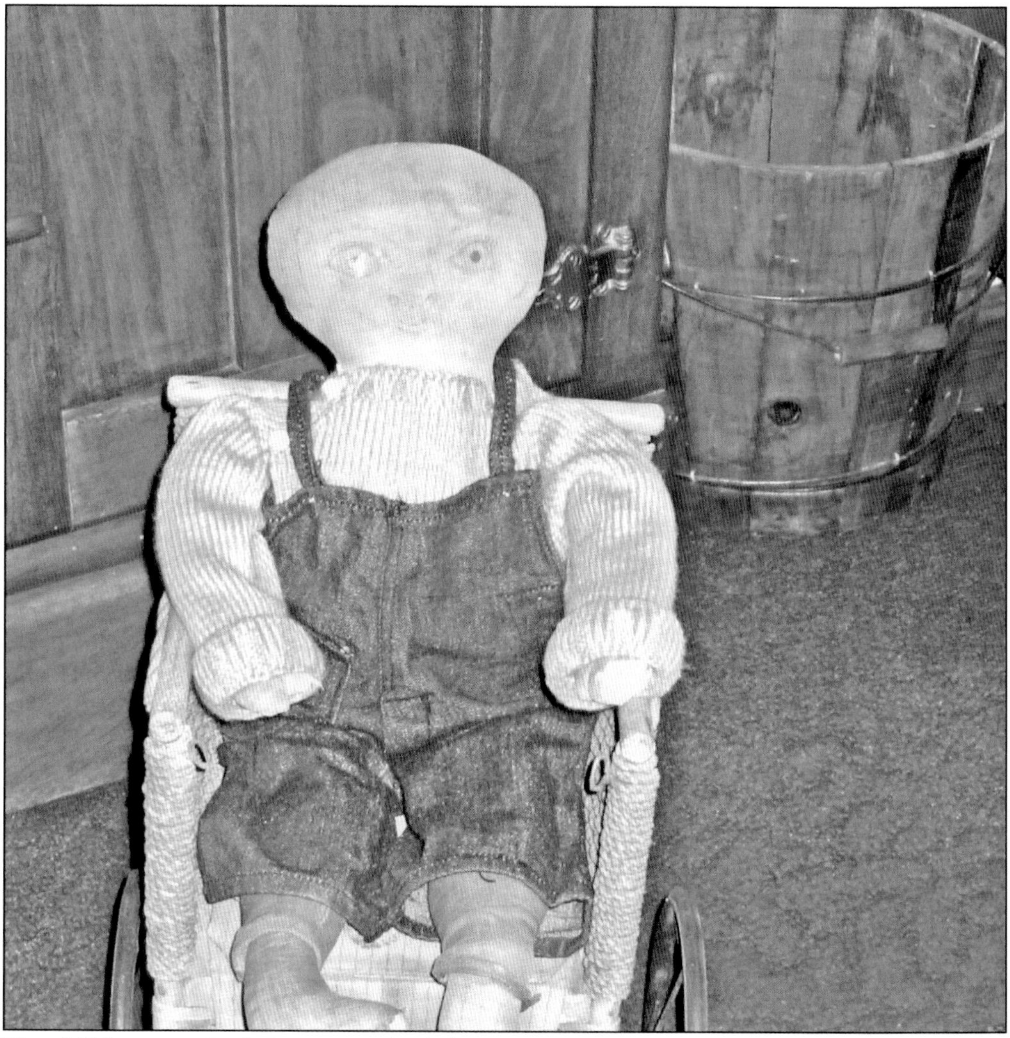

This doll, known as Little Susie, was a birthday present to Hanna Poffenberger on her first birthday. Now more than 90 years later, Susie shows the result of much care and love. The overalls the doll is wearing are of particular interest, as they were specially made for the doll at the Barnhart Overall Factory that was once located in Williamsport on the corner of E. Potomac and N. Artizan Streets, which later became Red Barron furniture. (Courtesy Williamsport Town Museum.)

Four

The C&O Canal

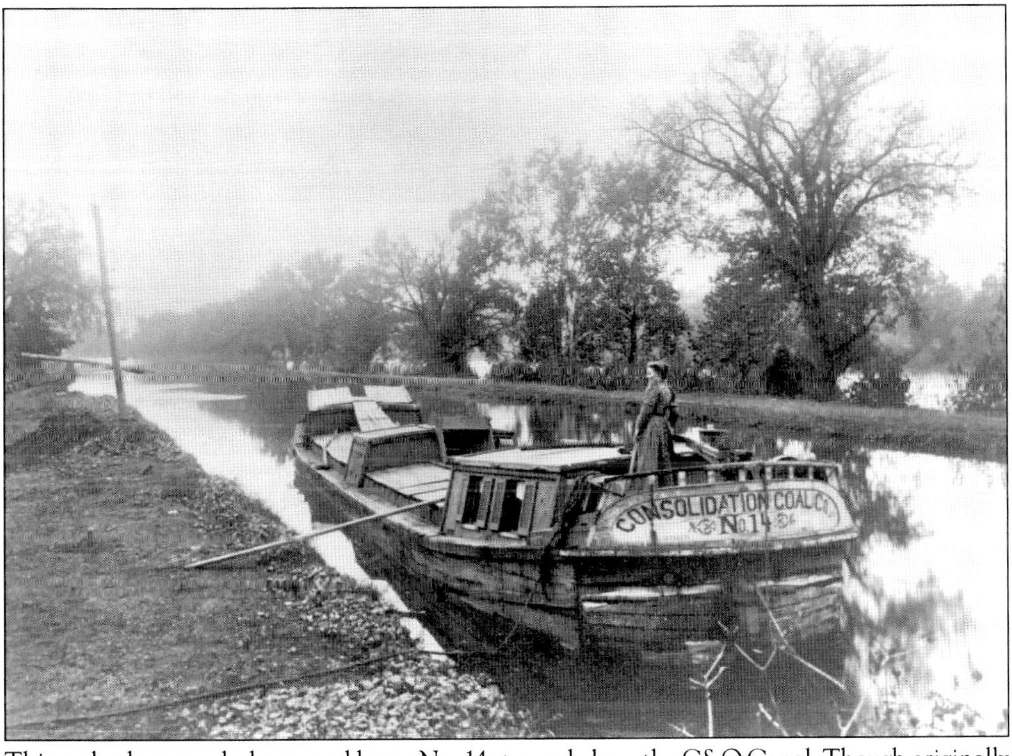

This early photograph shows coal barge No. 14 stopped along the C&O Canal. Though originally planned to extend all the way from Georgetown to the Ohio River near Pittsburgh, Pennsylvania, only about half the distance—as far as Cumberland—was completed. Chief cargoes included coal, grain, cement, lumber, bricks, and produce. (Courtesy Williamsport Town Museum.)

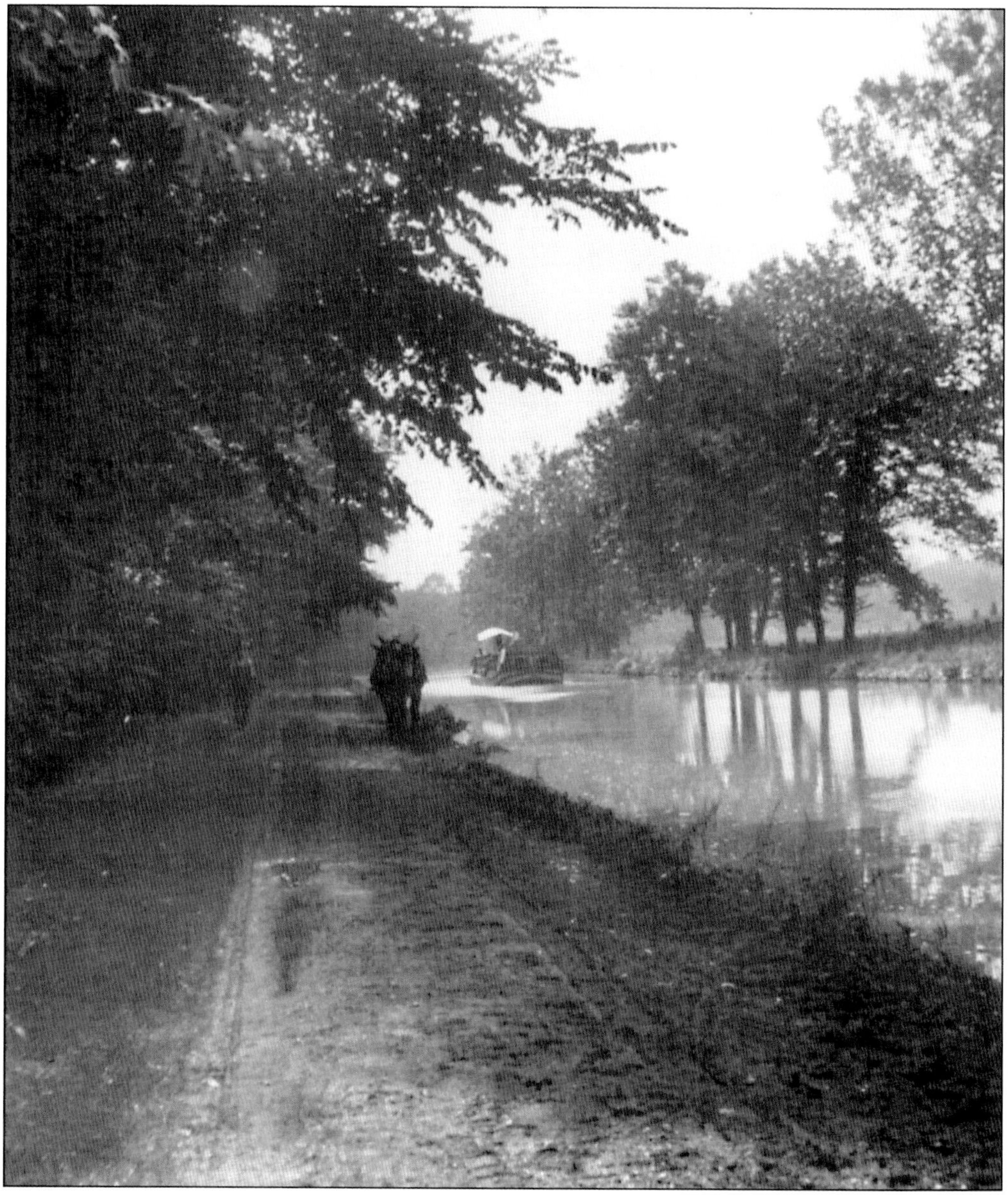

This 1920 shot shows a mule plodding along the peaceful C&O Canal towpath where the Hagerstown Water Plant now stands. (Courtesy *Maryland Cracker Barrel.*)

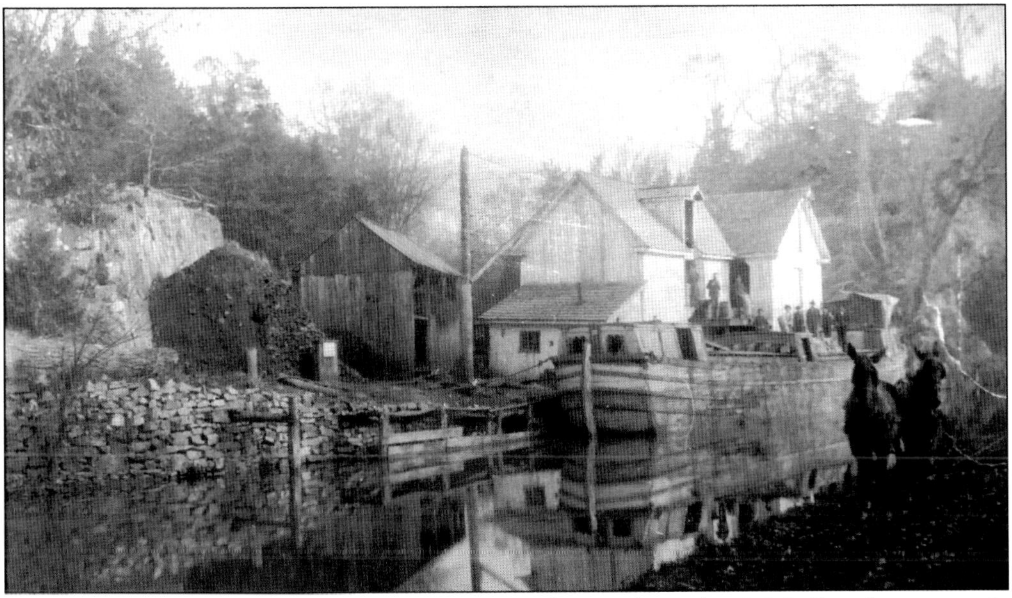

This *c.* 1890 photograph shows Abe Roth's warehouse along the C&O Canal just outside Williamsport in Pinesburg, Maryland. Take special note of the far right of the photograph, where two mules can be seen engaged in their task of pulling the canal barge. The canal mule could pull twice the load of a comparably sized horse and worked two eight-hour shifts every 24 hours. During rest periods, the mules were stabled in stalls at the forward end of the barge. (Courtesy Washington County Historical Society.)

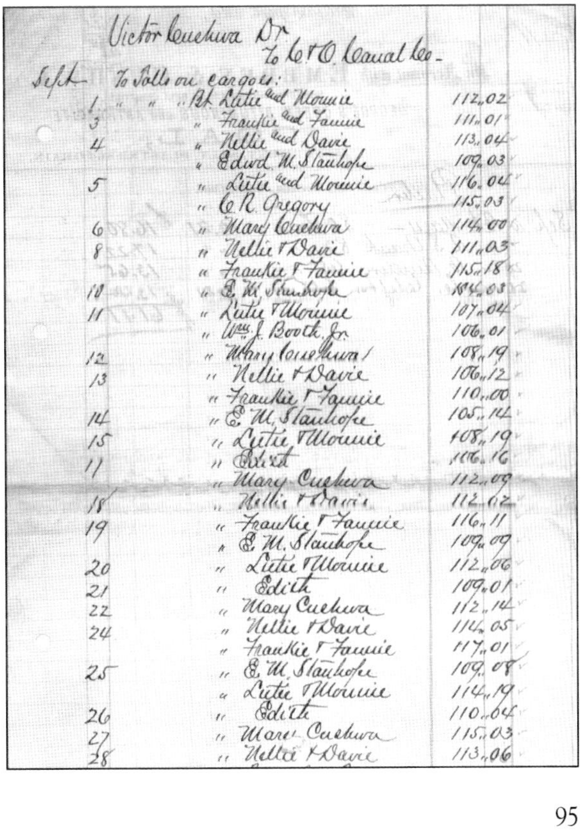

Victor Cushwa Dr
To C&O Canal Co.

Sept To Tolls on cargoes:

Day	Boat	Toll
1	" " Bt. Lutie and Monnie	112.02
3	" Frankie and Fannie	111.01
4	" Nellie and Davie	113.04
	" Edwd. M. Stanhope	109.03
5	" Lutie and Monnie	116.04
	" C.R. Gregory	115.03
6	" Mary Cushwa	114.00
8	" Nellie & Davie	111.03
	" Frankie & Fannie	115.18
10	" E. M. Stanhope	[illegible]
11	" Lutie & Monnie	107.04
	" Wm. J. Booth Jr.	106.01
12	" Mary Cushwa	108.19
	" Nellie & Davie	106.12
13	" Frankie & Fannie	110.00
14	" E. M. Stanhope	105.14
15	" Lutie & Monnie	108.19
	" Edith	106.16
17	" Mary Cushwa	112.09
18	" Nellie & Davie	112.02
19	" Frankie & Fannie	116.11
	" E. M. Stanhope	109.09
20	" Lutie & Monnie	112.06
21	" Edith	109.01
22	" Mary Cushwa	112.14
24	" Nellie & Davie	114.05
	" Frankie & Fannie	117.01
25	" E. M. Stanhope	109.08
	" Lutie & Monnie	114.19
26	" Edith	110.04
27	" Mary Cushwa	115.03
28	" Nellie & Davie	113.06

This manifest shows a listing of cargo tolls for canal boats from the Cushwa wharves in 1883. Note that the boats each have special names, as opposed to the boat number that would later supersede the individual boat naming. (Courtesy Western Maryland Room Washington County Free Library.)

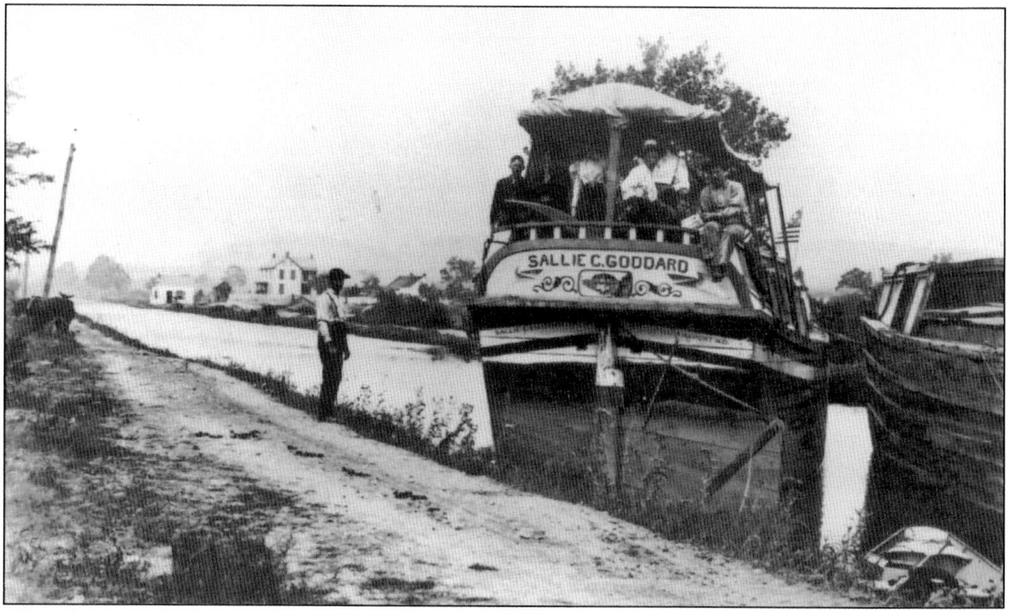

This photograph shows a late-19th-century boat moored on the towpath. The boat, the *Sallie C. Goddard* of Williamsport, Maryland, was named for the owner's daughter. (Courtesy C&O Canal National Historical Park Headquarters.)

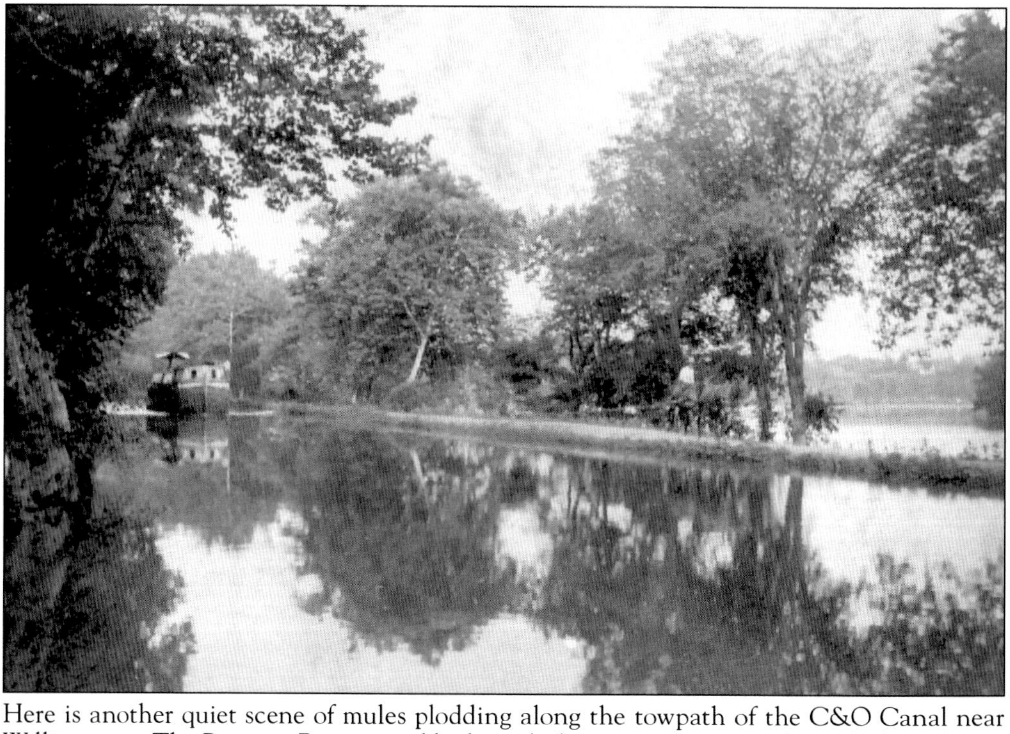

Here is another quiet scene of mules plodding along the towpath of the C&O Canal near Williamsport. The Potomac River is visible through the gap in the trees. The mules bred for use on the canal were smaller than those bred for farming, usually no more than 12 to 14 hands high, so that it could fit into the stable with its low ceiling at the front end of the barge. (Courtesy Williamsport Town Museum.)

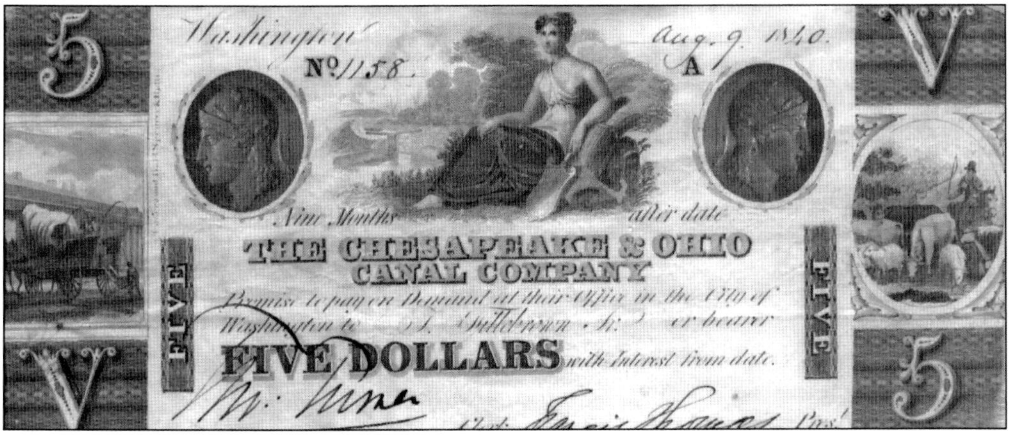

Prior to the Civil War, the United States did not have a true national currency—paper money was issued by state banks. Some of these banks helped finance canal construction. While intricately engraved, the money was easy to counterfeit. This C&O Canal banknote dated August 9, 1840, was good for "Five Dollars with interest." Note the intricate artwork adorning the note. (Courtesy Western Maryland Room Washington County Free Library.)

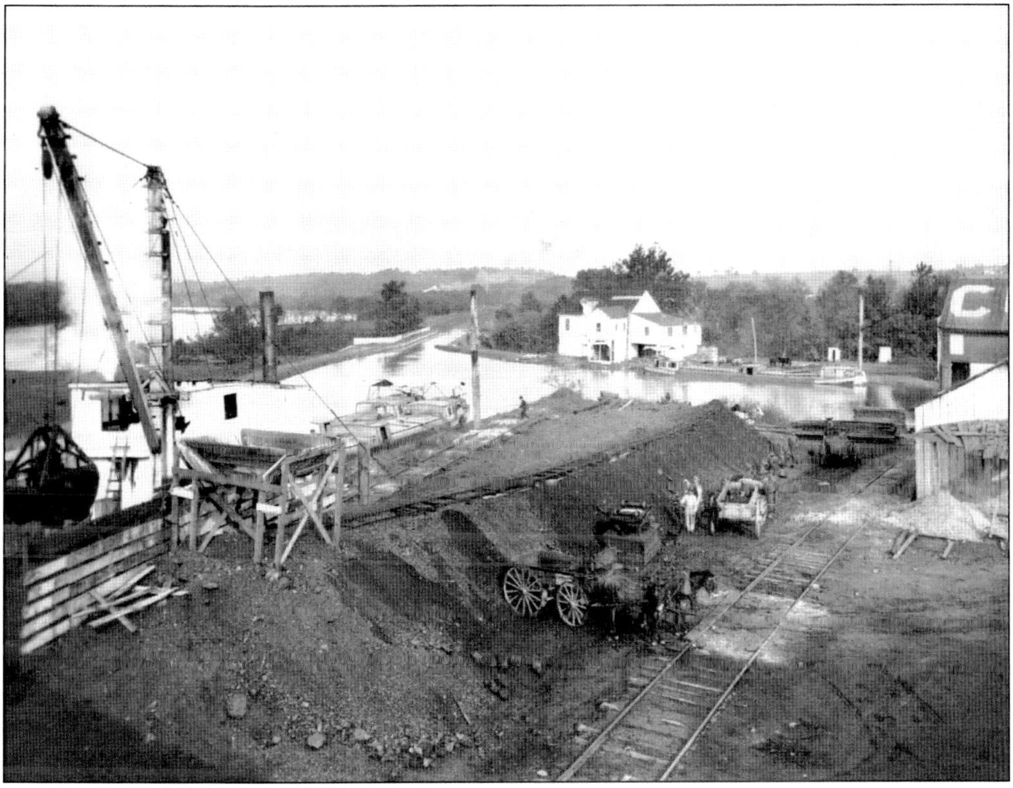

Here is a close-up view of the Cushwa Basin showing empty, mule-drawn wagons ready to be loaded with coal. The large building with the "C" on the far right is still in existence and now serves as the C&O Canal Visitor Center. The white building in the center is no longer standing. The aqueduct can be seen to the left of the white building. (Courtesy C&O Canal National Historical Park Headquarters.)

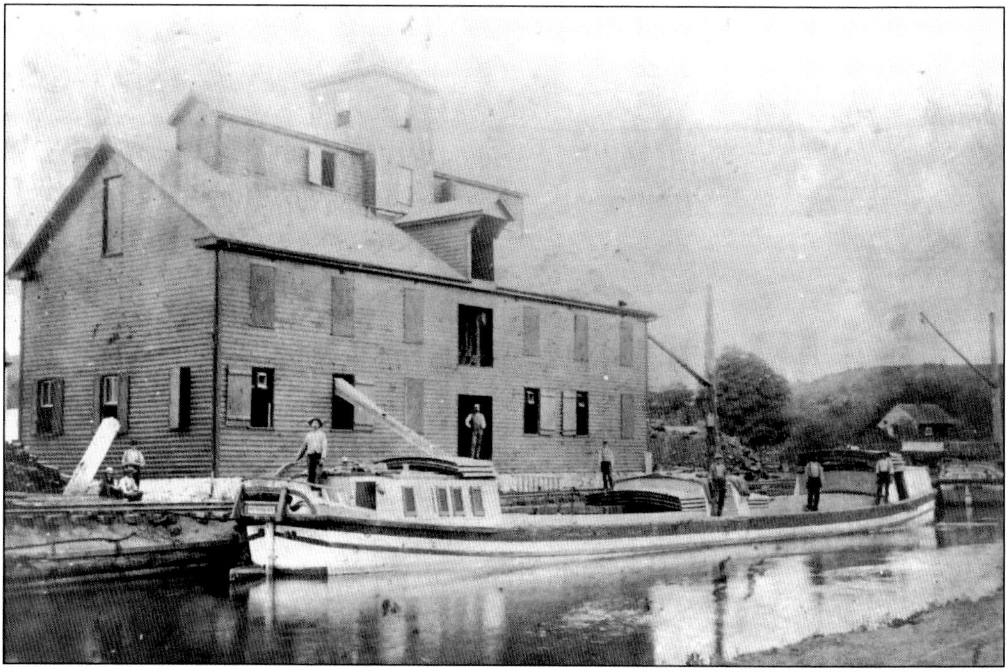

This canal boat is loading at Darby Mill, an old landmark near Lock No. 44 in Williamsport, Maryland. The mill was destroyed by fire in 1920, just four short years before the canal closed. Shown in the photograph from left to right are "Pots" Corby (sitting), George Lake, Eugene Ardinger, "Wash" Taylor, F. H. Darby (in doorway), Ruby Darby, Harry Prior, John Ream, and unidentified. (Courtesy C&O Canal National Historical Park Headquarters.)

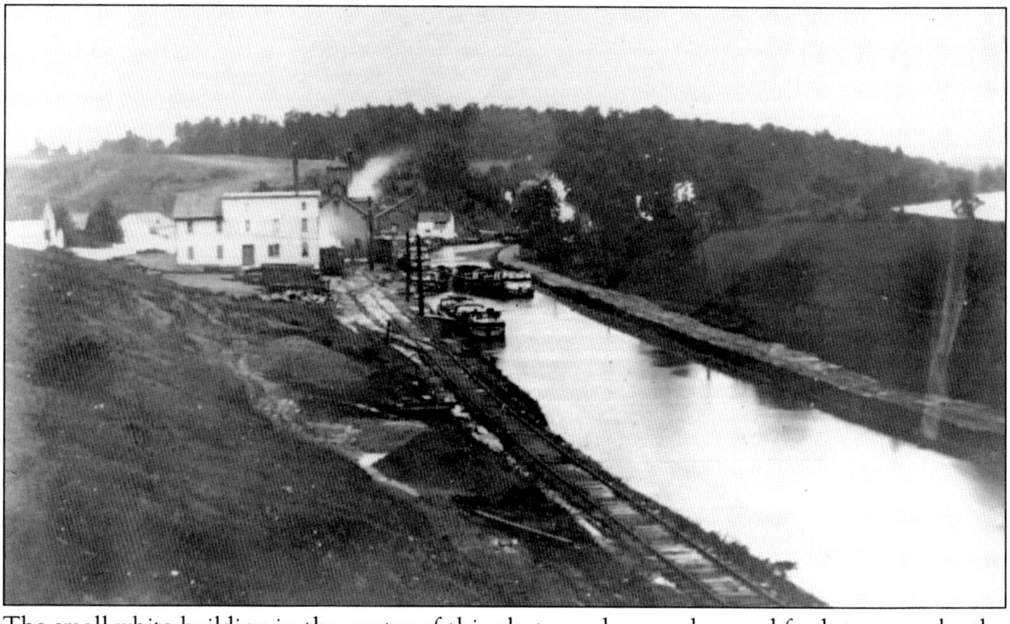

The small white building in the center of this photograph was a hay and feed store run by the canal company. Canal boat operators obtained feed for the mules there. The larger building in the foreground on the left is Darby's Mill. This photograph dates sometime prior to the destruction of the mill in 1920. (Courtesy C&O Canal National Historical Park Headquarters.)

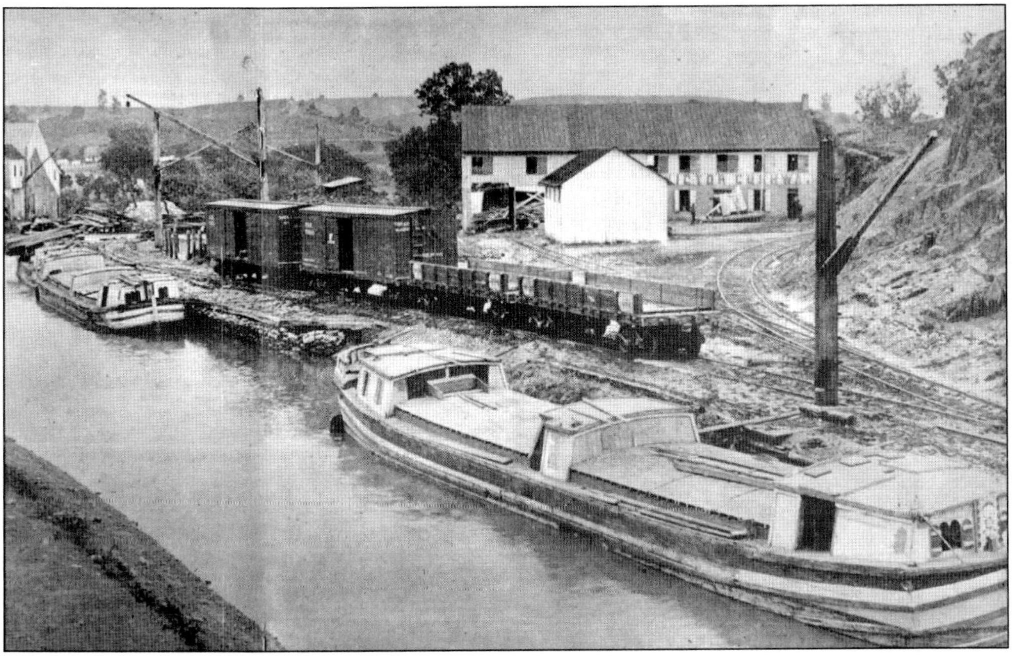

This 1875 photograph taken at the Victor Cushwa plant in Williamsport shows canal boats docked right next to their main competition, the railroad cars. Coal from Maryland and West Virginia mines near Cumberland, Maryland, was transferred from canal boats to Western Maryland Railroad cars at Williamsport. (Courtesy *Maryland Cracker Barrel.*)

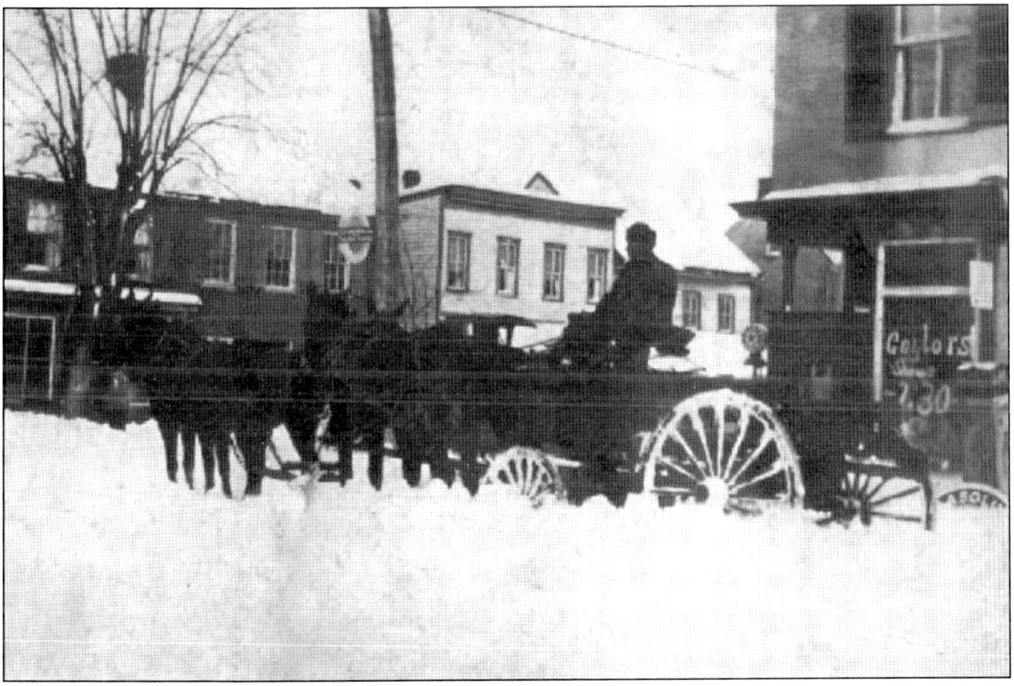

Here we see Harry McElroy delivering coal from the Cushwa Coal Yards on January 30, 1918. He is using the transportation of the day, a four-mule-team wagon. Look at that snow the wagon is moving through. (Courtesy Williamsport Town Museum.)

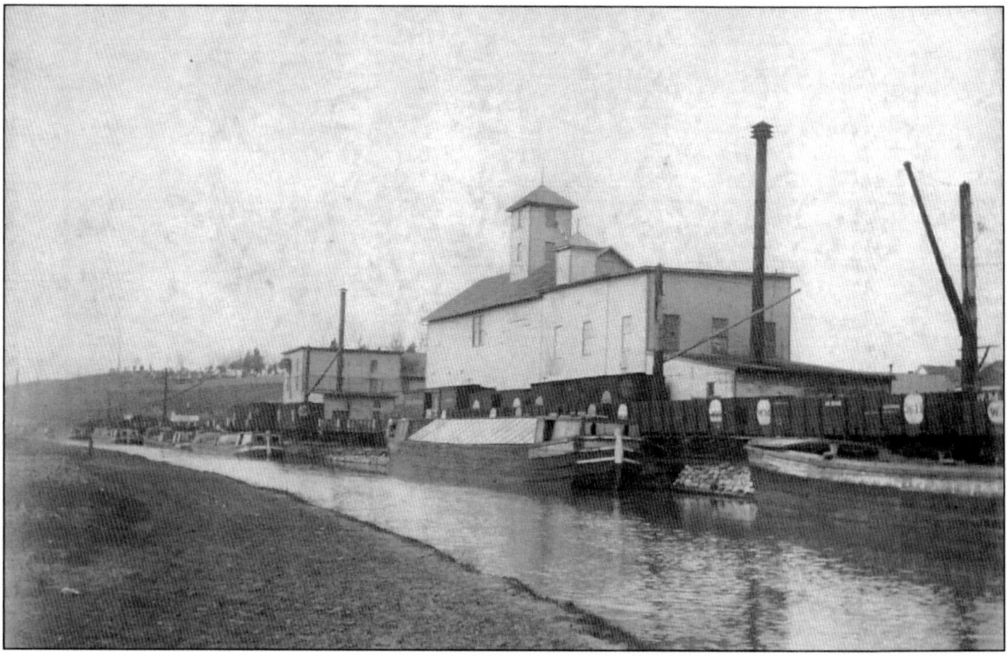

The angle this photograph was taken from *c.* 1901 shows a wider view of the canal than is usually seen. In the forefront is a boat being loaded from the grain elevator, while a line of canal boats and Riverview Cemetery, just visible on the hill, can also be seen in the background. (Courtesy Western Maryland Room Washington County Free Library.)

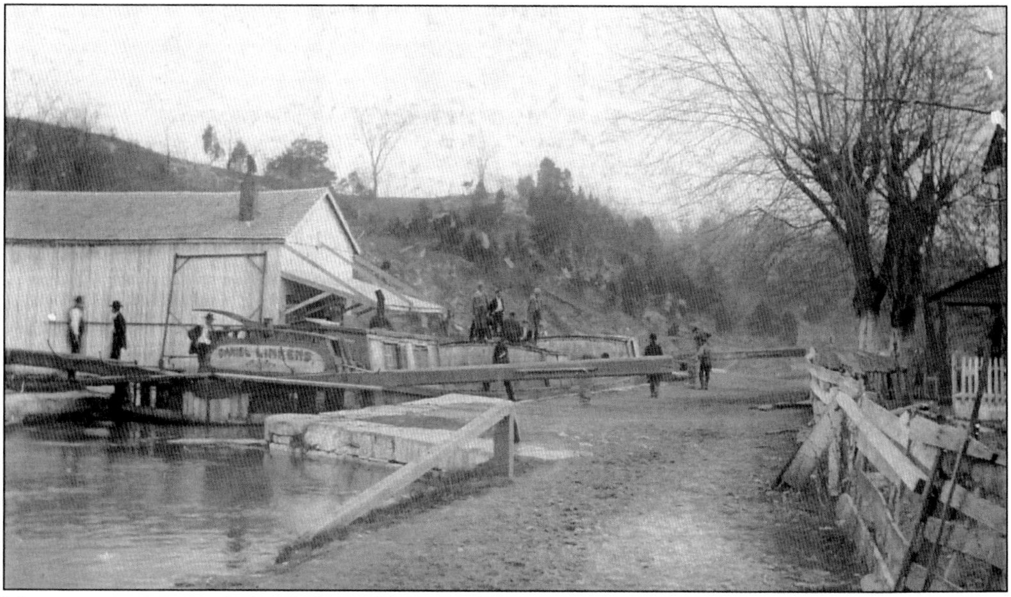

Here is a good view of a loaded canal boat in the Williamsport Lock (No. 44) *c.* 1901. The porch of the lock house itself can be seen on the right. The white building on the left, which is no longer standing, served as a feed store for the boatmen. Note that this photograph was taken prior to the days of the Consolidated Coal Company and their numbered boats. This boat clearly has its own name, the *Daniel Linkens*, instead of the later-standardized number only. (Courtesy Western Maryland Room Washington County Free Library.)

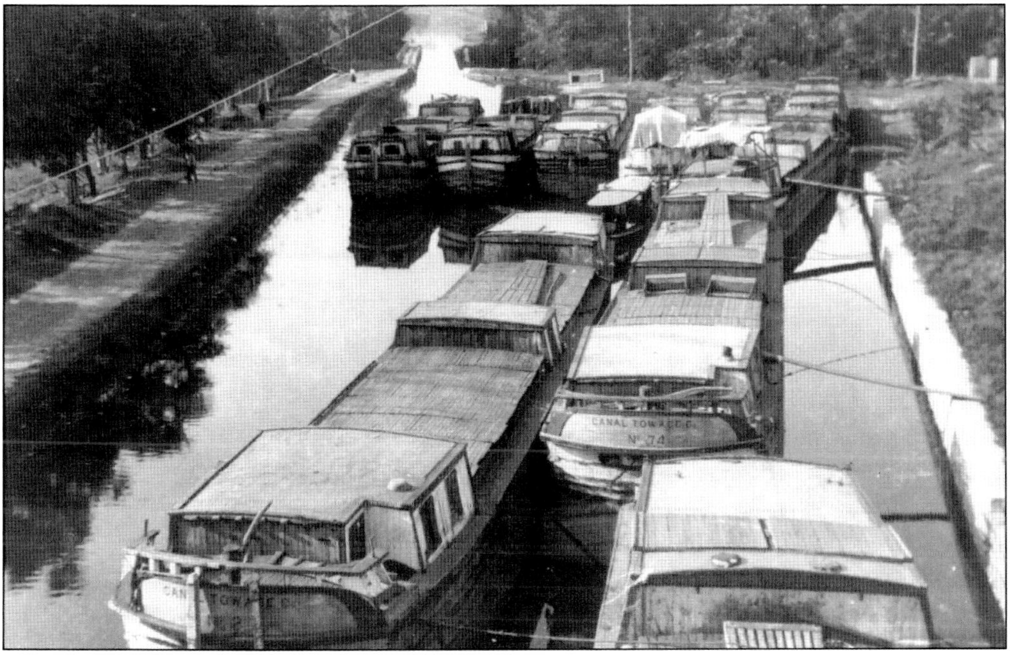

Here is a crowd of boats in the Cushwa basin *c.* 1920–1922. Note that the boats are now simply numbered as Canal Towage Company boats, and gone are the days of the unique names owners gave their boats. The Conococheague Creek Aqueduct can be seen in the background. (Courtesy Williamsport Town Museum.)

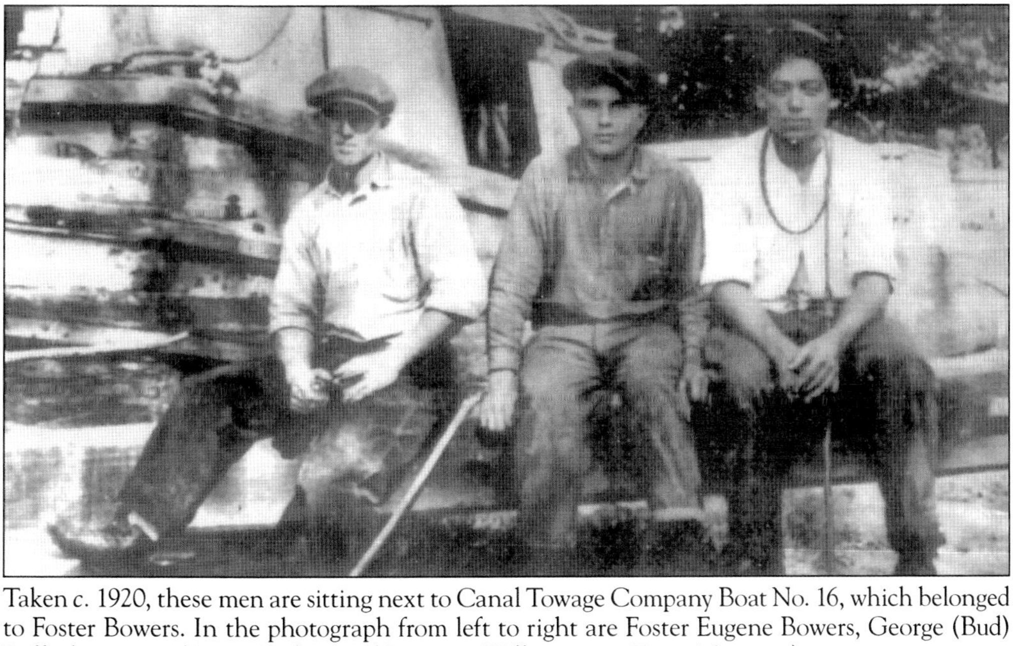

Taken *c.* 1920, these men are sitting next to Canal Towage Company Boat No. 16, which belonged to Foster Bowers. In the photograph from left to right are Foster Eugene Bowers, George (Bud) Poffenberger, and Max Anderson. (Courtesy Williamsport Town Museum.)

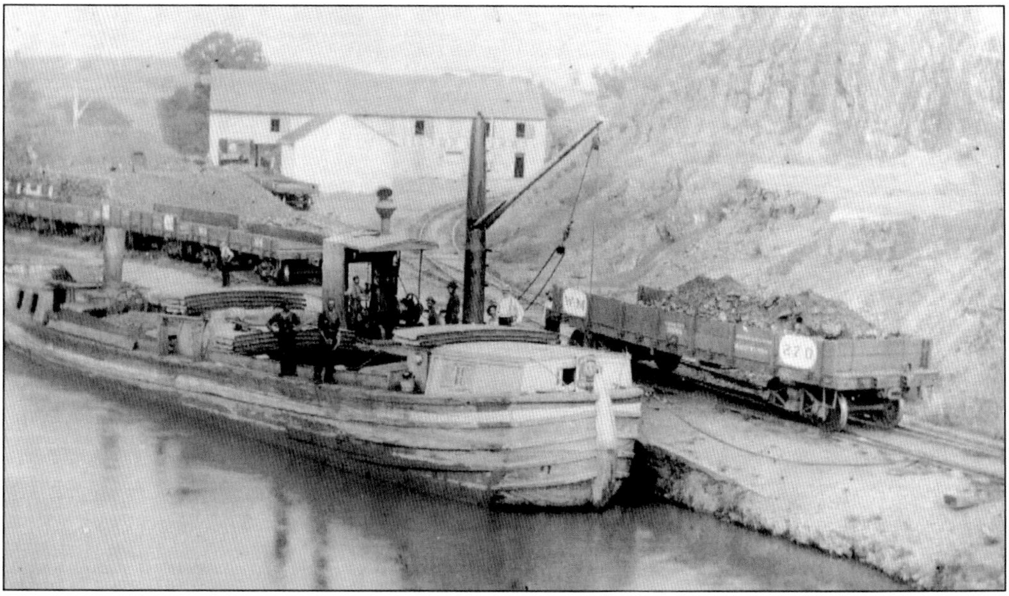

This photograph shows one of the rare steam-driven canal boats from around 1885. The canal company tried several steamboats as an experiment but abandoned the idea when it was discovered the boat's high speeds produced a wake that caused excessive washing of the banks of the canal. The steam stack can be seen rising up from the middle of the boat in the picture. Also, note the advertisement on the bow of the boat for Bartholomew's lager beer. The steam hoist in the picture lifted the bucket while loading the boat, but it was the manual force of the men that pulled it to the right or left as required. (Courtesy C&O Canal National Historical Park Headquarters.)

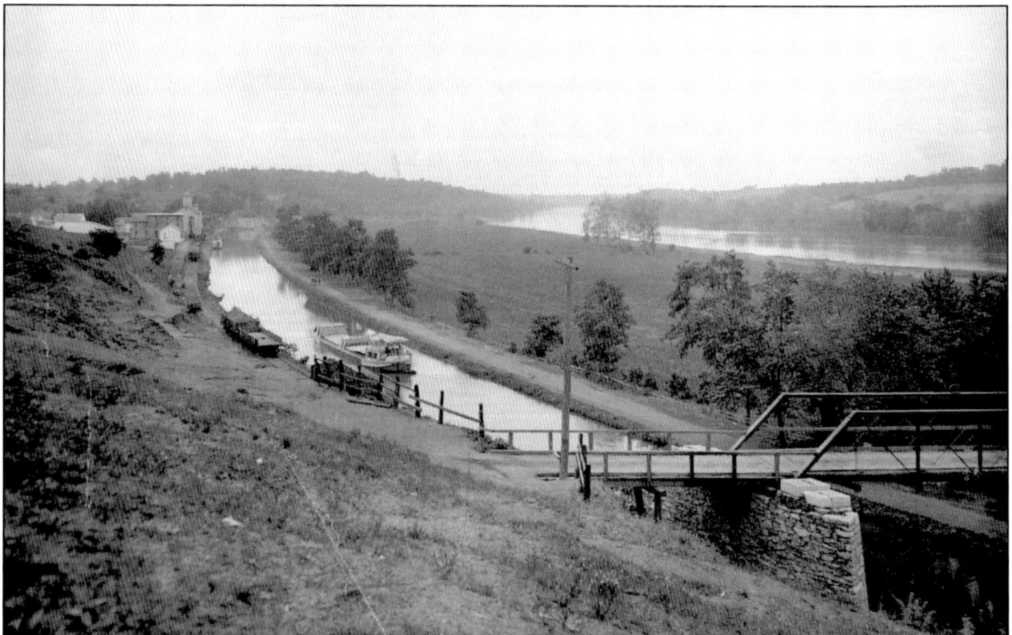

This view shows Williamsport looking down from Doubleday Hill. The Bollman Bridge is in the foreground, and Lock House No. 44 is on the right in the distance. Note the boat in the canal and the river itself off to the right. (Courtesy C&O Canal National Historical Park Headquarters.)

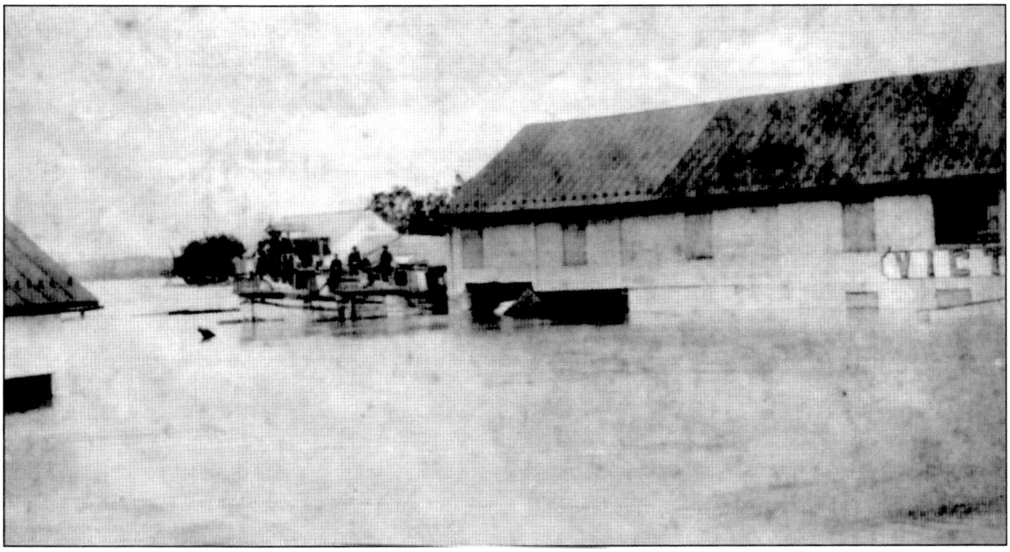

This photograph was taken June 1, 1889, after the historic May 31, 1899, flood. The photograph shows how high up the side of Cushwa's the floodwaters had climbed. Some men sitting on a canal boat are in the background. (Courtesy Williamsport Town Museum.)

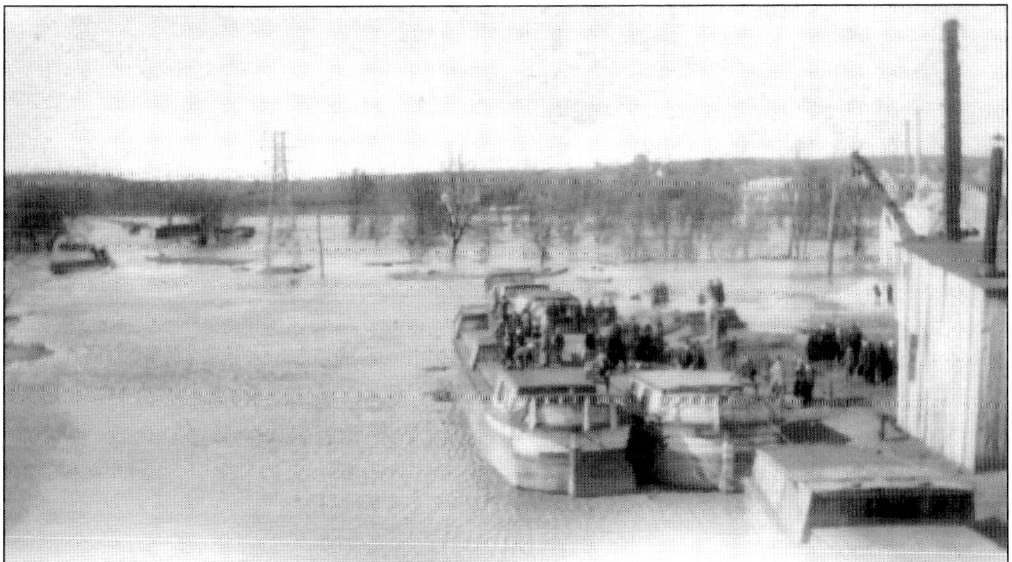

Here is the canal and a few boats during another flood, this time on March 30, 1924. The two floods of 1924 (the other was on May 13, 1924) were a result of heavy spring rains and melting snow. (Courtesy Western Maryland Room Washington County Free Library.)

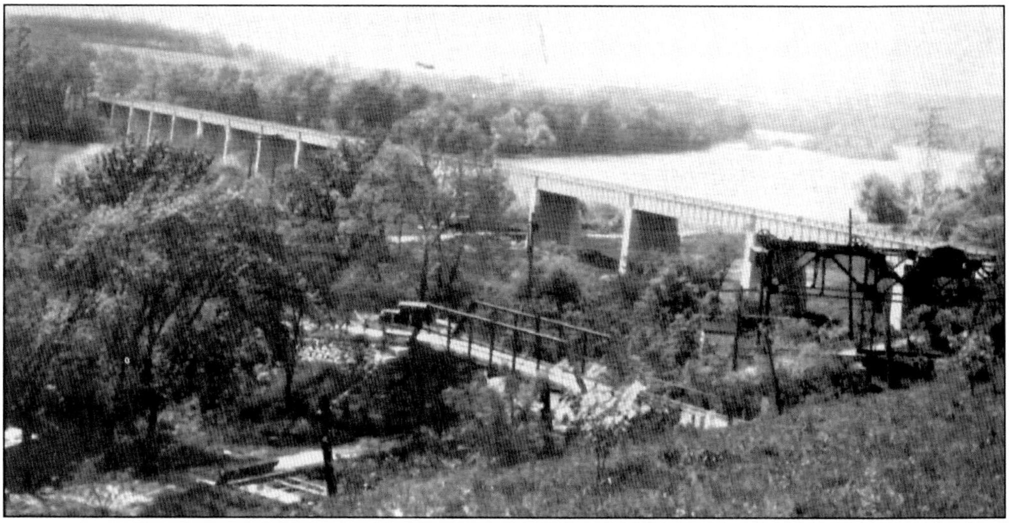

Here is a "before" shot of the Potomac taken in July 1935 that shows the normal level of the river. (Courtesy *Maryland Cracker Barrel*.)

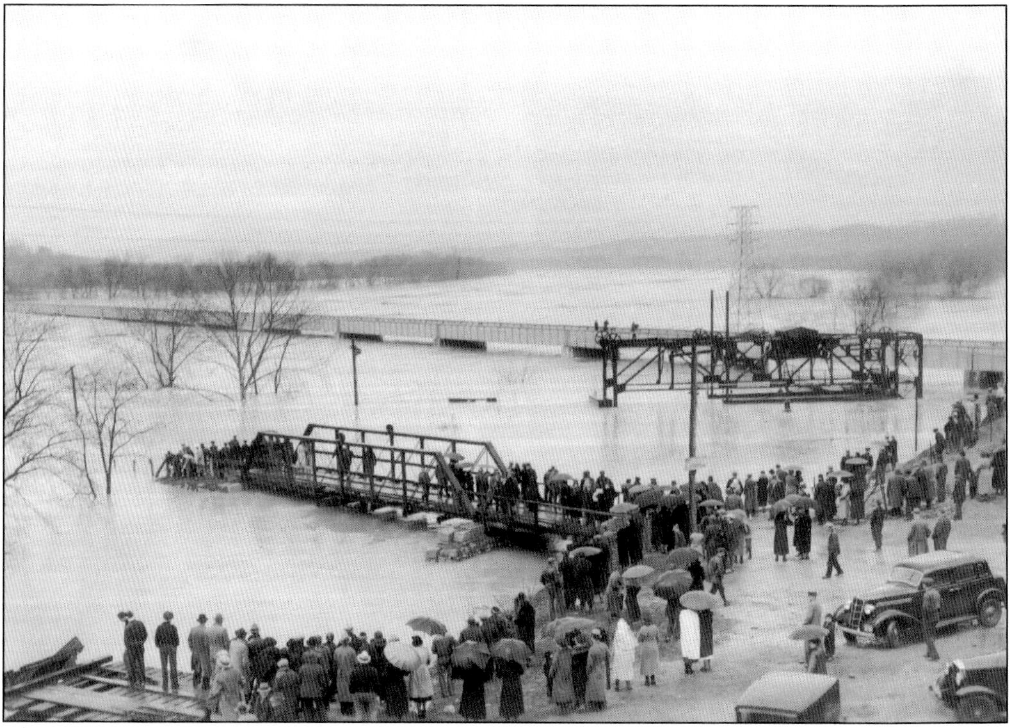

This is an "after" shot of the same location shown above. Taken during the flood of 1936, the area would be unrecognizable if not for the bridge tops showing above the water. (Courtesy Williamsport Town Museum.)

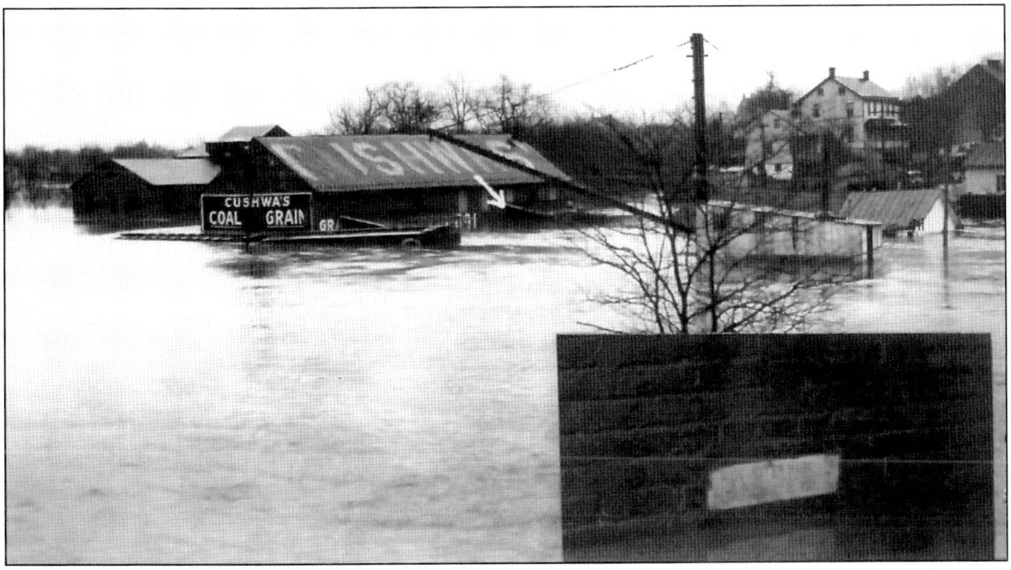

This photograph, showing Cushwa's during the 1936 flood, includes an inset photograph showing a plaque mounted on the building illustrating the height the water had reached on May 31 during the Great Flood of 1889. The white arrow in the middle of the main photograph indicates the location of the plaque. (Courtesy Williamsport Town Museum.)

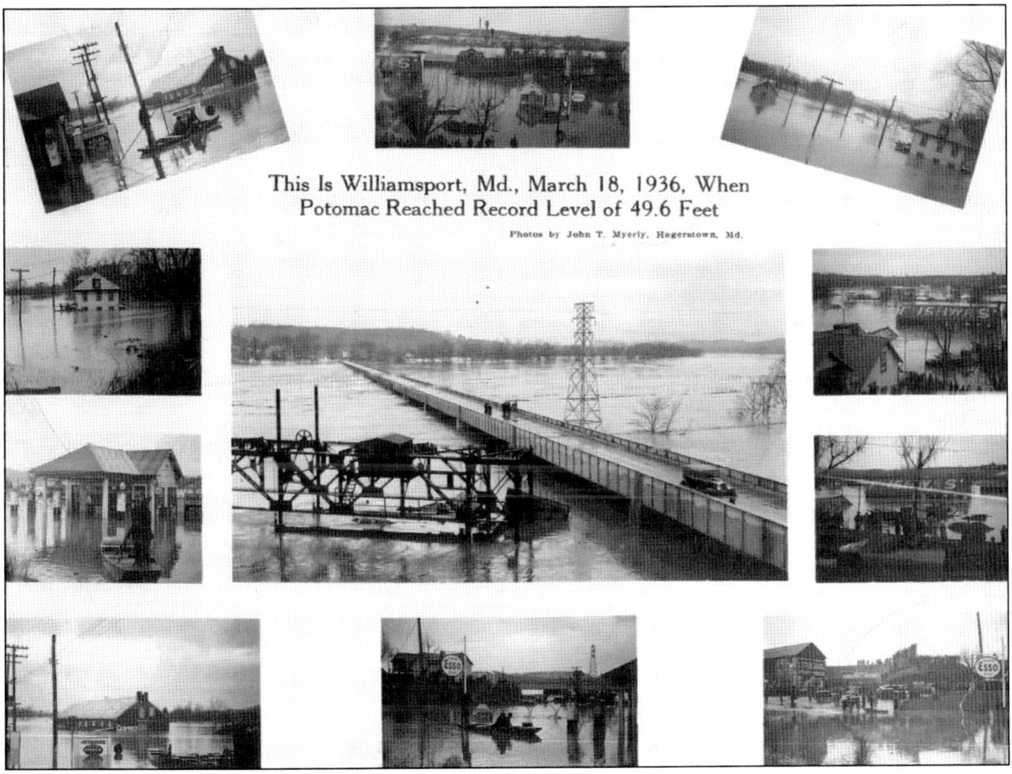

Here is a collection of photos taken by John T. Myerly of Hagerstown, issued as one large photograph, showing images around Williamsport after the March 18, 1936, flood. (Courtesy Williamsport Town Museum.)

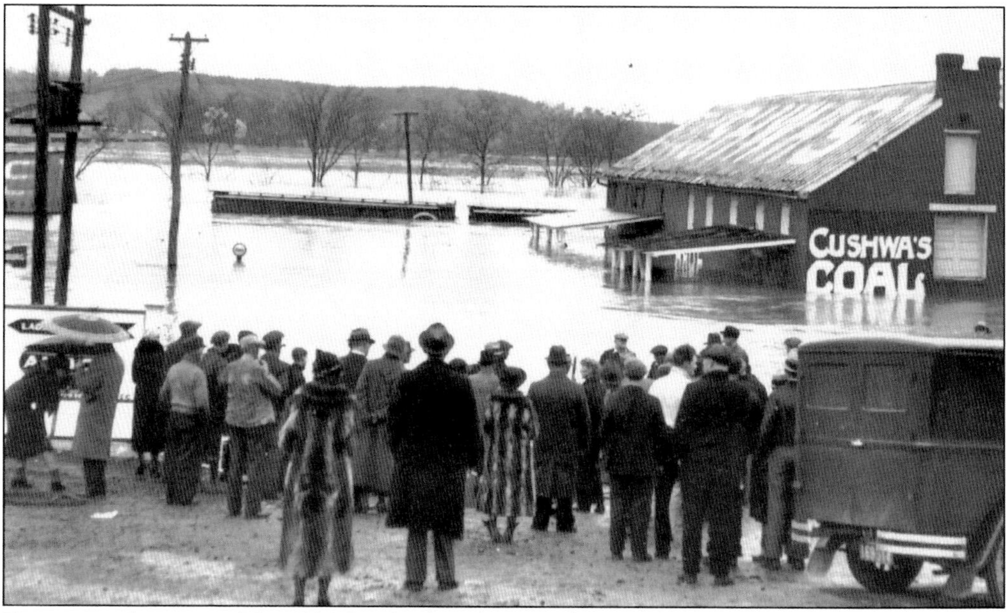

Here is another view of the 1936 flood. This photograph was taken at the foot of Potomac Street, where today the road turns into the C&O Canal Visitor Center parking lot to the right. Those long black shapes in the middle of the photograph are the tops of railroad cars that are almost completely under water. It must have still been raining when everyone turned out to view this scene, as the umbrellas to the left indicate. (Courtesy C&O Canal National Historical Park Headquarters.)

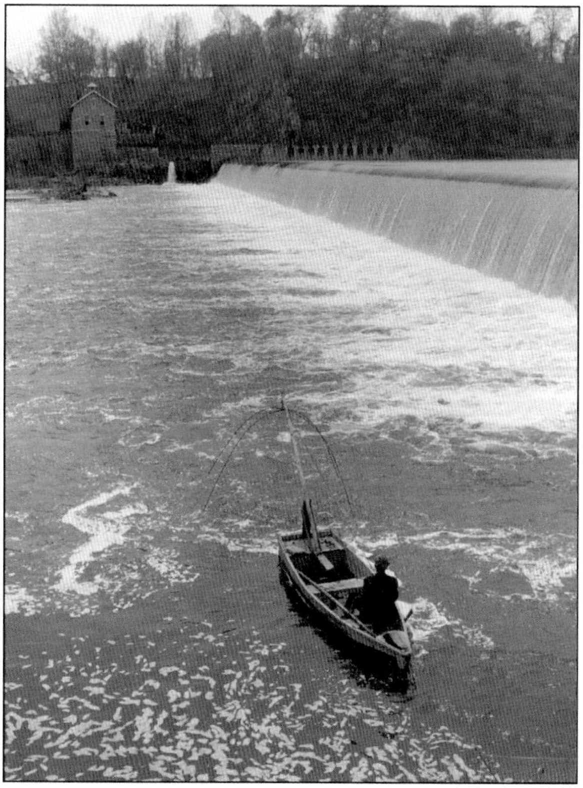

Not far from Williamsport, the canal arrives at Dam No. 4. This gentleman in his small boat is fishing with a net at the dam. The building seen across the water is an early electric power plant built by the Martinsburg Power Company in 1909 on the West Virginia shore. The company had a lease agreement for water rights with the C&O Canal for the sum of $500 a year. (Courtesy C&O Canal National Historical Park Headquarters.)

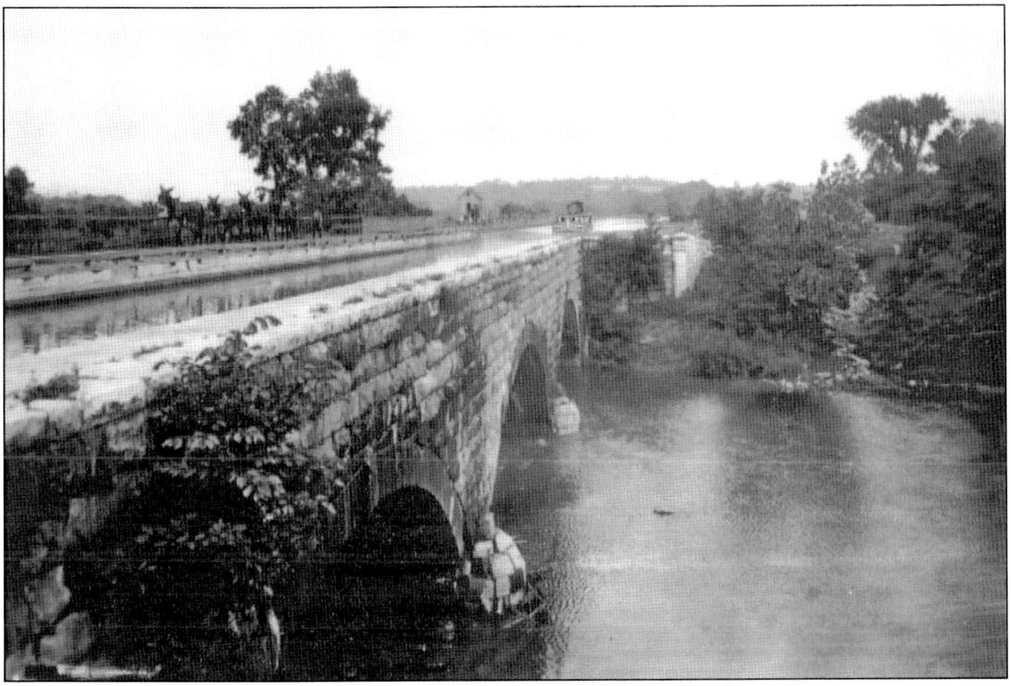

This vintage postcard shows the mules on the left pulling a canal boat through the Conococheague Aqueduct. Listed on official C&O Canal surveys as Aqueduct No. 5, the aqueduct was constructed of locally mined blue limestone in 1834 by Byrne and Company, the same builders of the Monocacy Aqueduct, which opened just the year before in 1833. (Courtesy C&O Canal National Historical Park Headquarters.)

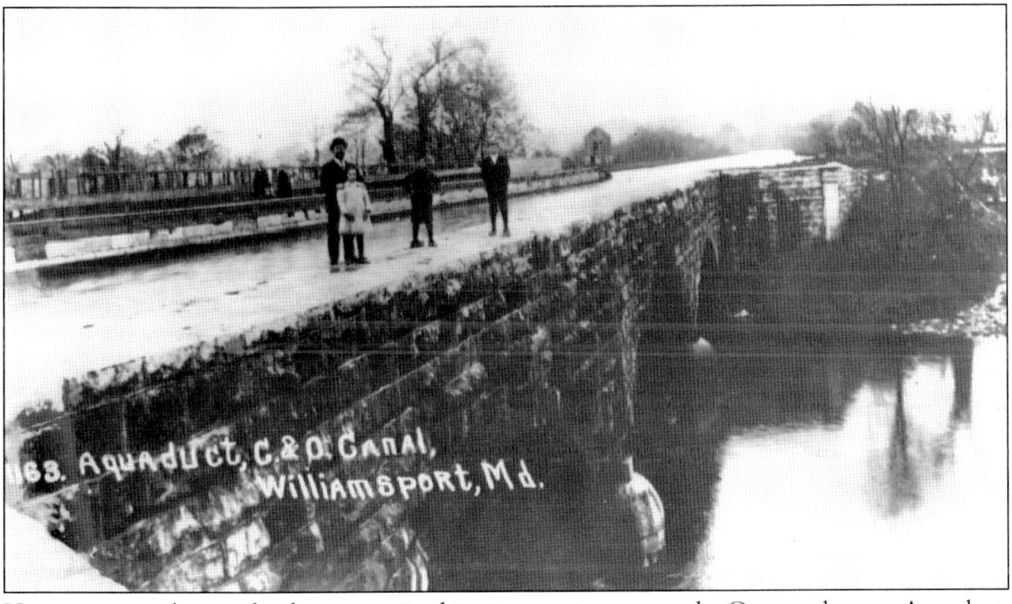

Here some people pose for the camera in this vintage view out on the Conococheague Aqueduct. The aqueduct was the focal point of Irish riots in 1834. The aqueduct served as the dividing line between two feuding segments of the Irish, and local militia patrolled the area hoping to keep the groups separated. (Courtesy C&O Canal National Historical Park Headquarters.)

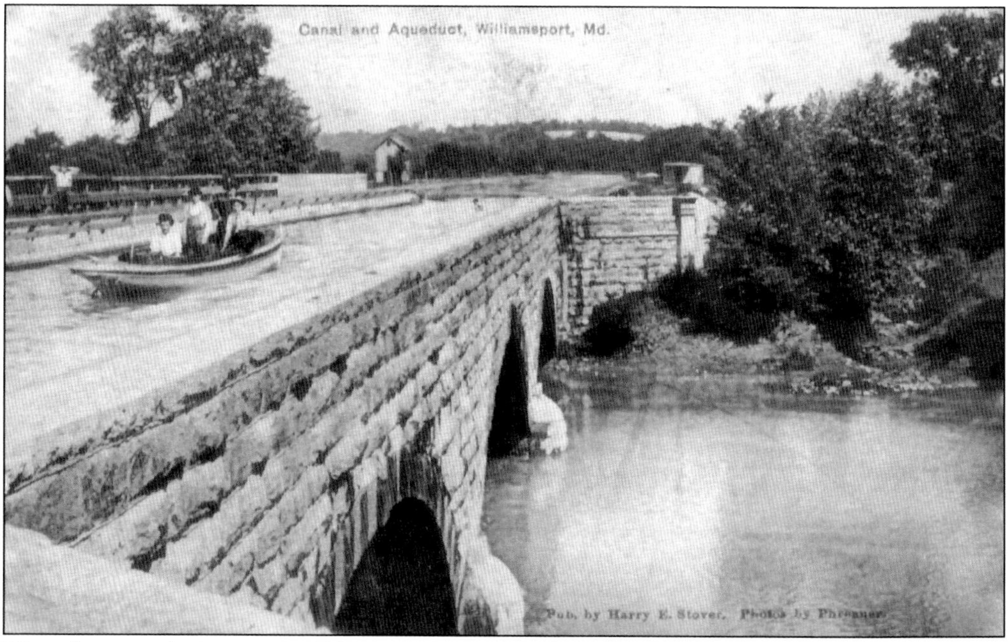

This photograph shows a small boat crossing over the Conococheague Creek at Milepost 100 via the Conococheague Creek Aqueduct. Blasting by Mosby's Raiders during the Civil War damaged part of the northwest end of the aqueduct. Today, remnants of the aqueduct can be seen at the Cushwa Basin in Williamsport. (Courtesy C&O Canal National Historical Park Headquarters.)

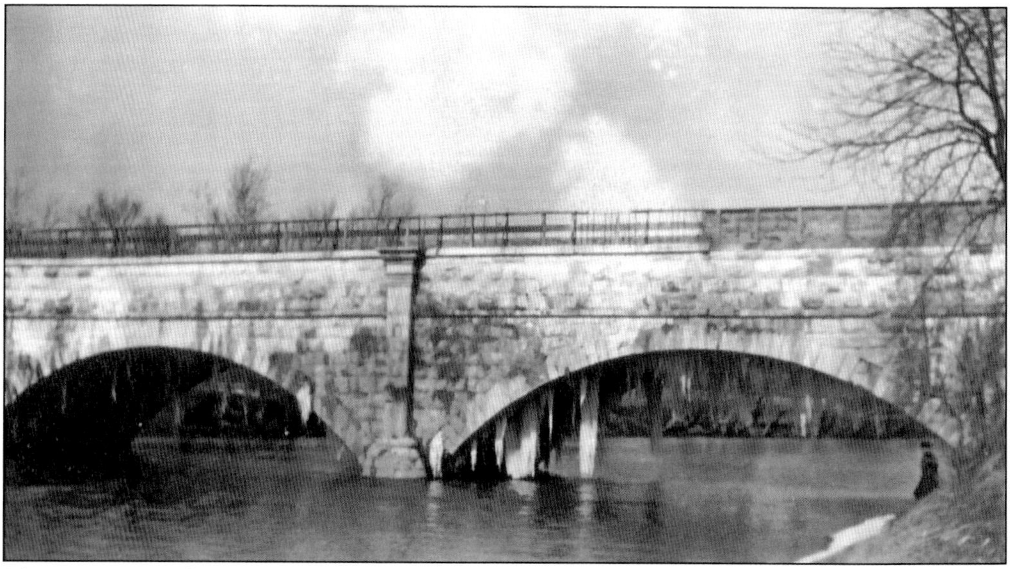

This is an unusual view of the Conococheague Aqueduct during the winter. Just look at the ice hanging down from under the arches. Unlike other county stone bridges built during the same period, each of the arches of the aqueduct has a keystone. (Courtesy Williamsport Town Museum.)

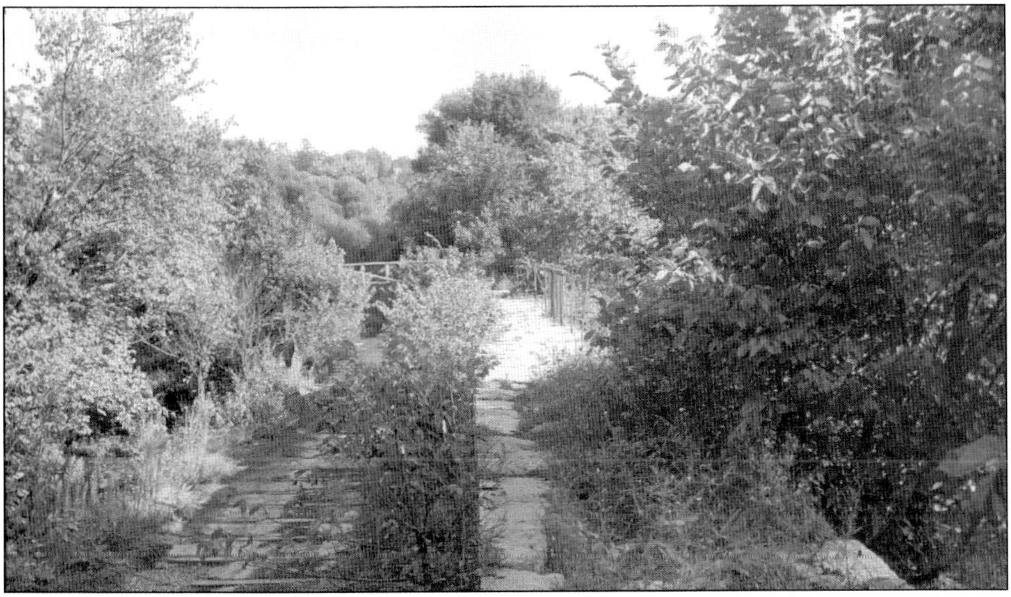

This photograph was taken on August 22, 1956, and shows the canal bed of the Conococheague Aqueduct years after it had fallen into disuse and disrepair. The canal bed would later be cleared of the overgrowth and weeds. Toward the center-back of the photograph, note the remnants of the old wrought-iron railings that once lined the aqueduct on the west side as a protection to crossing teams and pedestrians. The largest part of this iron guard was destroyed during the Civil War. (Courtesy C&O Canal National Historical Park Headquarters.)

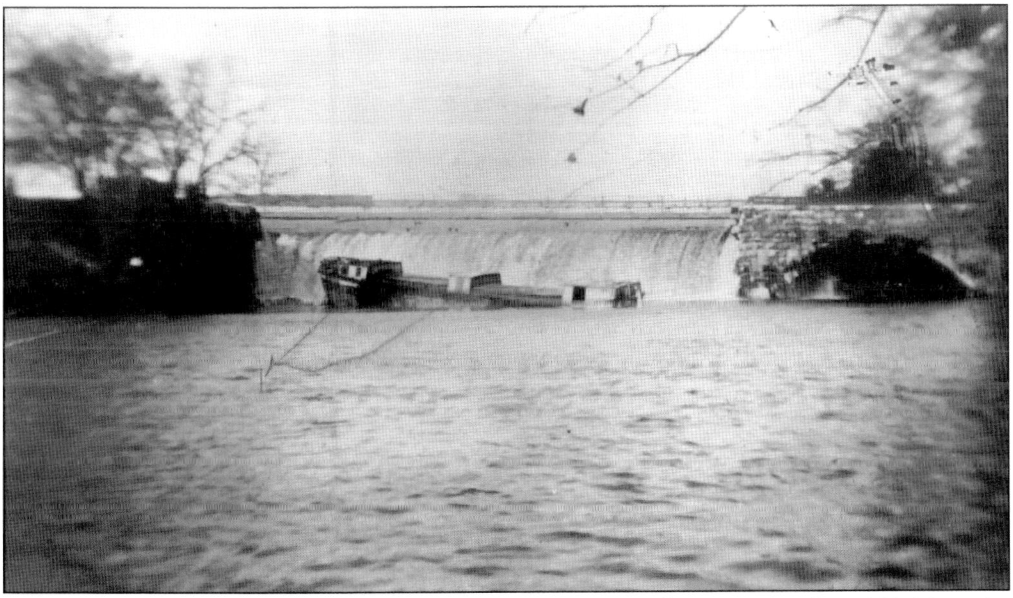

This close-up is of the Conococheague Aqueduct after its collapse on April 9, 1920. Note the water spilling out of the canal. The canal boat in the photo, captained by Frank Myers, was headed west when a very strong wind caught the light boat (not loaded with coal). It struck the upstream wall of the aqueduct and was dumped into the creek when the wall collapsed. Mr. Myers was able jump from the boat before it tumbled over. (Courtesy C&O Canal National Historical Park Headquarters.)

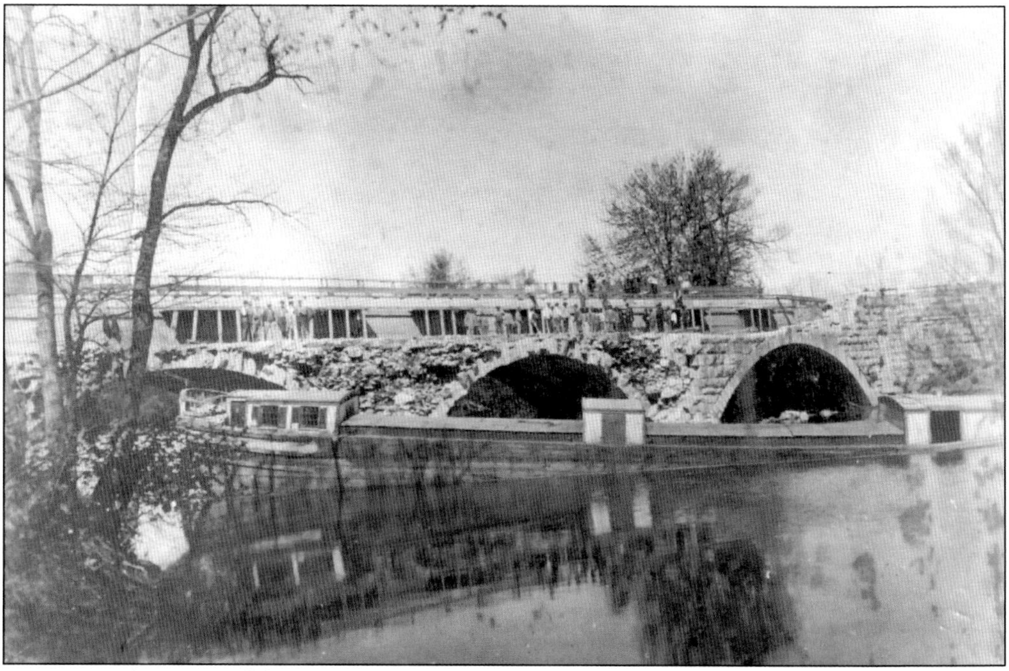

Here is another view of the collapsed wall of the Conococheague Aqueduct on April 17, 1920. The aqueduct is lined with groups of people looking at the canal barge that pitched down into Conococheague Creek. The toppled barge remained in the creek until the 1936 flood washed it away down the river. A wooden wall was constructed to keep the aqueduct and the canal in service after the 1920 incident. (Courtesy C&O Canal National Historical Park Headquarters.)

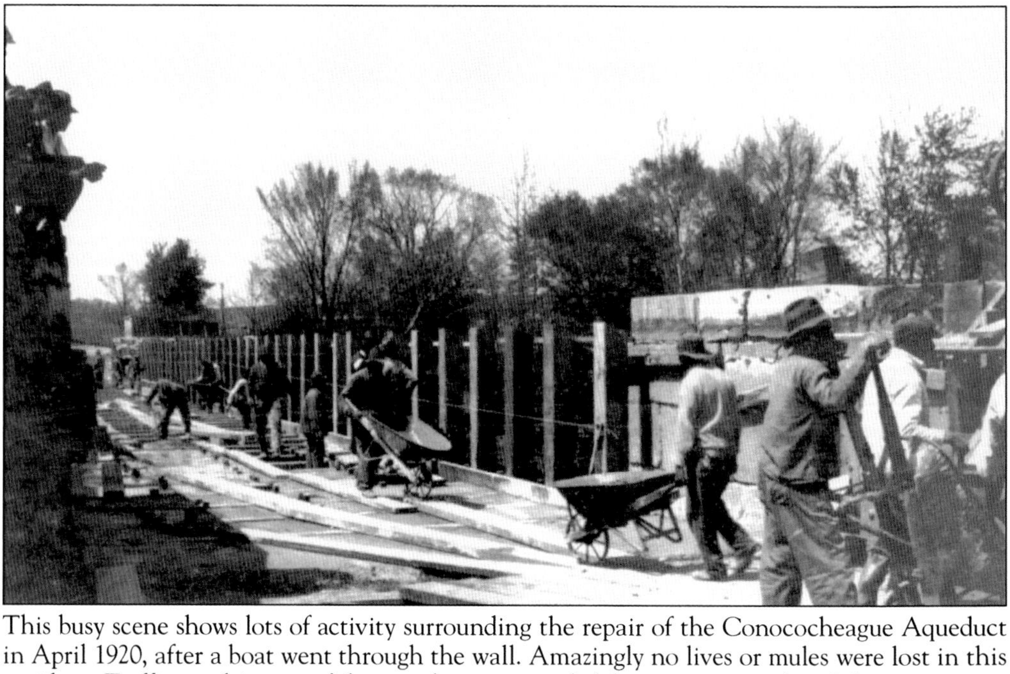

This busy scene shows lots of activity surrounding the repair of the Conococheague Aqueduct in April 1920, after a boat went through the wall. Amazingly no lives or mules were lost in this accident. Traffic on this part of the canal was suspended for over two weeks while repairs were undertaken. (Courtesy C&O Canal National Historical Park Headquarters.)

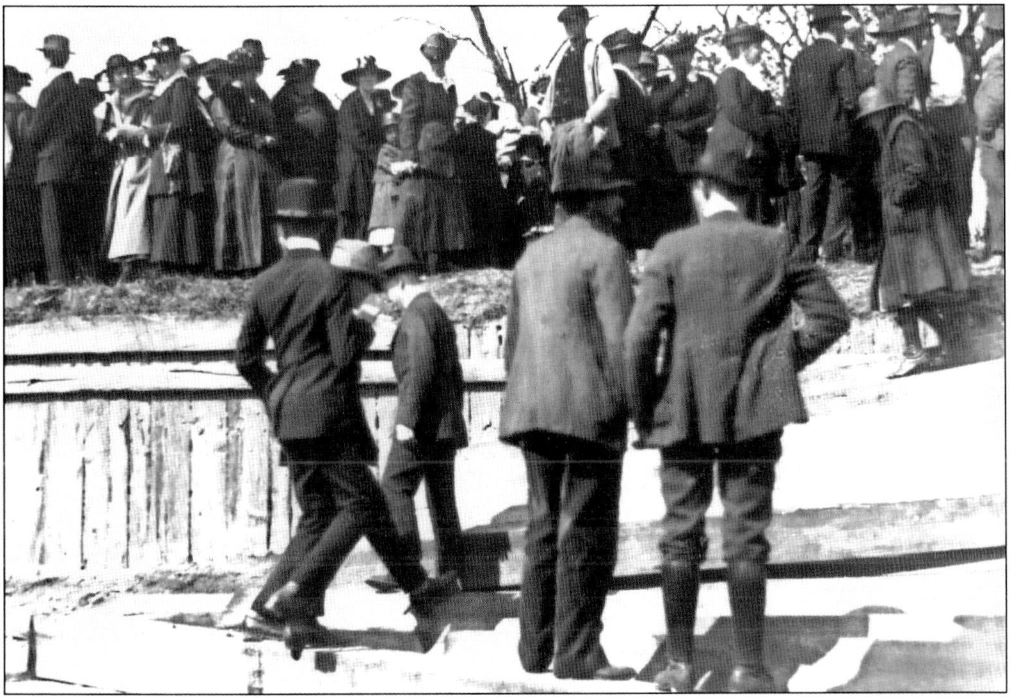

The canal-boat accident at the aqueduct brought out the crowds, as this additional picture from April 1920 shows. Everyone came down to view the scene and watch as the repair work took place. One woman holds her daughter close behind her to keep her from falling into the aqueduct. (Courtesy C&O Canal National Historical Park Headquarters.)

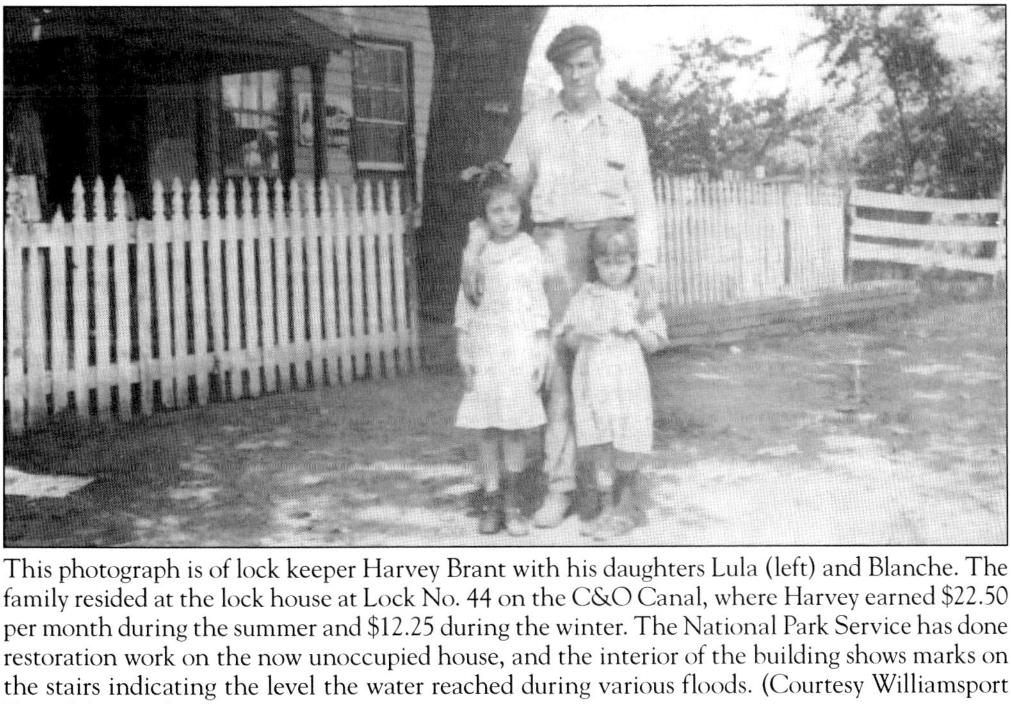

This photograph is of lock keeper Harvey Brant with his daughters Lula (left) and Blanche. The family resided at the lock house at Lock No. 44 on the C&O Canal, where Harvey earned $22.50 per month during the summer and $12.25 during the winter. The National Park Service has done restoration work on the now unoccupied house, and the interior of the building shows marks on the stairs indicating the level the water reached during various floods. (Courtesy Williamsport Town Museum.)

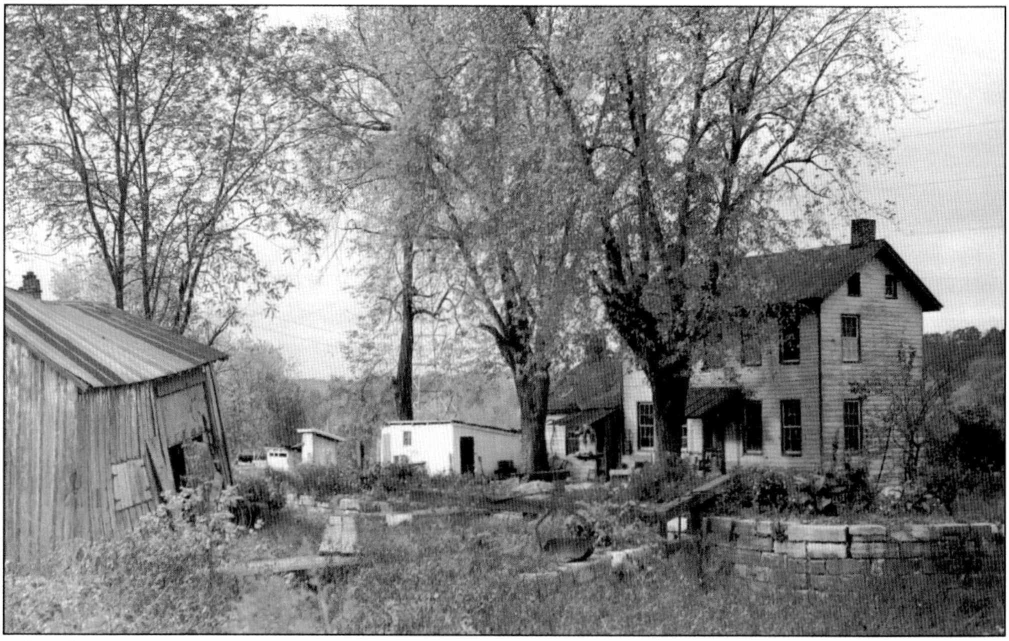

This photograph shows Lock No. 44 and the lock house as it appeared in the years after the canal closed. Harvey Brant became locktender in 1916 and continued to live in the house until 1961. He and his family recall the flood of 1924 that washed away much of the canal and resulted in its closure. The Brants also lived through the record-breaking flood of 1936, when water rose to cover the first two stories (each with nine-foot ceilings) and to a depth of two feet into the attic. Note how overgrown the canal is—the lock itself can just be made out in the right-hand foreground. (Courtesy C&O Canal National Historical Park Headquarters.)

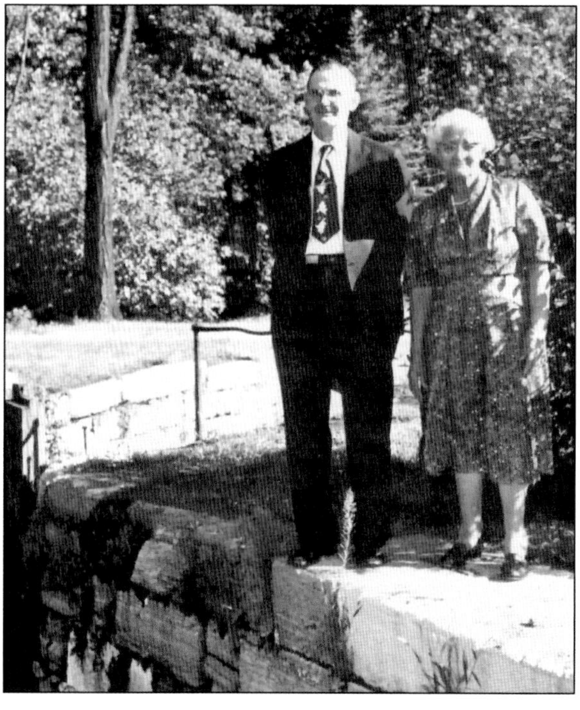

In 1962, just a year after leaving the lock house at Lock No. 44, Harvey and Sarah Brant had this picture taken near the lock. Note that the wooden gates were still in place at that time. Today there are paintings showing the canal and lock house on the walls of the Williamsport McDonald's on U.S. Route 11 near Interstate 81. (Courtesy *Maryland Cracker Barrel.*)

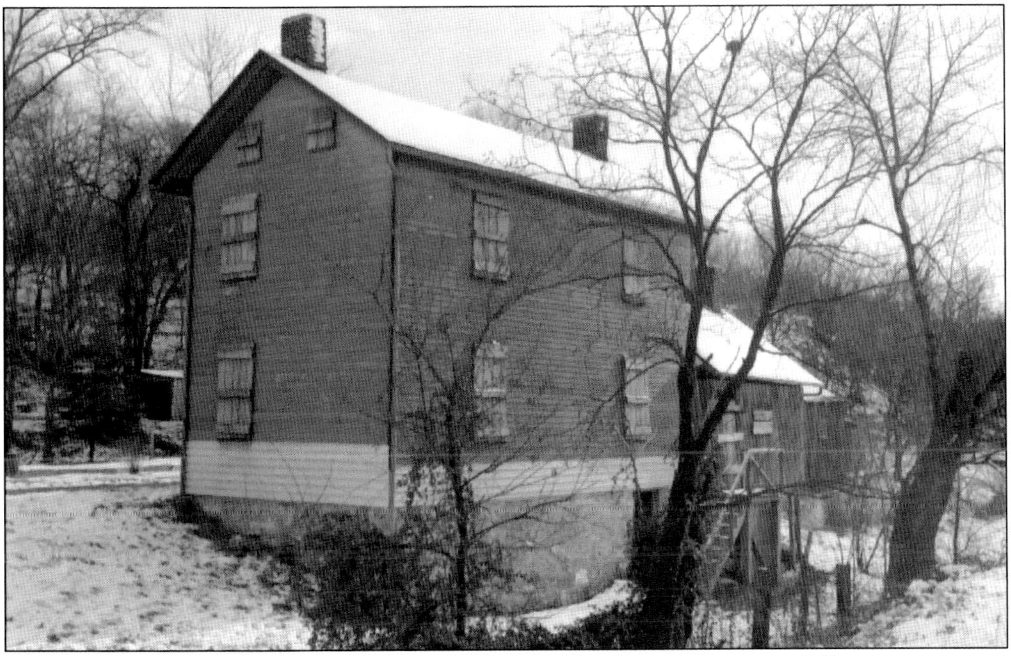

This photograph of the rear view of the lock house at Lock No. 44 gives a different perspective on the house. The home was no longer occupied, and the windows were shuttered at the time of this winter photo. Imagine when the floodwaters reached all the way to the attic level. (Courtesy C&O Canal National Historical Park Headquarters.)

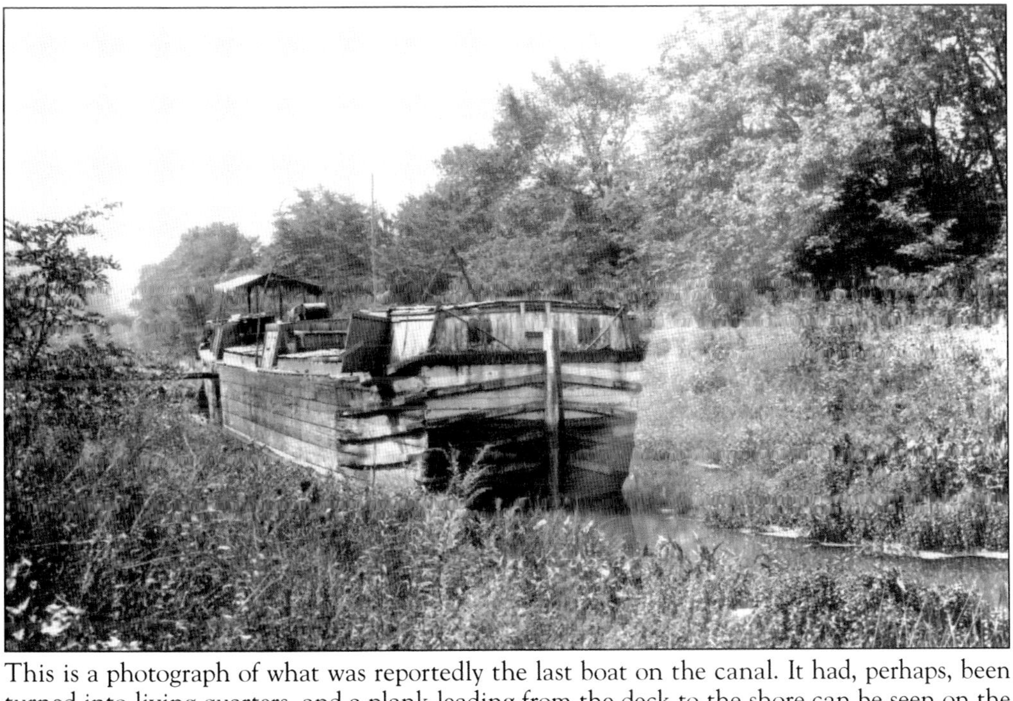

This is a photograph of what was reportedly the last boat on the canal. It had, perhaps, been turned into living quarters, and a plank leading from the deck to the shore can be seen on the left. The boat was swept away during the 1936 flood. (Courtesy C&O Canal National Historical Park Headquarters.)

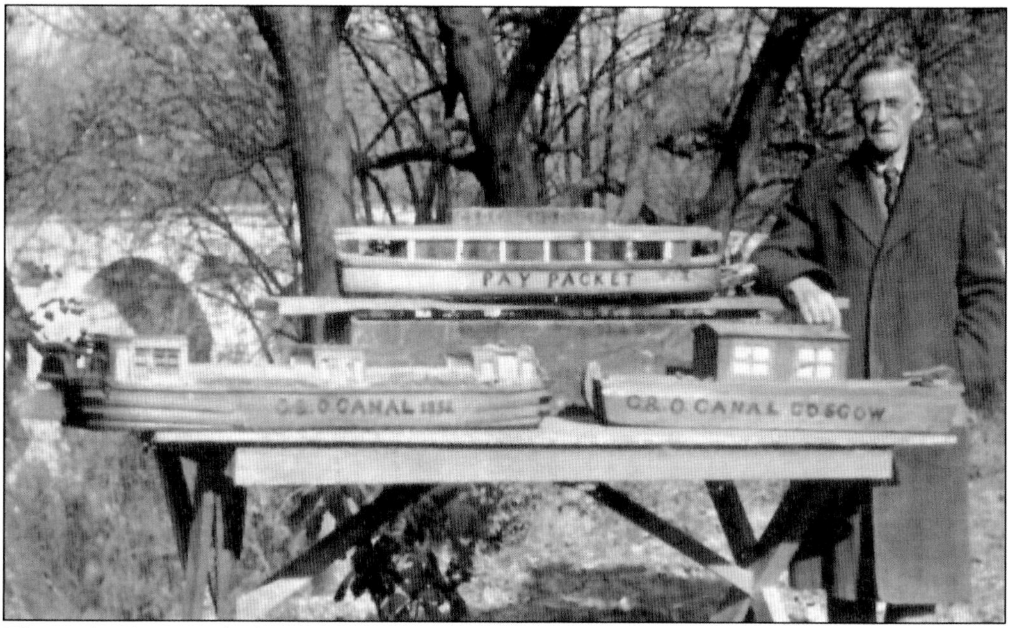

This 1954 photograph shows Joseph D. Grove of Williamsport, Maryland, posing with models of three different types of canal boats that traveled along the canal—a pay packet boat, a work scow, and the standard cargo boat. He made all three of the boats by hand in 1930. (Courtesy Western Maryland Room Washington County Free Library.)

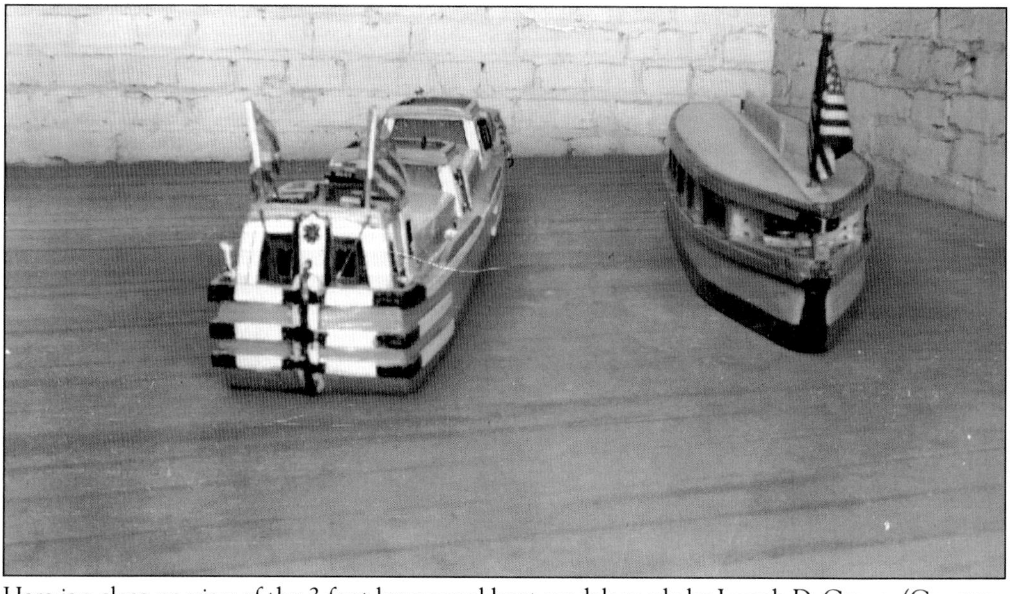

Here is a close-up view of the 3-foot-long canal boat models made by Joseph D. Grove. (Courtesy C&O Canal National Historical Park Headquarters.)

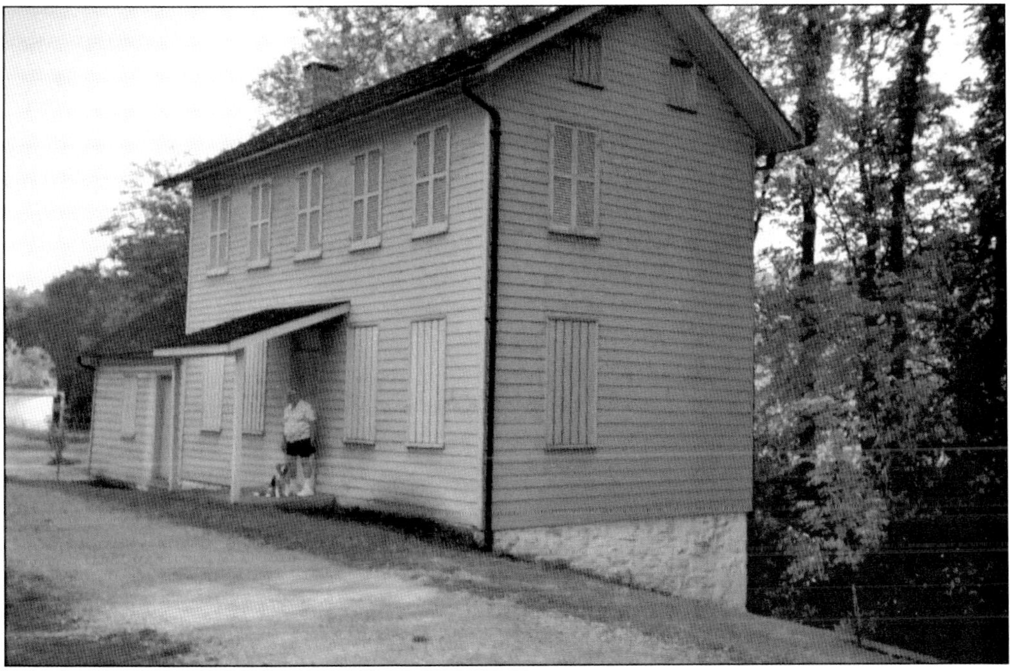

This photograph shows a current-day view of the now unoccupied Lock House No. 44. The interior of the building has marks on the stairway to the second level indicating the height water had reached during various floods. (Courtesy Mary H. Rubin.)

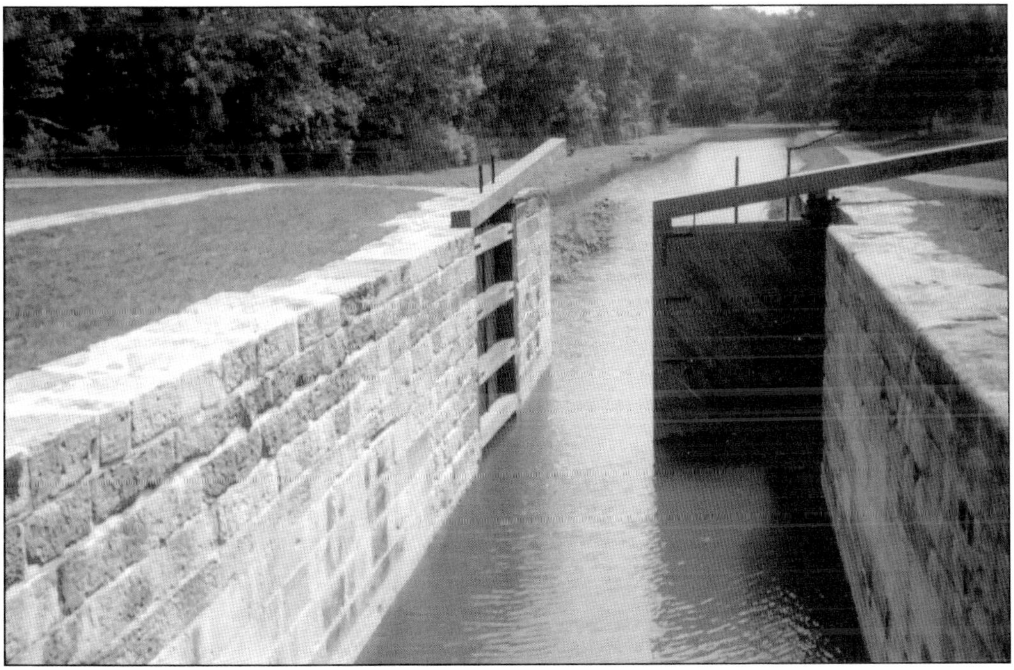

Here is a current view of the restored lock and gates at Lock No. 44 in Williamsport. Note how the open side of the gate is flush with the lock walls. The indentation in the lock walls can be seen on the right by the closed gate. Canal barges just fit within the confines of the lock, so these gate indentations were necessary. (Courtesy Mary H. Rubin.)

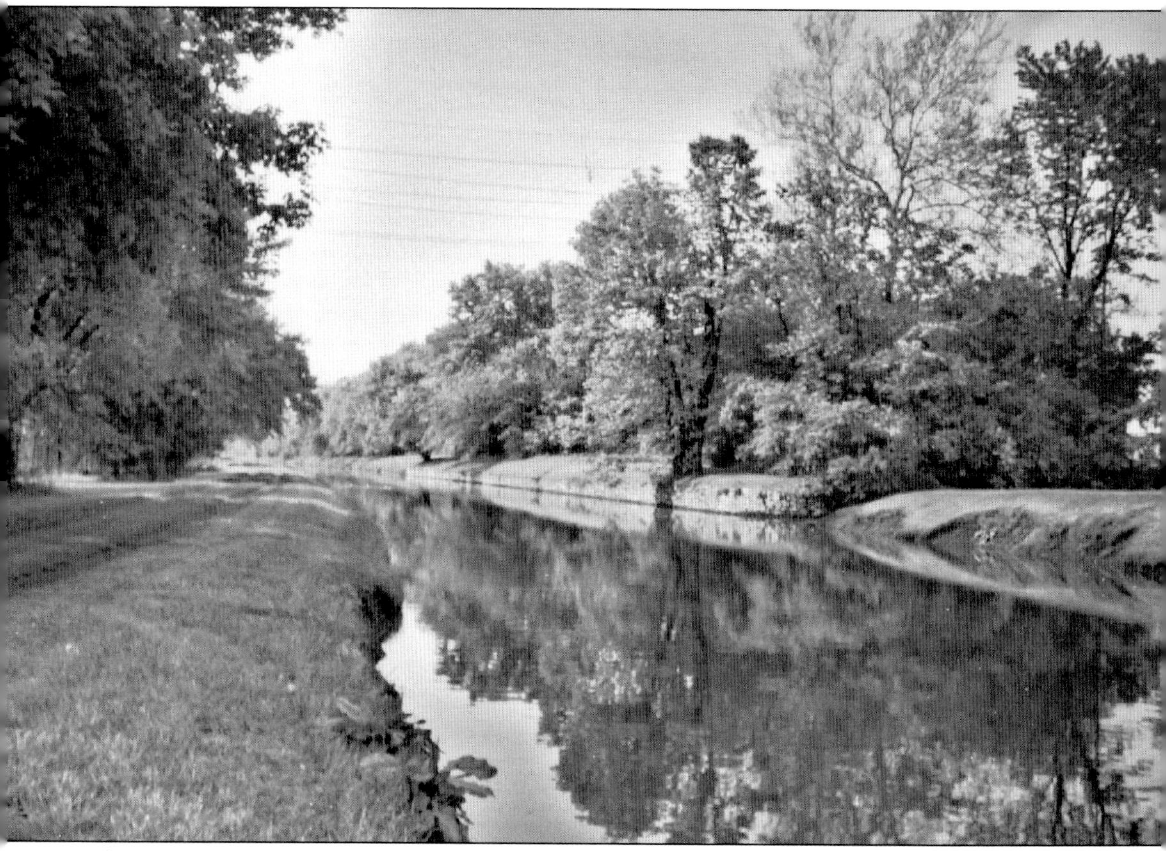

This peaceful scene shows the C&O Canal at Lock House No. 44 looking toward Williamsport. Though this is a modern day photo, you almost expect to hear the clip-clop of the mules and see a canal boat appear around the bend. (Courtesy Mary H. Rubin.)

Five

TRANSPORTATION

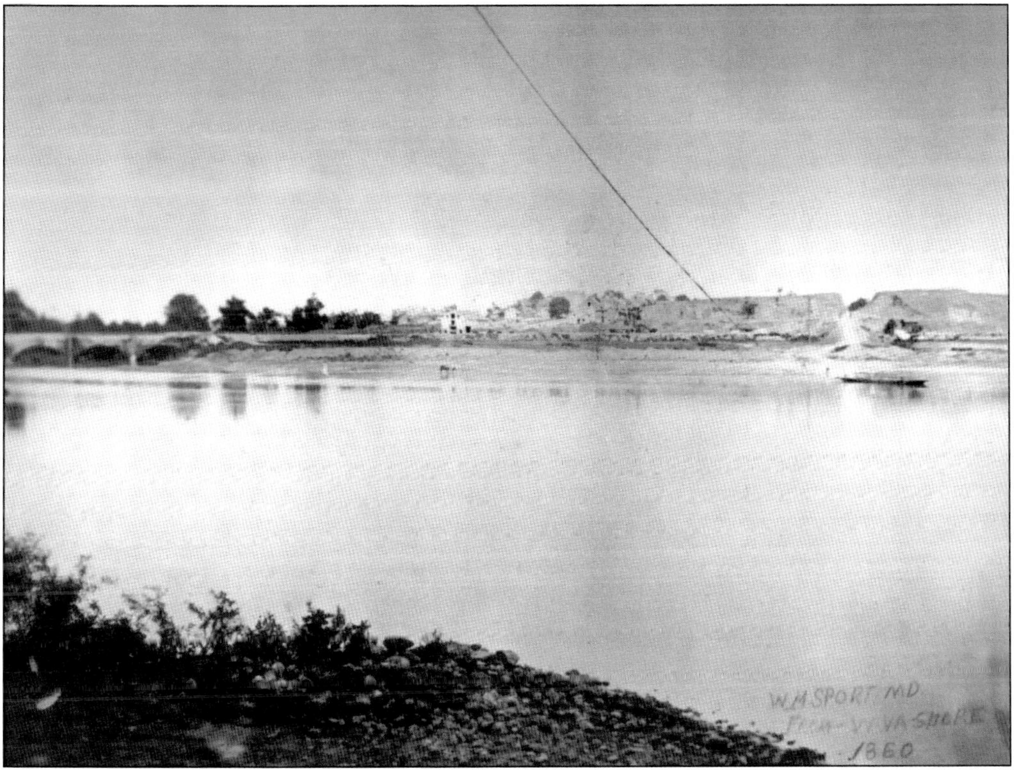

This 1860 photograph shows Williamsport as it appeared from across the Potomac River in what, at the time, was the state of Virginia. This same vantage spot is now located in West Virginia. Note the ferry line stretching across the river in the photo. The Watkin's Ferry, in operation from as early as 1748, was part of the Maidstone estate on the West Virginia shore and later operated as the Ardinger Ferry, in service from 1775 until 1909, when the bridge constructed across the river made the ferry crossing unnecessary. (Courtesy C&O Canal National Historical Park Headquarters.)

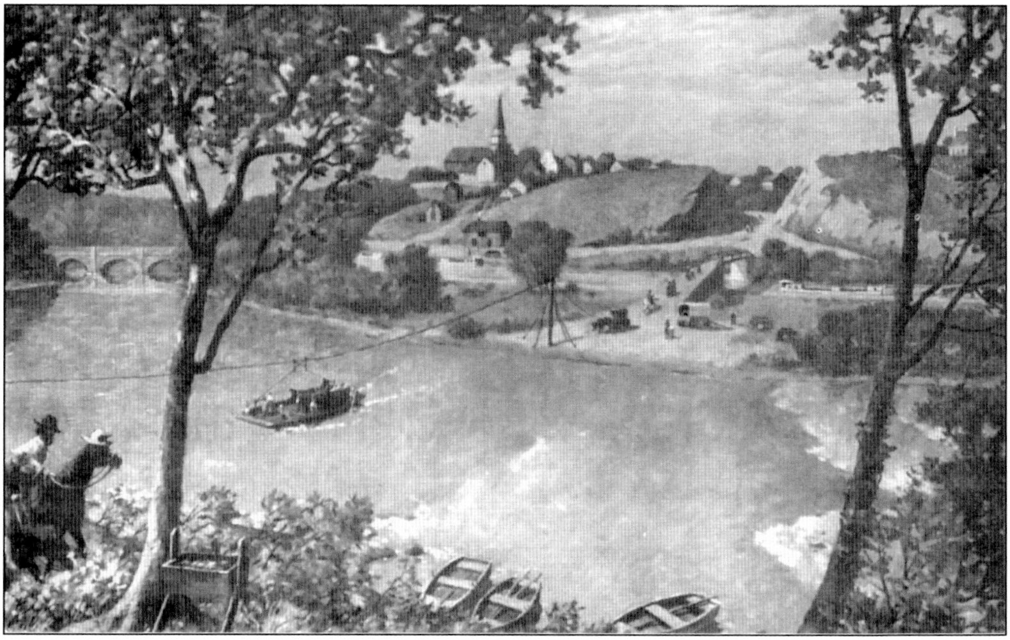

Before the construction of a bridge across the Potomac in 1909, the only method of passage from Williamsport to the West Virginia shore was by ferryboat. There's a canal boat in the middle of this oil painting of the ferry as well as the aqueduct on the left and a church spire dominating the Williamsport skyline. The painter also had a sense of humor; the horse on the far left is wearing a perky little hat with his ears stuck through. (Courtesy Williamsport Town Museum.)

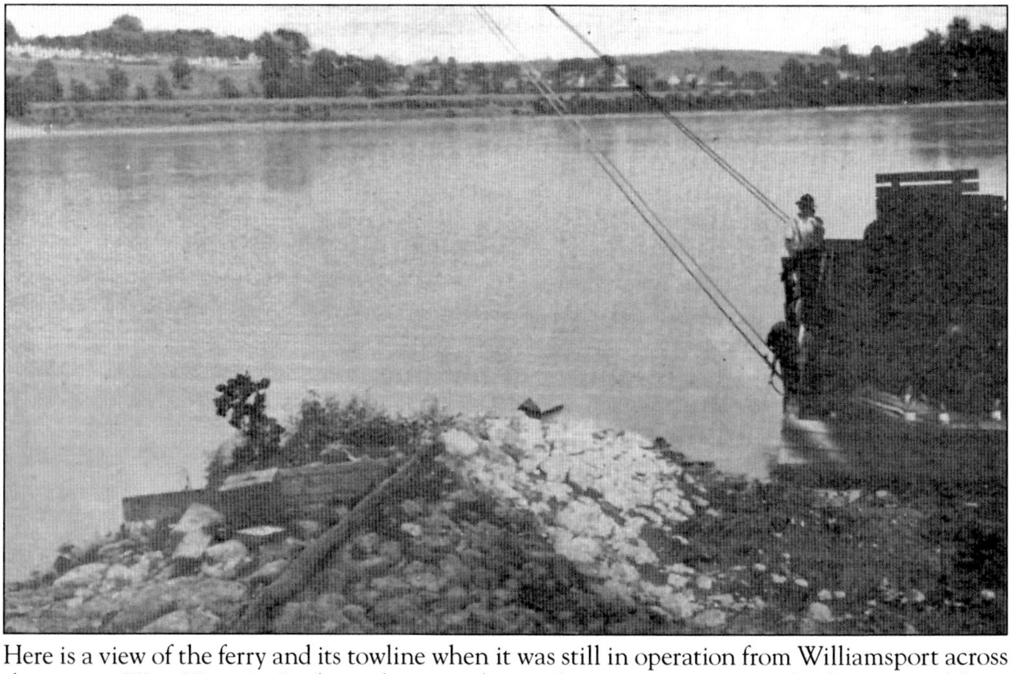

Here is a view of the ferry and its towline when it was still in operation from Williamsport across the river to West Virginia. In the early years, charges for transportation on the ferry ranged from 10¢ for passengers to 5¢ for cattle, 3¢ for sheep, and anywhere from 35¢ to $1 for wagons and sleighs. (Courtesy Western Maryland Room Washington County Free Library.)

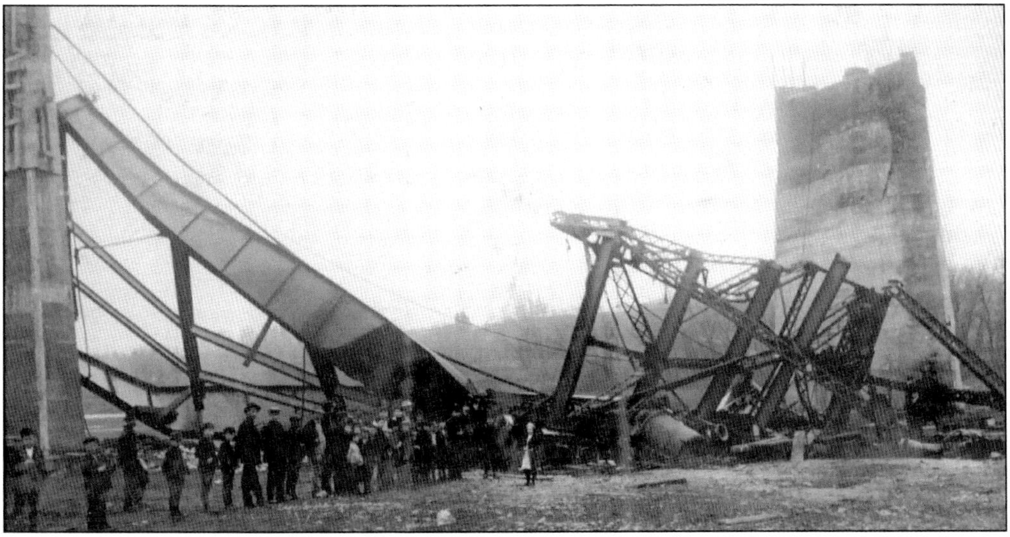

This December 16, 1908, photograph shows townspeople surveying the ruins of the damaged bridge over the Potomac. The bridge had crashed to the ground earlier that day, at 9 a.m. The plan was to build "a bridge of concrete, wide enough for a trolley track and a roadway to accommodate two or three teams and a sideway three feet wide." When a pier of the 70-foot-high bridge gave way during construction, eight workmen were killed, and work halted until the spring of 1909. (Courtesy Williamsport Town Museum.)

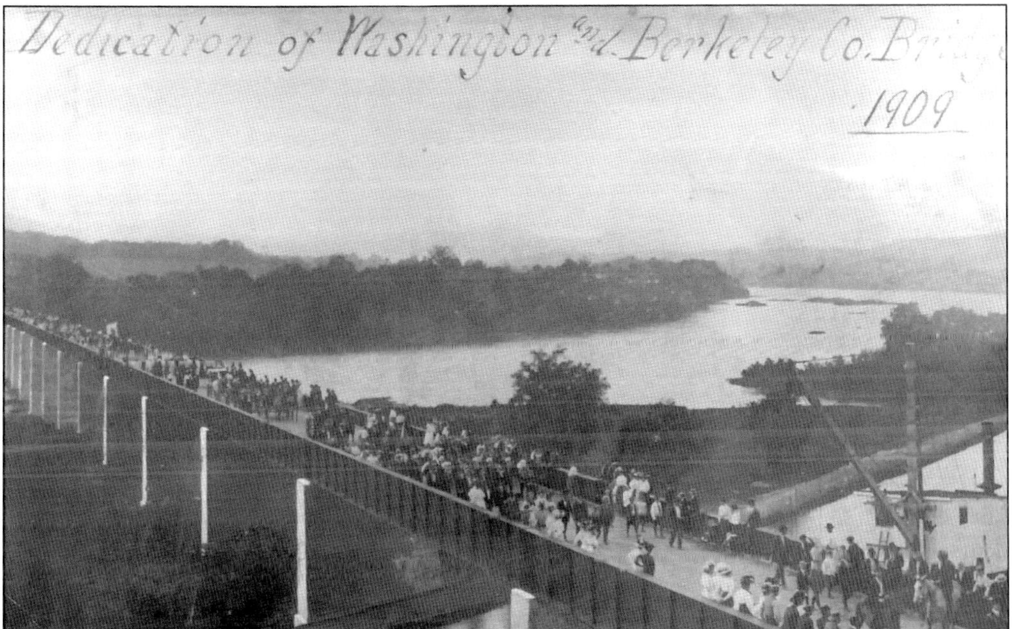

In 1908, determined citizens of Williamsport, Maryland, appealed to the county commissioners for a bridge across the Potomac from Williamsport to Berkeley County, West Virginia. The "Bridge for the Public," built at a cost of $100,000, was originally designed as a toll bridge, charging 25¢ for a horse-drawn wagon. The photograph above is from the August 10, 1909, dedication of the bridge. The U.S. Route 11 bridge underwent rebuilding between 1978 and 1979. (Courtesy Western Maryland Room Washington County Free Library.)

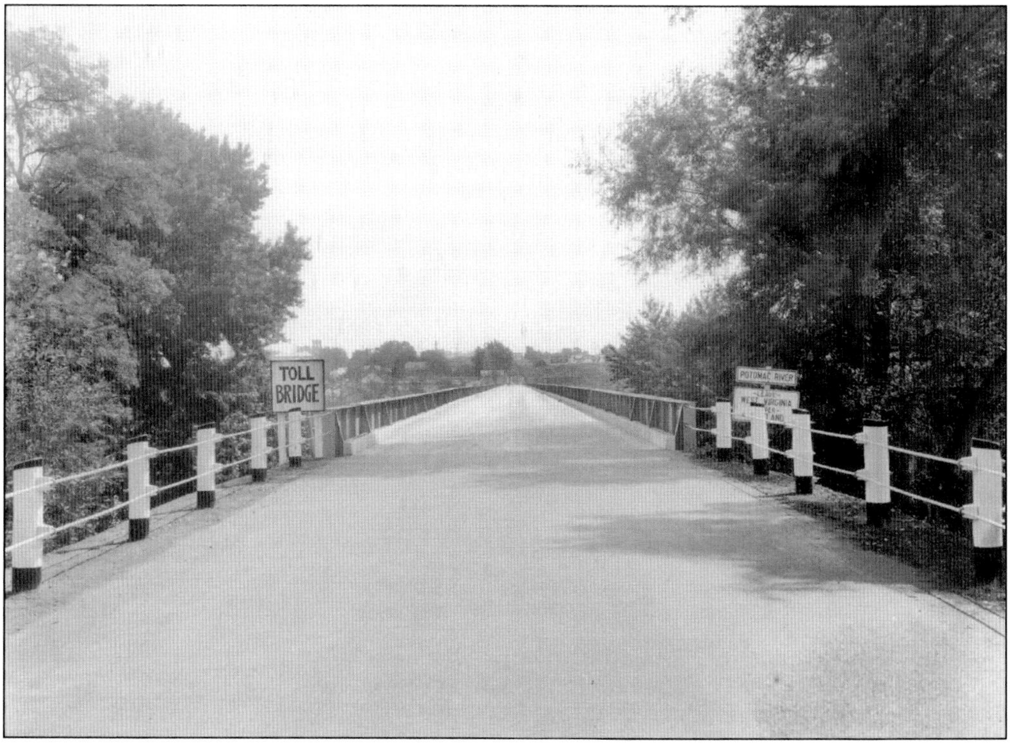

Here is the U.S. Route 11 bridge across the Potomac from the West Virginia side looking toward Williamsport. In the days of this photo, the bridge still charged a toll to cross. (Courtesy Williamsport Town Museum.)

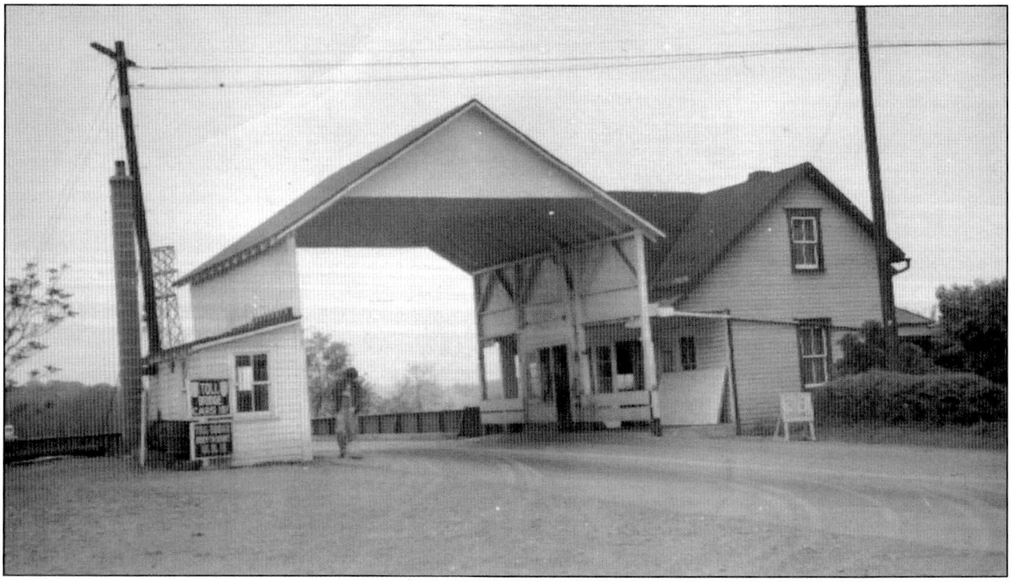

Here is a 1953 view of the tollgate house on the West Virginia side of the Potomac. The bridge was purchased by the state of Maryland in 1954, and it continued to operate as a toll bridge until 1958, when it was made toll free. (Courtesy Nelson Hause, Western Maryland Room Washington County Free Library.)

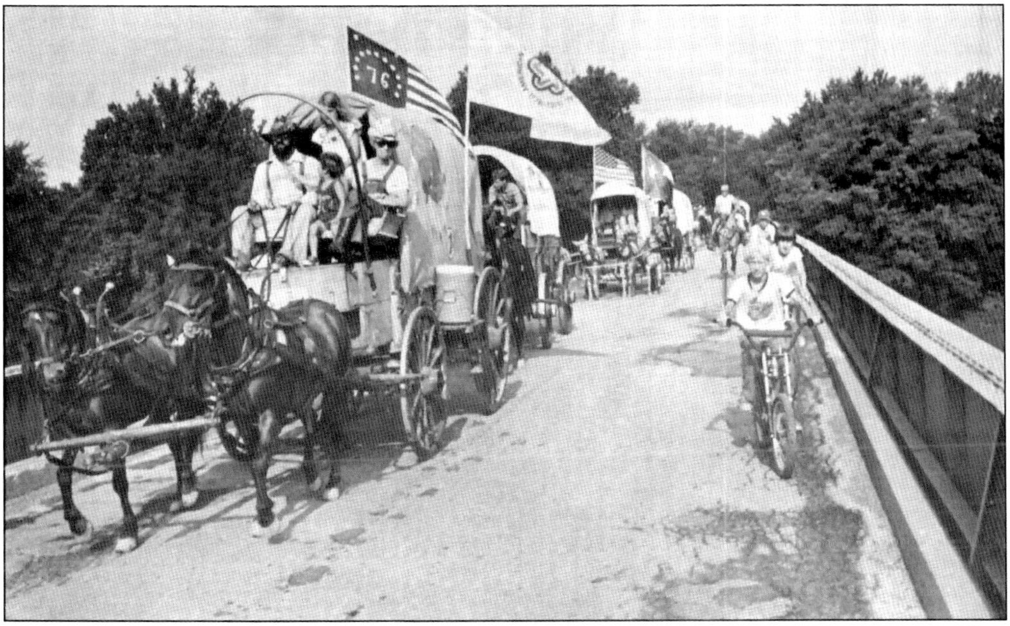

The U.S. Route 11 bridge has carried more than traffic through the years since it opened in 1909. The bridge has also been witness to history, as seen in this 1976 photograph, taken when the National Bicentennial Mule Train crossed the then well-worn roadbed. (Courtesy *Maryland Cracker Barrel.*)

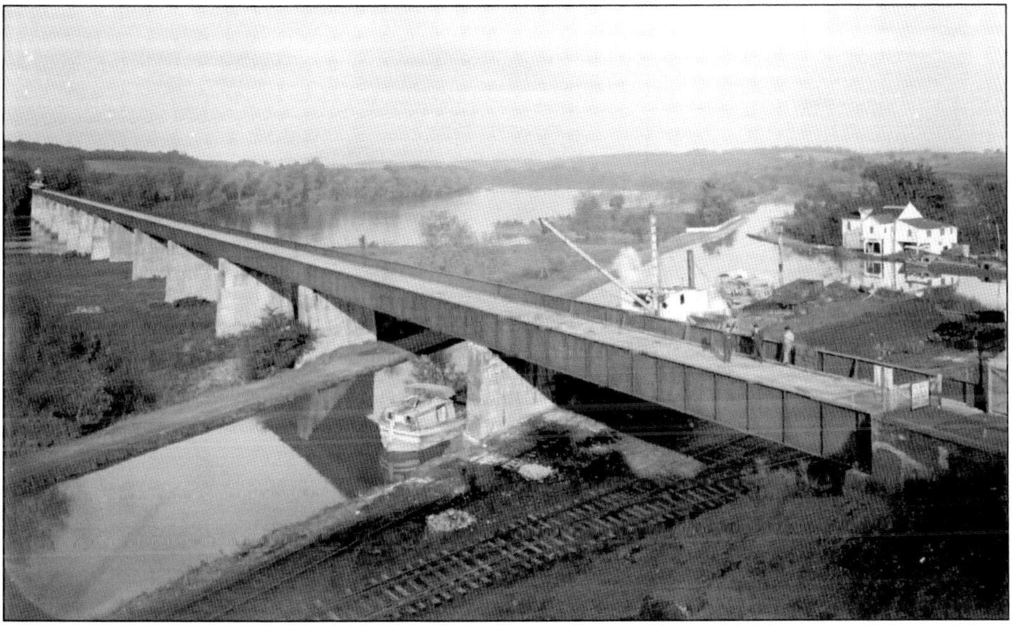

This c. 1920 Consolidated Coal Company photo shows the bridge across the canal and the Potomac from Williamsport, Maryland, to West Virginia. The bridge is said to be the only Potomac River bridge between Washington, D.C. and Cumberland to have survived the 1936 flood. Note the canal boat passing underneath the bridge and the rail tracks in the foreground. The modern U.S. Route 11 bridge now crosses at this point. Interstate 81 has its own busy bridge crossing within site. (Courtesy C&O Canal National Historical Park Headquarters.)

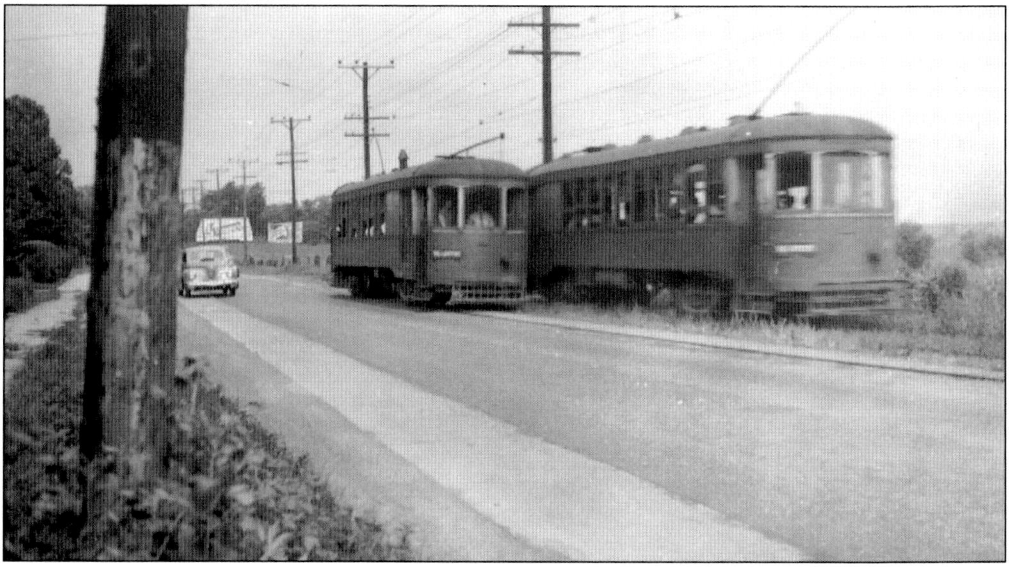

This photograph shows Virginia Avenue in Halfway's younger days. In this photograph is a passing siding for the trolleys that ran up Virginia Avenue the several miles from Hagerstown to Williamsport. Service between Hagerstown and Williamsport was inaugurated on August 8, 1896. (Courtesy Williamsport Town Museum.)

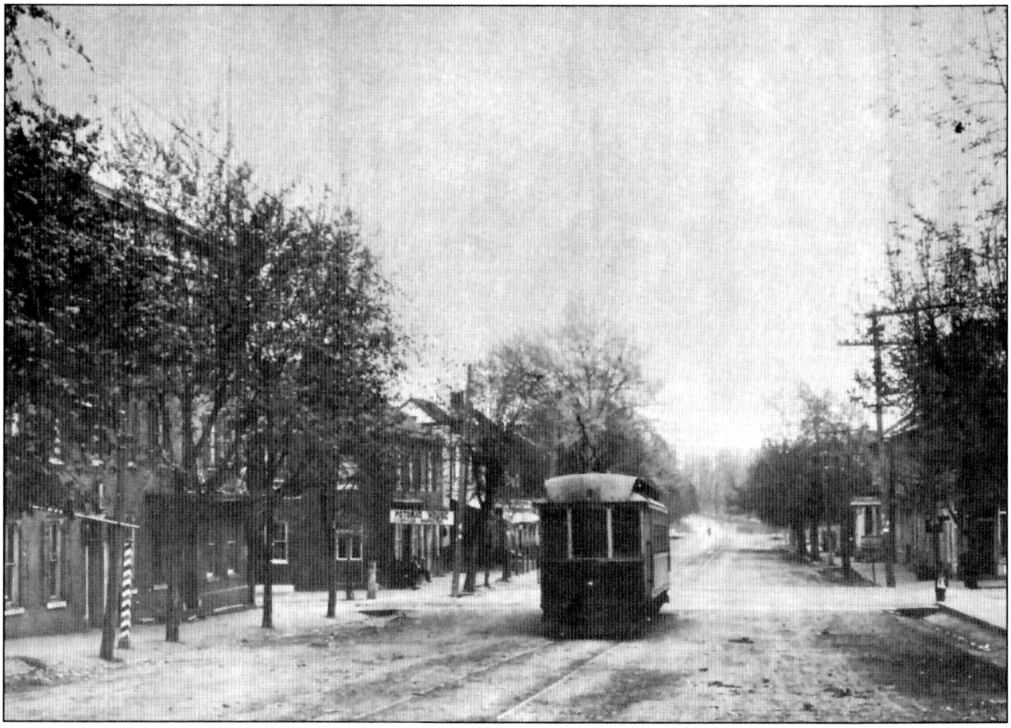

Here is another view of one of the beloved old trolleys rolling down the middle of Potomac Street *c.* 1910. When the Hagerstown Railway Company of Washington County was created in 1888, one of the conditions of the plans to begin service was that a line be constructed linking Hagerstown and Williamsport. (Courtesy *Maryland Cracker Barrel.*)

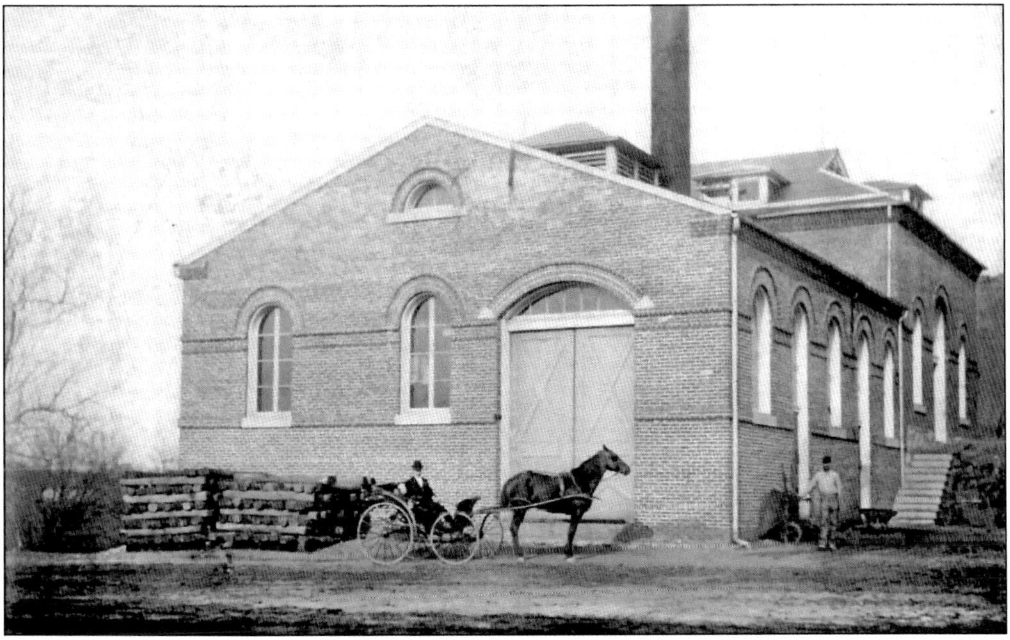

This trolley-car repair building is at the C&O Canal Cushwa Basin in Williamsport. The building served as the original powerhouse for the trolleys in the spring of 1896. Two years later, a plant was constructed in Hagerstown at the corner of Summit Avenue and Lee Street, and use of the Williamsport plant was discontinued. Today the building houses displays during the annual C&O Canal Days held in Williamsport every August. (Courtesy Western Maryland Room Washington County Free Library.)

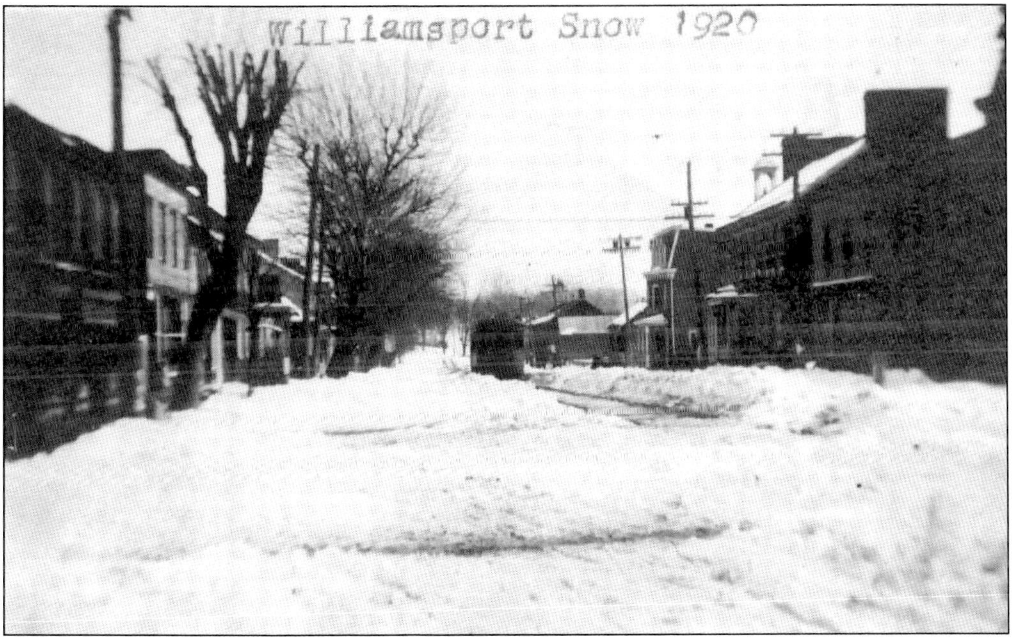

Here is one of the venerable old trolleys on its way through Williamsport in 1920. The Catholic church steeple can just be seen on the right. It looks like the snow on Potomac Street was only cleared far enough to allow the trolley to travel along its route. (Courtesy Williamsport Town Museum.)

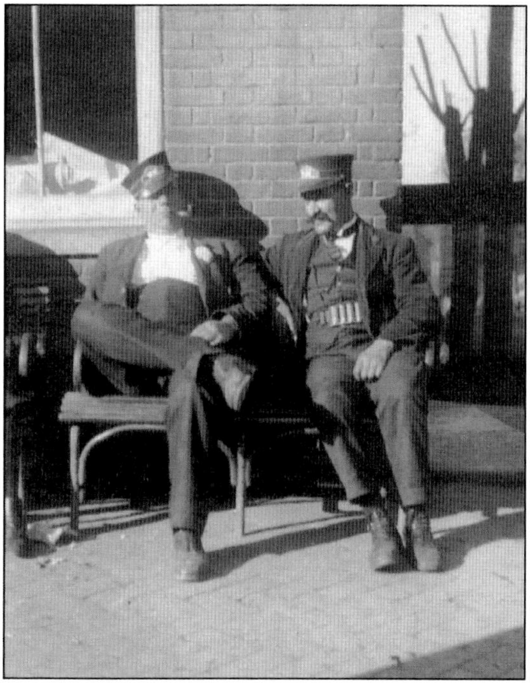

In this photograph, taking a break from their duties in 1915 are John Lowery and Bill Stouffer, conductors on the Hagerstown and Frederick Railways. In 1897, the speed limit for the trolleys was raised to 10 miles per hour, though they still had to slow down to six miles per hour at crossings. (Courtesy Williamsport Town Museum.)

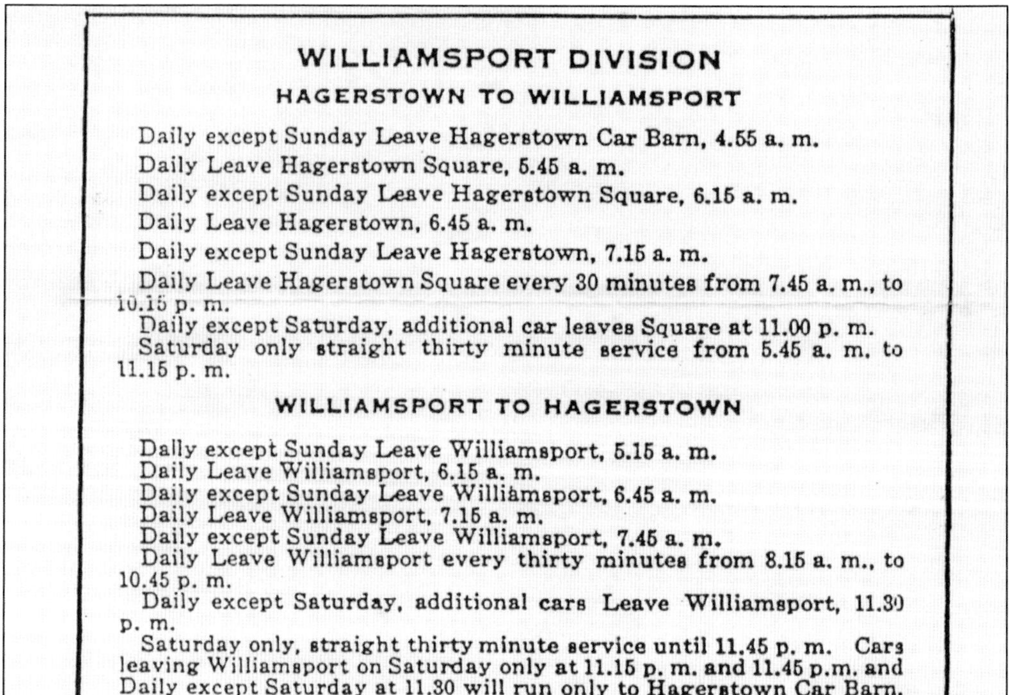

WILLIAMSPORT DIVISION

HAGERSTOWN TO WILLIAMSPORT

Daily except Sunday Leave Hagerstown Car Barn, 4.55 a. m.
Daily Leave Hagerstown Square, 5.45 a. m.
Daily except Sunday Leave Hagerstown Square, 6.15 a. m.
Daily Leave Hagerstown, 6.45 a. m.
Daily except Sunday Leave Hagerstown, 7.15 a. m.
Daily Leave Hagerstown Square every 30 minutes from 7.45 a. m., to 10.15 p. m.
Daily except Saturday, additional car leaves Square at 11.00 p. m.
Saturday only straight thirty minute service from 5.45 a. m. to 11.15 p. m.

WILLIAMSPORT TO HAGERSTOWN

Daily except Sunday Leave Williamsport, 5.15 a. m.
Daily Leave Williamsport, 6.15 a. m.
Daily except Sunday Leave Williamsport, 6.45 a. m.
Daily Leave Williamsport, 7.15 a. m.
Daily except Sunday Leave Williamsport, 7.45 a. m.
Daily Leave Williamsport every thirty minutes from 8.15 a. m., to 10.45 p. m.
Daily except Saturday, additional cars Leave Williamsport, 11.30 p. m.
Saturday only, straight thirty minute service until 11.45 p. m. Cars leaving Williamsport on Saturday only at 11.15 p. m. and 11.45 p.m. and Daily except Saturday at 11.30 will run only to Hagerstown Car Barn.

This schedule for the Williamsport-Hagerstown run of the Hagerstown & Frederick Railway went into effect on June 16, 1918. Note that the trolleys made runs to Williamsport on a much more frequent schedule than the buses do today . . . the first trolley left Williamsport as early as 5:15 a.m., and the last run at night was as late as 11:30 p.m. (Courtesy Williamsport Town Museum.)

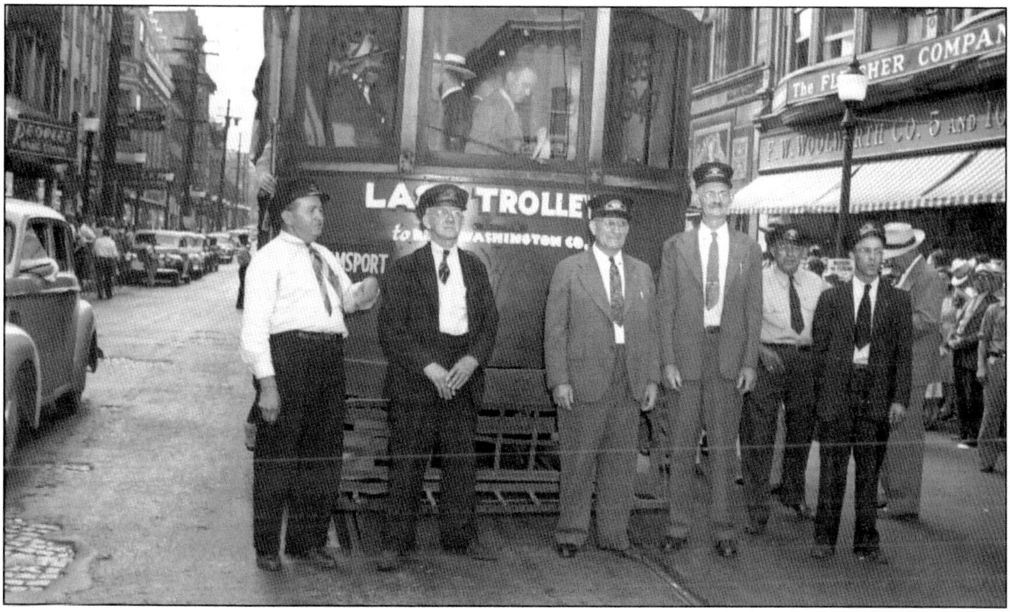

The trolley was a major fixture, and it provided an important link between downtown Hagerstown and the six-mile-distant Williamsport. In the 1920s, the growth in popularity of cars and buses resulted in a decline of trolley passengers, and service in the county was discontinued on the last of the routes in August 1947. That final run was from downtown Hagerstown to Williamsport. Here is that last trolley getting ready to make its run amidst much fanfare and ceremony. Pictured from left to right are Catfish Smith, Harry Walling, Ed Mundy, Ed Koogle, Charles Wolford, and Earl Kiser. (Courtesy Williamsport Town Museum.)

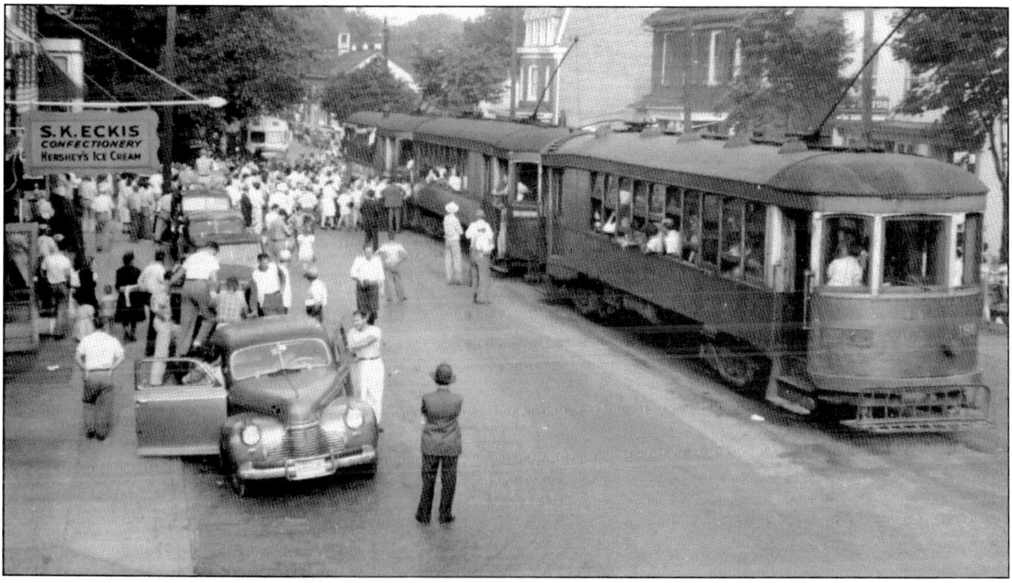

Here we see a mix of the old and new. The trolley cars are at the Williamsport end of the last trolley trip. On the left, at the rear of the trolley cars, is the front of the first bus that would begin service throughout town. After arriving in Williamsport via trolley, the official party boarded the bus for the return trip to the Hagerstown Square, thus inaugurating the buses on their first official trip. (Courtesy Williamsport Town Museum.)

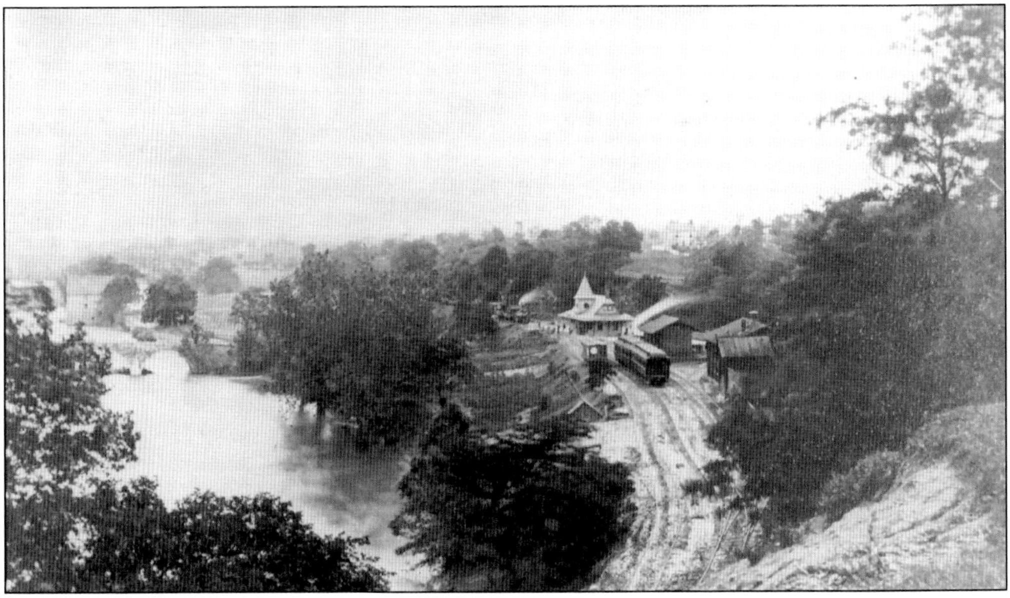

This June 5, 1889, image is of the old Williamsport station of the Western Maryland Railroad on Conococheague Street. Note the steam from two trains, one approaching from each end of the station. There is also a stone bridge on the left. This is just one of the stone bridges in Washington County, all built by army engineers. Construction of the rail line extension from Hagerstown to Williamsport began in the fall of 1871, and the first railway station, a one-room building, was constructed during the winter of 1872 on the west side of Conococheague Street. The station in this photograph was built in March 1877 on the east side of Conococheague Street. (Courtesy Western Maryland Room Washington County Free Library.)

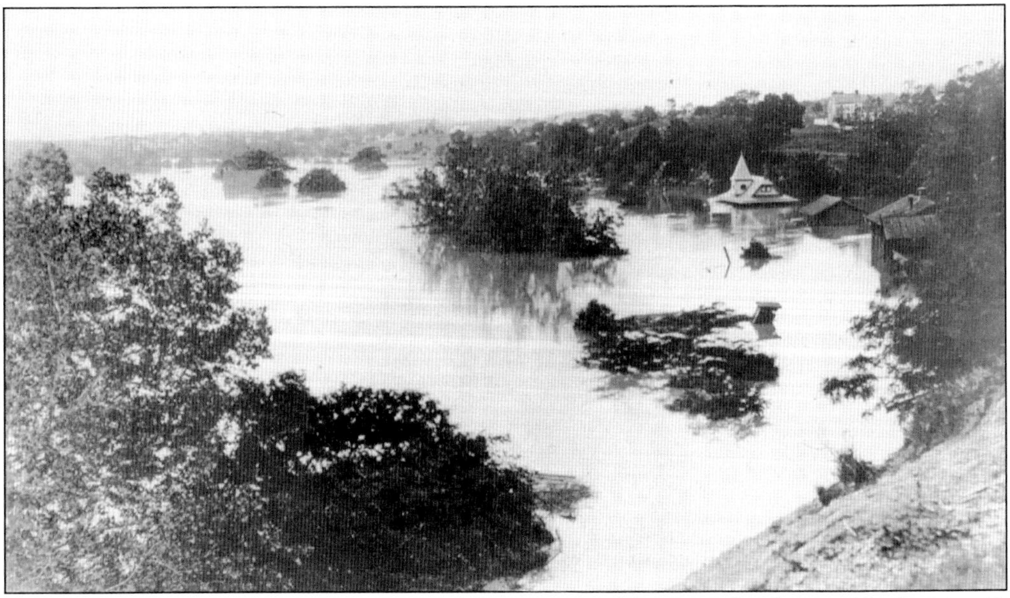

Here is that same Williamsport train station following one of the many floods (possibly the May 31, 1889, flood) that have hit Williamsport over the years. Just the very top of the Western Maryland railroad station can be seen above the floodwaters that reached 12 feet, and the tracks themselves are well under water. (Courtesy Western Maryland Room Washington County Free Library.)

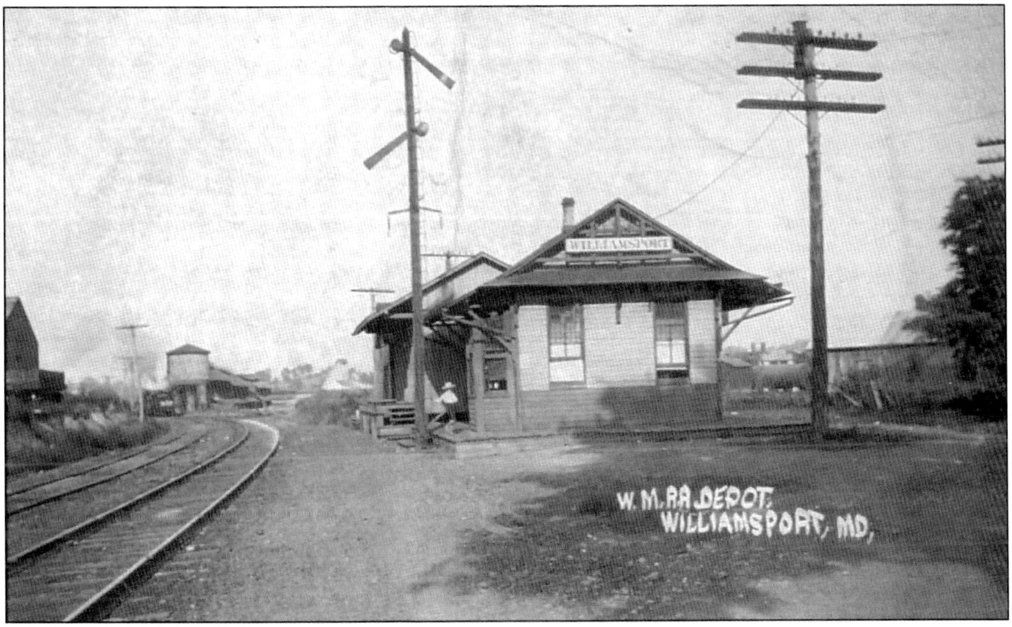

This photograph shows a wide-angle view of the Williamsport train station and tracks for the Western Maryland Railroad. The first railroad agent was Matthew McClannahan, and the first telegraph operator was Mary Clark. The first ticket sold from this station was to Waynesboro, Pennsylvania, and cost 75¢. (Courtesy Williamsport Town Museum.)

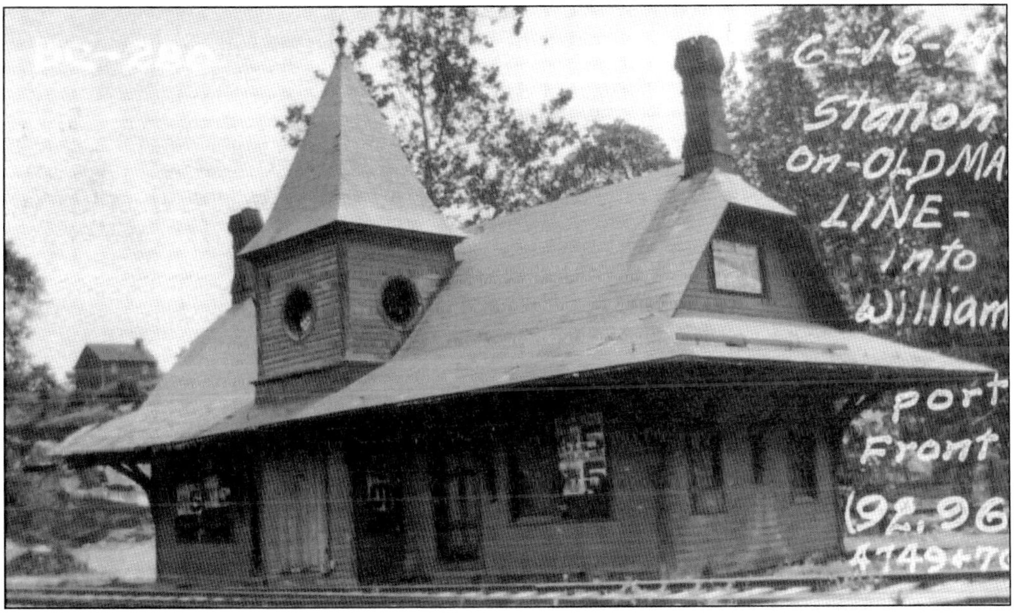

Williamsport was once a main stop along the railroad line, providing town residents with daily service to and from Baltimore as well as the transport of coal to Hagerstown from Cumberland via Williamsport. By 1917, however, when this photograph was taken, the Williamsport stop had already faded from importance, and its passenger station was boarded up and unused. (Courtesy *Maryland Cracker Barrel*.)

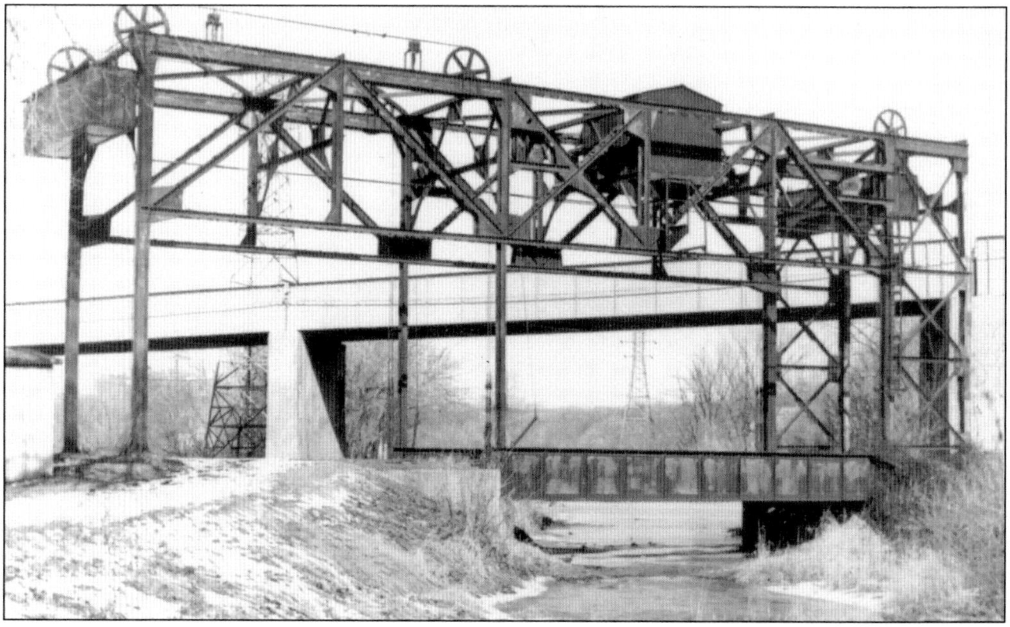

The odd-looking contraption in this 1930 photograph was a railroad lift-bridge over the C&O Canal in Williamsport, Maryland. Built in 1923–1924, the bridge cost the then-princely sum of $100,000, but because the trains quickly cut into the business of the canal, the bridge was never actually utilized. It can still be seen today near the Potomac Edison Plant and the Cushwa Basin on the canal in Williamsport, Maryland. (Courtesy Hagerstown Roundhouse Museum.)

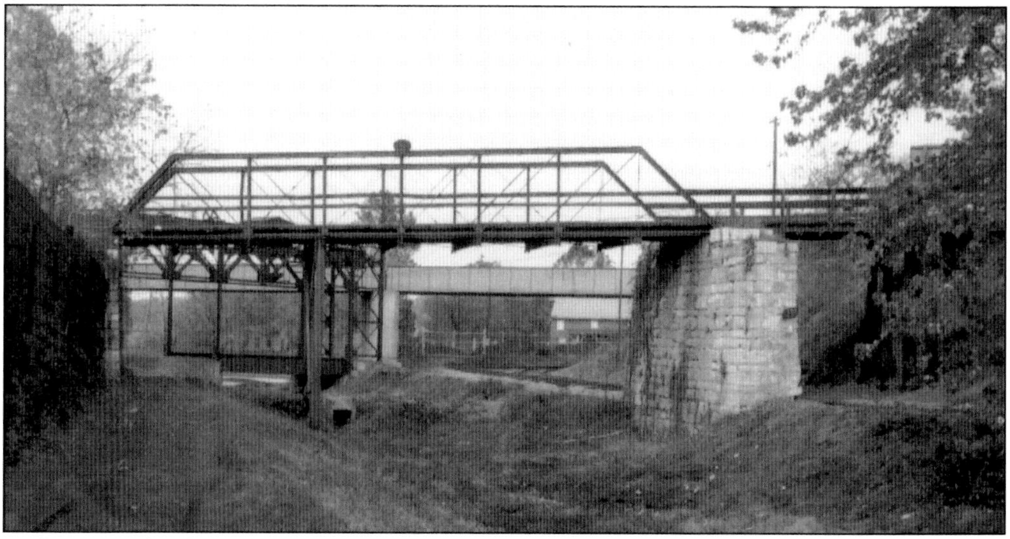

Built in 1879 by the Bollman Patapsco Bridge and Iron Works, Williamsport's Bollman Bridge leads over the canal bed and down to the Potomac Park area. The bridge, at the end of Salisbury Street, rests on piers of the bridge Gen. Robert E. Lee used to cross with his troops on the way to Gettysburg and during his retreat in 1863. Wendel Bollman, a Baltimore engineer, invented a system of iron bridge trussing, which was the first to be regularly used on rail lines throughout the United States. Of the approximate 100 bridges built by Bollman in the United States as well as Central and South America, only one other besides Williamsport's iron truss bridge still survives. (Courtesy C&O Canal National Historical Park Headquarters.)